Violent Interactions in the Mesolithic

Evidence and meaning

Edited by

Mirjana Roksandic

BAR International Series 1237
2004

Published in 2016 by
BAR Publishing, Oxford

BAR International Series 1237

Violent Interactions in the Mesolithic

ISBN 978 1 84171 596 4

© The editor and contributors severally and the Publisher 2004

Typesetting and layout: Darko Jerko

BAR Publishing is the trading name of British Archaeological Reports (Oxford) Ltd.
British Archaeological Reports was first incorporated in 1974 to publish the BAR
Series, International and British. In 1992 Hadrian Books Ltd became part of the BAR
group. This volume was originally published by Archaeopress in conjunction with
British Archaeological Reports (Oxford) Ltd / Hadrian Books Ltd, the Series principal
publisher, in 2004. This present volume is published by BAR Publishing, 2016.

Printed in England

BAR
PUBLISHING

BAR titles are available from:

BAR Publishing
122 Banbury Rd, Oxford, OX2 7BP, UK
EMAIL   info@barpublishing.com
PHONE   +44 (0)1865 310431
FAX   +44 (0)1865 316916
www.barpublishing.com

Contents

INTRODUCTION: HOW VIOLENT WAS THE MESOLITHIC, OR IS THERE A COMMON PATTERN OF VIOLENT INTERACTIONS SPECIFIC TO SEDENTARY HUNTER-GATHERERS?

Mirjana ROKSANDIC

Keywords: prehistoric warfare, traumatic injury, inter-personal violence,

Why another book on violence in prehistory? Do we have enough evidence to draw meaningful conclusions on the importance and meaning of violent interactions among sedentary and semi-sedentary hunter-gatherers of Europe? What methodological and theoretical questions do we hope to answer with this volume? Many questions on the evidence and meaning of confirmed violent interactions remain unresolved even as more and more books appear on the topic. This volume was prompted by my own research in the Iron Gates Gorge and the differences in patterns observed between sites on the right bank of the Danube – Vlasac, Lepenski Vir, Hajducka Vodenica, Padina, Velesnica, and Ajmana – and Schela Cladovei, a coeval site on the left bank belonging to the same cultural sphere. So far, the evidence for violent interactions on the right bank is very limited and spread over time, while the left bank shows such an extreme incidence of violent deaths as to be very puzzling. The papers presented here reflect a similar puzzlement felt by each of the participants while examining the evidence of trauma and possible or probable interpersonal violence.

1. MESOLITHIC

Mesolithic times have been signaled out as a period when the evidence for violence becomes far more common than in the earlier periods of human history (Frayer 1997, Thorpe 2000, Vencl 1999), to the point that it is taken as a confirmed fact by non-specialists (De Pauw 1998). But is it really so? What unequivocal evidence do we have to claim that the Mesolithic was more violent than previous periods? And if that indeed was true, what explanations can be offered? Is the violence related to sedentism, accumulation, prestige, or other elements of the *societal* structure (Pospisil 1994); or might it not be a sampling error stemming from the fact that we have far more skeletal remains from the Mesolithic than from the earlier periods? If indeed we can demonstrate higher levels of conflict in the Mesolithic than in previous periods, what happens later: more conflict, less conflict? Does violence – and more specifically organized violence – play an evolutionary role in creating large-scale aggregations with a centralized power structure (Carneiro 1994), is it the by-product of the centralization of power (Kang 2000) or should war and society be regarded as co-evolving as Kelly (2000) proposes?

This volume presents evidence of violent interactions in a group of societies conveniently defined as "Mesolithic:" three from different spots around Mediterranean: the *Iron Gates Gorge* (Serbia and Romania), the *Muge* and *Sado* valley shell middens (Portugal) and the recently excavated Iberomaurusien site of *d'Ifri n'Amar* (Morocco); earthen mounds from Eastern coast of Uruguay, the Epipaleolithic and Mesolithic sites in Ukraine, and a Neolithic site from China. Except for the latter, they have in common their "Mesolithic nature," defined here by a combination of economic practices (hunter-gatherers) and mobility patterns (semi-sedentary or sedentary), irrespective of the geographic area and temporal framework (Roksandic 2000: 4-6). For most of these populations, at some point in their history, contact with farming communities was possible (Lubell, Jackes, and Meiklejohn 1989, Radovanovic 1996a) even if it did not occur. Some of the groups participated in these communications through trade (evidenced by imports of non-local products) and possibly by other means. This period of latent and possible change had an important impact on the ideological integrity of these populations. In the case of the Iron Gates Gorge, it produced a stronger ideological integration of the community at a time when contact with farming societies became possible (Radovanovic 1996b, Radovanovic 1996c). It is often suggested that this kind of contact might have resulted in conflict through greater population pressure and territorial claims as well as other economic or ideological factors (as in Schela Cladovei). Our aim is to show whether or not we have evidence for that conflict in the archaeological and anthropological record of the sites presented.

2. INTERPRETATION OF ORGANIZED VIOLENCE

Another question of great importance to all of the participants in the volume is: How do we proceed from the evidence of an individual's violent interactions and death to interpretation of organized violence? And a step further in the same direction: Is all organized violence warfare? Indeed, how do we make this jump in interpretation based on skeletal data alone? The often cited massacre at Offnet (Frayer 1997) could have more than one explanation and could have involved more than one type of action. How do we interpret a cache of bones: 1) a simultaneous burial of body parts rescued after a massacre; 2) a simultaneous burial of war trophies; 3) a diachronous burial of decapitated individuals sacrificed to a bloodthirsty god; 4) a diachronous burial of skulls reflecting the cult of ancestors? Any of these explanations, and a score of others, is possible. Only careful excavation and documentation can give us sufficiently fine-grained resolution to allow reliable identification of the synchronicity of the burials, a crucial argument in the interpretation of a collection as deriving from a massacre. Unfortunately, for Offnet, and many other sites excavated earlier in the twentieth century, this is not an option.

If we accept that some of this evidence is strong enough to stand meticulous examination, is this indicative of organized violence? And further along the line of deduction, can it be interpreted as warfare? Ideally, only when we have answered all these questions in succession, and in the affirmative, can we presume to answer, by examining many of these individual societies, the question of whether the Mesolithic in general witnessed a higher incidence of warfare than previously. In that case, we can start building explanatory mechanisms for this elevated level of warfare. Unfortunately, we are still struggling to prove each case to be one of violence against a number of other possible explanations. Even where violence is proven beyond doubt, we have too little information to start delineating a picture of war and peace. Thus we are left with an examination of origins and causes of organized violence and a definition of warfare borrowed from the cultural anthropological literature. We propose that combining insights of cultural anthropology with skeletal evidence and contextual archaeological information will result in a more reliable picture of prehistoric warfare.

3. CULTURAL ANTHROPOLOGY ON ORIGINS OF WARFARE

After a period of relative neglect of warfare and violence in anthropology, there has been a revival of interest in theoretical questions regarding violent interactions in present-day small-scale societies and in archaeological populations. Recent editions – such as Reyna and Downs' series *War and Society* (in 5 volumes from 1992 to 1998), Haas' (1990) *Anthropology of War*, Ferguson's (1984) *Warfare, Culture and Environment*, to mention a few – confirm the growing interest in questions of war and warfare and the theoretical bases for understanding war and its impact on developing structures within societies. Walker (Walker 2001) laments the lack of significant contributions to the study of violence by anthropologists, as opposed to the importance it has for historians. Nevertheless, books like Kelly's (2000) *Warless Societies and the Origin of War*, Guilaine and Zammit's (2001) *Le sentier de la Guerre*, Carman and Harding's (1999) *Ancient Warfare*, and Keeley's (1996) *War before Civilization* – with their emphasis on understanding early prehistoric evidence – stem from the interest in discerning the predominance of violent interactions in the past that might help explain one of the most common but perhaps undesirable modes of human social behavior.

Warfare was always part of the explanatory mechanism for the archaeological record and has been invoked in interpreting a number of structures, arms, evidence of village burning, and evidence of multiple deaths. What is perhaps new in this recent attitude towards the study of past warfare is the quest for its origins, for an interpretation of its roots in human societies. The focus on non-state societies, whether contemporary or prehistoric, seems to represent a logical choice in such explanatory attempts. The evidence gathered from present day indigenous people practicing traditional ways of life, as well as historic accounts of these people, still provides the most immediate insight into the diversity of human responses. This evidence must be paramount. Considering these societies as pristine is *passé* (to use Reyna's words: 1994: xiii), and only very few anthropologists would claim that they afford "an intimate glimpse beyond history" (Chagnon 1977:xii). Direct ethnographic analogy is often misleading as it takes evidence out of its historical context. The recognition that these groups have their own history has to be the basic premise of all theory building and explanatory attempts (Ferguson 1992, Marshall Thomas 1994). "Wars are often fought locally, even world wars: they are conjunctural events" (Simons 1999: 92). This local and historical character has to be kept in mind in all attempts to understand war and its background. Haas (1999) has stated that we can only begin to understand the origins of war by identifying the repeating patterns of warfare in pre-state societies. Keeley shows that warfare is present in the archaeological record of non-state societies and he demonstrates (1996:175) that pre-state society warfare cannot be regarded as different in extent and lethality from wars between states. Nevertheless, Haas questions Keeley's contention that warfare is universal and a given and notes that Keeley "forces us to examine the critical question of why warfare appears and disappears at different times and places" (Haas 1999:13). Whether analyzing causes of war in human society in general, or searching for similar patterns and causes on a regional level, it is crucial to take an historical approach to warfare from its emergence to its resolution. That an historical approach is crucial is also stressed by ethnographic research (Ember and Ember 1997, Ferguson 1992) which shows that all present-day small-scale societies have to be seen in the context of their interactions with the state societies and global economy. Similarly, an understanding of Mongol nomadic warfare is possible only when it is seen in the context of the socio-political milieu of the sedentary farming state of China (Barfield 1994).

There is no doubt that every human being is capable of violent behavior. Socialization and learning help direct and channel this type of behavior. Certain instances will be praised, others shunned in any given group. Every individual in a given group has to find the modality that will fulfill both individual needs and social expectations in a particular situation, including violence. However, societies differ both in the amount and direction of violent behavior that is considered permissible or appropriate. Furthermore, war is "not related to violence as simply more of the same" (Kelly 2000): 21). This brings us to an important question in studying war: Can all violence be interpreted as warfare? When interpersonal violence in a studied group is rampant and involves more than one group perceived as a, more or less, coherent unit, do we need to draw a line between warfare and feuding? And even more importantly for this book, how do we distinguish between them in the archaeological record? If we decide that warfare does not appear before a certain level of socio-political complexity (such as the state) within any society is reached (Reyna 1994b), then all of the violence experienced by the non-state organized groups remains in the domain of "resolution of individual personal grudges" (Reyna 1994a). If we conceptualize war as restricted to centralized polities (Reyna 1994a:xiv) the question of warfare in the Mesolithic does not even arise.

The definition of warfare Reyna offers is based on its proximate (stated and real) causes and he resorts to "grudge-accumulation process" as the explanatory mechanism for protracted tribal fighting in which members of villages became involved in raids and battles (Reyna 1994b: 42). But can we really emphasize causal factors as the determinant in our definition of warfare, and which cause do we consider: the immediate proximate cause, or the underlying one? It is more than obvious that proclaimed causes that prompted states to declare war have rarely been anything but a propaganda tool aimed at the state population itself, the people who had to accept and support the war. The motives of the society (or rather its elite) are usually well hidden behind ideological proclamations aimed not so much at the enemy or future historians but at one's own population whose dissent has to be prevented. Thus Keeley (1996: 114) asks: "Should any motive *declared* by anyone be considered? Should motives be inferred from the operation, results, and effects of specific wars or acts of war?" (Emphasis L. K.). Predominant motives for pre-state warfare (based on cross-cultural studies reported in Keeley (1996: 200) are revenge for homicides and various economic issues (p.115). Personal aggrandizement – prestige – as a motive is actually more commonly associated with higher levels of political centralization (chiefdoms and states). Apparently, subjugation and tribute are the only motives absent in non-centralized polities (p.116), the major reason being that a kin militia (typical of non-state societies) has no means of maintaining violence beyond a few weeks. Even when continuous raids result in a gain of territory (a common enough motive) through the driving out of the opponents, this is not a form of control, but a dispersion (Carneiro 1994, Reyna 1994a). Keeley argues, however, that repeated violence can result in "gift" giving (or tribute), a form of tax similar to "extortion rackets exercised by urban gangsters, rural brigands and pirates in civilized societies." Thus the motives of the centralized versus non-centralized societies cannot be easily distinguished – they do not offer a good set of variables for defining warfare.

A definition of warfare offered by Kelly seems to be applicable to all levels of political centralization and offers a good working definition for examining prehistoric warfare. Kelly (2000) considers war (including feuds) to be grounded "in application of the principle of *social substitutability*" (p. 21). And further, "the principle that one group member is substitutable for another in these contexts underwrites the interrelated concepts of injury to the group, group

responsibility for the infliction of injury and group liability with respect to retribution" (*idem*: 5). All of this would distinguish it from murder, duels and capital punishment, since these are directed against the perpetrator of a crime.

The cultural anthropological literature on warfare is mostly concerned with its evolutionary significance summed up as "when it started and how can we end it." Cultural anthropologists consider that biology plays a relatively unimportant part in the emergence of war (Carneiro 1994), although proponents of evolutionary ecology maintain that warfare is based in maximizing inclusive fitness (Gat 1999, Gat 2000a, Gat 2000b) and can not be regarded as characteristic of humans since it is based in the common heritage of social animals from chimpanzees to wolves (Wrangham 1999). Another commonly evoked source of warfare, population pressure – prominent since Thomas Malthus' famous *Essay on the Principles of Population* (1798) as major predictor of frequency of war – is not supported by cross-cultural studies (Keeley 1996:118). Kang (2000) demonstrates that under certain historical circumstances, warfare can result from underpopulation caused by environmental stress. However, Kelly (2000:chapter 3) suggests that population density does play an important role if we limit the analysis to either segmented or non-segmented societies. Keeley (1996: 119) recognizes that some relationship between population pressure and frequency of warfare exists, however, this relationship is either complex or very weak or both and he concludes that: "warring societies are equally common and peaceable ones equally uncommon at any level of population density" (120). Along the same lines, Walker states that "throughout the history of our species interpersonal violence, especially among man, has been prevalent. No form of social organization, mode of production, or environmental setting appears to have remained free of interpersonal violence for long." (Walker 2001: 573). Since no form of social organization or mode of production can be causally linked with war or peace (Ember and Ember 1997, Otterbein 1997, Otterbein 2000), all societies will eventually indulge in war.

Much less often stressed is the fact that all these societies will know periods of peace and stability, and I would not necessarily agree that peaceable societies are as uncommon as they seem to be: the lack of diversity in responses offered by modern societies to stressors resulting in warfare could be obscuring a number of possible responses in the past. As noted by Kelly (2000: 11), the importance of studying peaceful societies cannot be over-emphasized, yet the literature on it is much less abundant than on the warring societies (Sponsel 1994).

Any of the above-mentioned factors: biological, ecological and cultural will not necessarily result in warfare if the society is unsegmented. Unsegmented hunter-gatherers have a low frequency of warfare as they lack organizational features associated with social substitutability that are conductive to development of group concepts. Segmented foragers, on the other hand, show much greater frequency of warfare: 16 out of 17 examined (Kelly 2000: 51). Thus recognition of group identity provides the best explanatory mechanism for the emergence of warfare. It is important to stress, however, that social structure in itself does not result in feuding or war. Certain external conditions will need to be imposed in order to generate warfare. Accordingly, Kelly states that "warfare is not an endemic condition of human existence but an episodic feature of human history (and prehistory) observed at certain times and places but not others" (2000:75).

4. GROUPS ARCHAEOLOGISTS STUDY

That local history has to be a component in understanding warfare is no less true for the groups archaeologists study. The examples presented in this volume are societies of relatively long duration, and local history spanning anywhere between 1000 to over 1500 years. Illustrative of the quality of evidence we are dealing with is the fact that we consider the sample size of 100 individuals from a single site of this period as substantial, and often make inferences based on less than 20 individuals. Given concerns about preservation bias, inability to detect soft tissue wounds as causes of (violent) death (Jackes, this volume, Cunha, this volume), and the near impossibility of distinguishing between violence and accident, we are left with an even more difficult question. If we can indeed recognize the evidence for violence, how can we interpret it: are we dealing with short episodes of unresolved conflict with high mortality rates, or a constant but low rate of "endemic" warfare? And furthermore, if we can ascertain a case of intertribal warfare can we consider the group (or as is currently done for the whole era of the Mesolithic) as warlike? Could not the sporadic episodes of – even organized – violence, be just what they seem to be: episodes of stress resolved through conflict without further impact on the society and its long-term history?

5. PAPERS IN THIS VOLUME

No lower or upper limit for the length of the articles was imposed, and the number of illustrations was left open to participants. This is reflected in individual papers. My editorial impact on the papers was minimal. Most of the comments on the first drafts of each paper were derived from the internal review process. I am most grateful to the participants in the volume who took time to review the articles and I hope that it created dialogue and helped exchange ideas. The internal review process was followed by an anonymous external review. The book presents an array of personal experiences, attitudes, interpretations and different positions proposed by the authors and while I do not necessarily endorse all of them, I appreciate the opportunity to offer them in one volume.

The first paper by Tracy Rogers examines our ability to determine warfare from the skeletal record from the perspective of a forensic anthropologist. Unfortunately, a growing number of forensic cases involving war dead from 20th century civil wars and mass burials, offers insights into the ways in which inter-personal violence is identified (cause), analyzed (mode), and interpreted (manner) in a modern context, and provides some recommendations for incorporating these analyses into the study of ancient aggression. Rogers concludes that, given the variety of reasons for engaging in warfare, it is unrealistic to expect warfare to exhibit a single diagnostic pattern in the bioarchaeological record. Modern warfare evidence exhibits greater variability in injury patterns and victim demography than homicide, which is a potentially useful indicator of warfare in past populations. The author stresses that our potential to recognize violence and infer warfare in the bioarchaeological record has to proceed through contextual analysis of: (1) the nature of conflict; (2) the type and seriousness of injuries sustained; (3) the demography of war dead; (4) the number of fatalities; and (5) the burial context. Since analysis of modern warfare and homicide demonstrates the potential scope of characteristics that may apply to ancient warfare, Rogers calls for a broader perspective to the study of conflict in past populations.

The further we go into the past, increasingly longer time sequences are collapsed, and the resolution we deal with becomes very coarse. We have to rely on any available evidence. What evidence can be accepted as sufficient for the definition of warfare and can absence of evidence be interpreted as the evidence of absence, these are the questions Mary Jackes attempts to answer through examination of different regions where she has first hand experience as both a cultural and biological anthropologist. Her understanding of trauma in the Portuguese Mesolithic series favours accidents over violence and warfare as explanatory mechanisms. A situation of undoubted extreme interpersonal violence in Kenya is shown to relate to within-population conflict caused by external pressures. Striking differences between known ethnohistoric data for North American groups of the Northeast Woodlands and the corresponding skeletal material bring forward in this chapter the full scale of ambiguity and difficulties in interpretation of prehistoric violence. That the problems become aggravated by excavation and curatorial practices is, alas too common knowledge for all of us, and we often have to "make do" with what little evidence we have. Osteological material from a Neolithic Chinese site which is the final focus of the paper, provides clear physical evidence of violence, despite the lack of archaeological recognition of conflict, thus pointing to the need to be wary of the interpretations in this sensitive area of anthropological study. Jackes concludes that we need to avoid simplistic explanations for evidence of violence and calls for the setting of that evidence within a broad context – one with chronological and social/geographical depth and breadth. Jackes concludes that, since there are inevitable political and judgmental overtones additional to osteological interpretations in the examination of violence in any given society, we must be extremely careful when making broad statements regarding violence in a society – we must be sure that we are being strictly neutral.

The third paper, by Eugenia Cunha, Claudia Umbelino and Francesca Cardoso brings more data on the Portuguese Mesolithic sample: the material from Muge housed in the

Porto Museum and the less known material from the shell middens of the Sado valley. It complements the information on Portugal given in the previous paper and concludes, along the same lines, that we do not have any reasonably strong indication that violence amounted to warfare at the sites of either the Muge or the Sado valley in the Mesolithic. Even though some trauma is present and some of it can be interpreted as violent trauma there is nothing that would suggest elevated levels of interpersonal or intertribal violence or warfare.

In the fourth paper we stay in the same general area and move south from the Iberian Peninsula to Morocco. Ben-Ncer brings us an interesting case of decapitation and dismemberment of a small child within the context of Iberomaurisien with some additional evidence of non-lethal conflict from the well-known site of Tafarault. The author examines two alternative explanations: that the child was killed by decapitation, or decapitated and dismembered after death. While I would not necessarily regard this decapitation in the same light as the author, since burial rituals are varied and not always conforming to present-day ideas of what constitutes a 'proper' burial, the case is interesting and confronts us with a number of questions: What was the purpose of this act? Burial ritual? Exorcism? Sacrifice? Given the most orderly burial of other young children, why was this child singled out? Are we dealing here with the phenomenon of substitutability indicating warfare by Kelly's standards discussed above, or could this be explained as evidence of for example witchcraft, among a number of other possible options. Given the sporadic evidence of non-lethal violence from Tafarault, warfare is an unlikely interpretation, however, as Mary Jackes has shown in this volume, since absence of evidence can not be regarded as evidence of absence, we can only hope for more material to come out of the new excavations currently underway in Morocco.

With the fifth paper we move to the Iron Gates Gorge Mesolithic material of Lepenski Vir type. Traumatic lesions caused by violence are presented in detail with all additional demographic and archaeological data from the burial context. They are contrasted with the evidence from Schela Cladovei, a coeval site on the left bank of the Danube. The likely cases of violence on the right bank of the Danube are few and randomly distributed throughout the three periods examined, while violence is more rampant at Schela Cladovei and tightly clustered in terms of absolute chronology. The dates for the Schela sample are on the borderline between the Pre-contact Mesolithic and the times when the contact with Neolithic farmers becomes possible, while most of the violent episodes on the right bank of the Danube fall into pre-contact times. Their random distribution and lack of special burial treatment indicates that the inter-personal violence does not amount to feuding or warfare (as discussed above) while the left bank data indicate an episode of conflict restricted in time. There is no indication that warfare was endemic in the Iron Gates Gorge Mesolithic. Furthermore, it cannot be associated with the stress caused by advancing farmers, as most of it happened when the contact was non-existent or at best sporadic and did not result from any major movement of populations.

Choyke and Bartosiewicz's article on osseous projectiles brings another aspect of inquiry that has not been performed on any of the Mesolithic series previously discussed. Both stone and bone projectiles are found embedded in human bone at Mesolithic sites. Stone projectiles predominate because of either their greater functional value or different taphonomic properties. In the case of the Swiss Late Neolithic site the authors discuss taphonomy, typology and function of bone projectiles and examine their potential role in hunting *versus* warfare. While the authors conclude that a distinction between hunting implements and arms can not be made on the basis of typology, and while taphonomy plays an important role in the frequency of bone projectiles at different sites, especially excavation and collection strategies, these objects should be routinely examined in the context of warfare. The expediency of the bone artifact production argues for their remaining in situ in case of conflict where they could indicate an attack from the outside group. The authors compare frequencies of bone projectiles in Lepenski Vir sites and their Swiss Neolithic site. While a greater percentage of osseous projectile points within the bone artifact assemblage from Lepenski Vir and other Iron Gates Gorge Mesolithic sites could be interpreted as showing evidence of possible warfare, the authors caution that different collection practices (namely large number of small bone artifacts collected through sieving in the Swiss Neolithic) could have produced this unbalanced picture. More research in this domain, from and around the sites where defense structures confirm the existence of conflict is needed to shed more light on these numbers.

Lillie presents us with a critical overview of the published sources relating to three Epipalaeolithic cemeteries from the Dnieper Rapids region of Ukraine, and outlines the evidence for violence that has been recorded on the human skeletal remains from these sites. The skeletal evidence suggests that the increased use of the bow and arrow in hunting was accompanied by its increased use in inter-group violence. The osteological and lithic analyses carried out by Russian researchers on Epipalaeolithic skeletal remains, highlight a prevalence of injury unattested to in the later Mesolithic and Neolithic cemeteries from this area, studied by Lillie. The restructuring of the fauna and flora in the steppe and forest-steppe zones of Europe at the transition to the Holocene period appears to have resulted in the potential for conflict over access to certain resources among the indigenous hunter-gatherer populations. In effect, the early absolute dates from Vasilyevka III, alongside the relative dates for Voloshkoe and Vasilyevka I, suggest that the inter-group violence potentially highlights the early stages of territoriality when regional groups would have competed for a preferred location, primarily for the exploitation of freshwater resources. Once these territorial rights were established, it appears on the current evidence, that the need for violent conflict to maintain them was unnecessary throughout the subsequent Mesolithic, Neolithic and Eneolithic/Copper Age periods in this region. While environmental changes can be regarded as the underlying cause, social restructuring seems to be the explanatory mechanism for the violence at the particular time.

In the last article Pintos Blanco discusses what he sees as evidence of interpersonal violence recovered from the burials of a group of complex semi-sedentary hunter-gatherers of Uruguay known in the literature as 'the culture of mound constructors' (*la cultura de los constructores de cerritos*). This culture of long duration represents increasing segmentation of the society and 'monumentalisation of death.' While cut marks, secondary burials and burnt bones brought forward by the author could be explained as easily within the context of burial ritual, the author suggests that they might be expressing situations of inter or intra community struggles. The evidence is interpreted in the context of both the underlying environmental and the superimposed cultural features: changes in diet and eventual adoption of food production, accompanying variations in lithic and ceramic technology, and increased monumentalization indicating increased territoriality and segmentation of the society. The author proposes a positive correlation between the process of space hierarchization through monument construction (earthen mounds), the monumentalization of death, the evidences of violent human interactions, and increase in production (processing cost, diversification of diet, domestication). The notion that segmentation of society plays a crucial role in interpersonal violence is furthered, and although the evidence of violent interactions itself is less than ideal, a strong case is built on the bases of the archaeological evidence.

CONCLUSION:

As a framework for this volume, I defined Mesolithic societies as sedentary or semi-sedentary prehistoric hunter-gatherers with no temporal or geographical limitations usually associated with this term, allowing for comparisons between temporally and geographically remote regional groups. While the number of societies presented could have been much larger, the articles in this volume present a number of different approaches, focuses and expertise. What seems to unite them is the call for minute examination of osteological evidence and broad understanding of contextual data.

Returning to the question we asked at the very title of this introduction: "is there a common pattern of violent interactions specific to sedentary hunter-gatherers?," we have to answer that in general Mesolithic societies differ little in the amount of violence from other small-scale societies. Where evidence of violence amounts to conflict between distinct groups (warfare), it is temporally restricted and dependent on local histories. In that respect it does not differ from any other period and any other form of subsistence pattern or social organization. While sedentism and territoriality could have played important roles in an increased incidence of warfare, the beginning of conflict between groups as defined by Kelly (2000:21), is grounded "in [the] application of the principle of *social substitutability*," and cannot be placed in the Mesolithic. Furthermore there is no evidence that the Mesolithic was either more or less violent than other periods of human (pre)history.

Authors address

Mirjana Roksandic, Ph.D.
Department of Anthropology and Religion
University of Toronto at Mississauga,
3359 Mississauga Road North,
Mississauga, Ontario, Canada l5l 1C6
mroksand@utm.utoronto.ca

Bibliography

BARFIELD, T. J. 1994. "The Devil's Horsemen: Steppe Nomadic Warfare in Historical Perspective," in *Studying War. Anthropological Perspectives*, vol. 2, *War and Society*. Edited by R. E. Downs, pp. 157-184. Amsterdam: Gordon and Breach Publishers.

CARMAN, J., and A. HARDING. Editors. 1999. *Ancient Warfare, Archaological Perspectives*. Phoenix Mill: Sutton Publishing Ltd.

CARNEIRO, R. L. 1994. "War and Peace: Alternating Realities in Human History," in *Studying War. Anthropological Perspectives*, vol. 2, *War and Society*. Edited by R. E. Downs, pp. 3-28. Amsterdam: Gordon and Breach Publishers.

De PAUW, L. G. 1998. *Battle Cries and Lullabies : Women in War from Prehistory to the Present*. Norman: University of Oklahoma Press.

EMBER, M., and C. R. Ember. 1997. "Violence in the Ethnographic Record: Results of Cross-Cultural Research on War and Agression," in *Troubled Times: Violence and Warfare in the Past*, vol. 3, *War and Society*. Edited by D. W. Frayer, pp. 1-20. Amsterdam: Gordon and Breach Publishers.

FERGUSON, R. B. Editor. 1984. *Warfare, Culture, and Environment. Studies in Anthropology*. Orlando: Academic Press.

FERGUSON, R. B. 1992. "A Savage Encounter: Western Contact and Yanomami War Complex," in *War in the Tribal Zone: Expanding States and Indigenous Warfare, School of American Research Advanced Seminar Series*. Edited by N. L. Whitehead, pp. 199-228. Santa Fe, New Mexico.: School of American Research Press,.

FRAYER, D. 1997. "Ofnet: Evidence for a Mesolithic Massacre," in *Troubled Times: Violence and Warfare in the Past*, vol. 3, *War and Society*. Edited by D. W. Frayer, pp. 181-216. Amsterdam: Gordon and Breach Publishers.

GAT, A. 1999. The Pattern of Fighting in Simple, Small-scale Prehistoric Societies. *Journal of Anthropological Research* 55:563-583.

GAT, A. 2000a. The Causes and Origins of "Primitive Warfare." Reply to Ferguson. *Anthropological quarterly* 73.

GAT, A. 2000b. The Human Motivational Complex: Evolutionary Theory and the Cause of Hunter Gatherer Fighting. *Anthropological Quarterly* 73:20-34.

HAAS, J. Editor. 1990. *The Anthropology of War. School of American Research Advanced Seminar Series*. Cambridge: Cambridge University Press.

KANG, B. W. 2000. A Reconideration of Population Pressure and Warfare: A Cprotohistoric Korean Case. *Current Anthroplogy* 41:873-881.

KEELEY, L. H. 1996. *War before civilization*. New York: Oxford University Press.

KELLY, R. C. 2000. *Warless Societies and the Origin of War*. Ann Arbor: University of Michigan Press.

LUBELL, D., M. Jackes, and C. Meiklejohn. 1989. "Archaeology and Human Biology of the Mesolithic-Neolithic Transition in

Southern Portugal: a Preliminary Report," in *The Mesolithic in Europe: Papers Presented at the Third International Symposium, Edunburgh 1985*. Edited by C. Bonsall, pp. 632-640. Edinburgh: John Donald Publishers Ltd.

OTTERBEIN, K. F. 1997. The Origins of War. *Critical Review* 11:251- 277.

OTTERBEIN, K. F. 2000. A History of Research on Warfare in Anthropology. *American Anthropologist* 101:794-805.

POSPISIL, L. 1994. "I am Very Sorry I cannot Kill You Anymore: War and Peace among the Kapauku," in *Studying War. Anthropological Perspectives*, vol. 2, *War and Society*. Edited by R. E. Downs, pp. 113-126. Amsterdam: Gordon and Breach Publishers.

RADOVANOVIC, I. 1996a. *The Iron Gates Mesolithic*. Ann Arbor: University of Michigen Press.

RADOVANOVIC, I. 1996b. "The Lepenski Vir Culture: a Contribution to Interpretation of its Ideological Aspects," in *Zbornik radova posvecenih D. Srejovicu*. Beograd: Centar za arheoloska istrazivanja Filozofskog fakulteta u Beogradu.

RADOVANOVIC, I. 1996c. Mesolithic/Neolithic Contacts: a Case of the Iron Gates Region. *Porocilo o raziskovanju paleolitika, neolitika in eneolitika v Sloveniji* XXIII:39-48.

REYNA, S. P. 1994a. "A mode of Domination Approach to Organized Violence," in *Studying War. Anthropological Perspectives*, vol. 2, *War and Society*. Edited by R. E. Downs, pp. 29-65. Amsterdam: Gordon and Breach Publishers,.

REYNA, S. P. 1994b. "Studying War, and Unifinished Project of the Enlightenment," in *Studying War. Anthropological Perspectives*, vol. 2, *War and Society*. Edited by R. E. Downs, pp. i-xvi. Amsterdam: Gordon and Breach Publishers,.

ROKSANDIC, M. 2000. Between Foragers and Farmers in the Iron Gates Gorge: Physical anthropology Perspective. *Documetna Prehistorica* XXVII:1-100.

SPONSEL, L. E. 1994. "The Mutual Relevance of Anthopology and Peace Studies," in *The Anthropology of Peace and Nonviolence*. Edited by T. Gregor, pp. 1-36. Boulder: Lynne Rienner.

THORPE, N. 2000. Origins of War. Mesolithic Conflict in Europe. *British Archaeology*:9-12.

VENCL, S. 1995. Interprétation des blesseurs causés par les armes au Mésolithique. *L'Anthropologie* 95:219-228.

VENCL, S.1999. "Stone Age Warfare," in *Ancient Warfare, Archaological Perspectives*. Edited by A. Harding, pp. 57-73. Phoenix Mill: Sutton Publishing Ltd.

WALKER, P. L. 2001. A Bioarcheological Perspective on the History of Violence. *Annual Review of Anthropology* 30:573-596.

WRANGHAM, R. W. 1999. Evolution of Coalitionary Killing. *Yearbook of Physical Anthropology* 42:1-30.

RECOGNIZING INTER-PERSONAL VIOLENCE: A FORENSIC PERSPECTIVE

Tracy ROGERS

Key words: inter-personal violence, manner of death, warfare

1. INTRODUCTION

The recognition of inter-personal violence in modern human remains is the responsibility of the coroner/medical examiner, pathologist and forensic anthropologist. The coroner/medical examiner is legally responsible for establishing: (1) the identity of the deceased, (2) the circumstances surrounding the death, (3) where death occurred, (4) when death occurred, (5) why and how the individual died. The pathologist and forensic anthropologist examine the remains to provide the coroner with information about the identity of the deceased, the cause, manner and mode of death.

These three concepts are fundamental to all modern death investigations. Cause of death refers to the disease or injury responsible for initiating the chain of events that result in a fatal outcome. Death may follow immediately after the precipitating event, or may be a prolonged process that does not occur until many years later, e.g., injuries producing a coma (Sauer, 1984). Manner of death refers to the type of death, e.g., homicide, suicide, accident, natural causes, or undetermined (Mann and Owsley, 1992). Mode of death is the method by which the individual's life is ended, e.g., shooting, strangling. Determining the cause of death involves the identification and documentation of traumatic injuries with respect to vital organs. The mode of death is established through analysis of the injuries, and manner of death is determined through the interpretation of the location and patterns of injuries, the circumstances of the case and the context of the scene.

This paper outlines the way in which inter-personal violence is identified (cause), analyzed (mode), and interpreted (manner) in a modern context, and provides some recommendations for incorporating these analyses into the study of ancient aggression. Once interpersonal violence is identified, the nature of the violence can then be addressed. Anthropological analyses of warfare and violence demonstrate the importance of the social context to our understanding of the cause, particular forms, and instances of violence (Carman, 1997; Simons, 1999). Walker (2001) suggests that modern data concerning physical manifestations of interpersonal violence can provide a baseline against which bioarchaeological evidence for ancient violence can be measured. In this paper modern warfare data will be used to demonstrate the contextual specificity of injury patterns and the variation that occurs in related factors such as the demographic profile of war casualties, the use of torture, and the disposition of the remains, that make it difficult to develop a definitive model for recognizing warfare in the bioarchaeological record.

2. CAUSE AND MODE OF DEATH

Pathologists are the recognized authority on cause of death. They are required to describe the soft tissue changes to vital centres of the body, such as the heart or brain, which lead to the death of the individual. Accurate assessment of the cause of death is often not possible based on skeletal evidence alone, since some fatal injuries do not affect bone and, conversely, some massive bone injuries are not fatal (Sauer, 1984; Stewart, 1979). For example, an individual who fell from a great height may suffer several broken bones, including a fractured skull and broken ribs, but could survive long enough to develop a fatal case of pneumonia, if the fractured rib punctured a lung. In this case, the proximate cause of death is pneumonia, but the ultimate cause of death is the fall. Depending on the nature of the fractures, it may be possible to establish that a fall occurred, but it would not be possible to diagnose the proximate cause of death on the basis of skeletal evidence.

Whether or not the injury is fatal, it is the forensic anthropologist's job to identify, describe and record bone trauma. The number of lesions, the location of injury (bone, side, aspect, surface), the size of the wound, the shape of the wound, the presence of foreign matter, and the relationship of bony injury to important anatomical structures, help the pathologist determine the cause of death. Differentiating antemortem and perimortem injury from postmortem damage is a crucial aspect of this analysis. Weapon injuries are easily distinguished from incidental or taphonomic factors (Berryman and Symes, 1998; Houck, 1998; Quatrehomme and Iscan, 1999; Sauer, 1998; Wakely, 1997), but the nature of broken bone can be more difficult to decipher.

In life and during the immediate post-mortem interval, when bone is considered "fresh" or "green", the presence of collagen allows bone to respond to trauma in an elastic manner. Damage to green bone produces edges that are frayed and sometimes incompletely fractured (hinge fracture) with attached fragments or flakes. Concentric fractures and radiating fractures are also indicative of fractures to fresh bone. In contrast, postmortem damage to bone lacking collagen is characterized by clean-edged, right-angled fractures (Galloway, 1999; Walker, 2001). See Roksandic this volume for further discussion.

Establishing the type of trauma, angle of entry of bullets or instruments, the direction and force of blows, and the patterns and timing of events contributes to the determination of mode and manner of death (Walsh-Haney, 1999). In the absence of soft tissues and blood stains on bone that are evident in the recently dead, mode of death is considerably easier to establish than cause of death. Mode of death refers only to the method by which the death is achieved, stabbing, strangling, etc. It does not depend on contextual information, or interpretation to the same degree as manner of death and is, therefore, less ambiguous. Of the three, cause, mode and manner of death, mode will be the easiest parameter to establish in an archaeological context.

Detailed descriptions of bone trauma can be found in several excellent sources (Galloway, 1999; Lovell, 1997). The following is a brief summary and description of antemortem injuries that can be observed on bone, with particular emphasis on those relating to inter-personal violence.

I. Fracture

A) Blunt trauma/impact

Usually directed at the head, blunt trauma can occur as the result of punching, kicking or hitting, with or without the help of an instrument such as chains wrapped around the fist, a hammer, club, or any sufficiently hard object (stone, wood, bone). Blunt injuries can also occur when an individual falls against an object, e.g., tripping and hitting one's head. Blunt force trauma is characterized by a point of impact surrounded by concentric fractures and, depending on the force behind the blow, the presence of radiating fractures extending away from the point of impact (Berryman and Symes, 1998; Galloway, 2000).

B) Sharp trauma

Sharp trauma involves an edged instrument and is further divided into:

Incised wounds - these are cuts or slashes from an edged instrument. Commonly cut bones include: ribs and face, forearm and hands (defense wounds), and cranial vault. In cases of dismemberment, cut marks may be found near joints (Reichs, 1998; White, 1992). Cut marks produced by metal blades result in relatively shallow v-shaped incisions with smooth sides and, occasionally, a slight ridge oriented parallel to the cut (Merbs, 1989; Sauer, 1984). See White (1992) for a description of non-metal instruments.

Stab wounds - are caused by sharp points. A distinction should be made between penetrating wounds, which merely enter a structure and perforating wounds which pass all the

way through. The appearance of stabbing injuries varies depending upon: (1) the characteristics of the instrument, e.g., shape of blade, single or double edges, length, sharpness; (2) the manner of attack , e.g., struggling or immobile victim, strength of attacker, angle of attack; (3) area of the body involved, e.g., in hard tissue the wound is usually smaller than the size of the blade because bone will give way under stress and then return as much as possible to its original state, some bones will fracture (rib) while others will perforate (scapula); and (4) bone characteristics, e.g., thickness and density.

Chop wounds - deep gaping wound, resulting from the impact of a heavy, sharp edged instrument such as an axe or machete. Chop wounds are easily distinguished from cut marks as follows:

1. The bone exhibits a smooth, flat, cut surface where the blade enters. If the angle of entry is greater than 90 [a], the obtuse surface will be smooth and the acute surface rough, ending in fractured bone.

2. At the margin of the acute surface, the outer bone layer detaches to form thin flakes. These flakes are usually missing in archaeological remains, but are retained by the periosteum in recent cases.

3. Large fragments may fracture away from beneath the bone as the blade passes through it (Wenham, 1989).

Cleaver trauma is characterized by a clean entry, approximately 1.5 mm wide at the midpoint. Chops made with a cleaver, perpendicular to the long axis of the bone, are incapable of penetrating the entire bone. Instead, kerf floors are produced. A kerf is the groove made by a cutting tool and the kerf floor refers to the point at which the cut terminates. Cleaver wounds do not produce radiating fractures at the entry site, but sometimes result in fractures from the kerf floor. Striations left on the bone by the blade are oriented perpendicular to the kerf floor (Humphrey and Hutchinson, 2001).

C) Tension

Tension fractures refer to the pulling action of ligaments that cause tubercles and trochanters to break away from the main body of the bone, e.g., Osgood-Schlatter's disease (Ortner and Putschar, 1985).

D) Compression

Crushing due to sudden, excessive impaction can produce compression fractures, e.g., jumping from a height (Ortner and Putschar, 1985).

E) Torsion

The twisting of long bones results in torsion fractures, e.g., skiing accidents involving the tibia, or fractures of the humerus caused by wrenching the upper arm in cases of child abuse (Brogden, 1998). Since the stress occurs in a spiral direction, the fracture line also spirals (Ortner and Putschar, 1985).

F) Flexion

The most common type of fracture results from bending. Parry fractures are defense wounds observed on the forearm of individuals trying to protect themselves from a blow. Parry fractures occur on the mid to distal end of the ulna and, depending on the force of the blow, may also be observed in the corresponding locations on the radius (Ortner and Putschar, 1985).

G) Shearing

Opposite forces applied to bone produce a shearing fracture, e.g., Colles fractures of the distal radius result from the force of an extended arm meeting the force of the ground during a fall (Ortner and Putschar, 1985)

II. Burns

Burns can be the result of high temperature, corrosive agents or friction. Deliberate burning in a forensic context is most often used in an attempt to destroy the body/evidence, or to mask the identity of the remains, rather than as a means of killing someone. In deliberate attempts to kill by burning, e.g., of witches, or arson combined with immobilization of a victim, the cause of death is typically asphyxiation. Socially sanctioned cremation is common in both modern and archaeological contexts, but the possibility of using fire to destroy an enemy's remains should not be overlooked. Burned remains should be carefully examined for evidence of trauma. In some cultures, cremation was reserved for those dying in battle, and in others it was common to set fire to enemy structures (Zimmerman, 1997), which could have contained people at the time. Proper analysis of cremated and burned bone is, therefore, integral to the analysis of warfare.

The characteristic marks left by knives and cleavers are largely unaffected by fire and are easily recognizable, but the damage caused by cleavers leaves the bone susceptible to cracking and fragmentation near the chop mark. The bone may fragment in such a way that only one side of the v-shaped mark is retained. Fractured surfaces of cremated bone may exhibit the characteristically smooth point of entry, or the roughened surface caused by the wrenching action of the blade as it is removed from the bone. Glancing blows produce oblong lesions with shallow angles of entry. Direct blows produce semicircular marks with steeper angles of entry. Fractured edges should be carefully examined to ensure that fragmentation of the bone is not masking evidence of trauma (de Gruchy and Rogers, 2002).

III. Electrical injuries

Electrical injuries can be produced by electrocution or lightning. Electrical injuries can be distinguished from other forms of burning by the localized nature of the damage. The force of the charge leaving the body can fracture long bones, burning the exit wound from the inside out. Electrical injuries are of little concern for archaeological analyses of warfare, but deliberate application of electricity is a form of torture used on victims of modern warfare. Electrical currents induce muscle contractions causing bone fractures, e.g., in ribs, and soft tissue injuries, with secondary degenerative changes in bone (Vogel, 2003).

IV. Firearms

Firearms injuries can be distinguished from blunt trauma by the presence of entrance or exit wounds, the absence of a point of impact, and the degree of fragmentation. Entrance wounds are beveled internally, with the exception of angled entries, which produce a beveled channel. Exit wounds are beveled externally. Firearms usually produce radiating fractures that move faster than the speeding bullet, thus the exit wound could intersect a radiating fracture line. Concentric heaving fractures, or hoop fractures, are produced by the force of the gases expelled by the gun (Byers, 2002).

V. Asphyxiation

Asphyxiation may result from a foreign body in the trachea, strangulation, postural asphyxia, smothering, or hanging. Only strangulation and hanging can produce damage to cartilage and bone. Depending on the nature of the strangulation, with thumbs, or by garroting, analysis may or may not reveal fractures of the hyoid, thyroid or cricoid cartilage. Hanging may produce similar damage, depending on the placement of the knot, with the possible addition of a fractured dens of the axis (Pollanen and Chiasson, 1996).

Asphyxiation is an unlikely cause of death during war. It is unreliable, putting the attacker and victim in close contact for an extended period of time, is dependent on the attacker being stronger than the victim and on the victim's inability to escape from the attacker. While it may be used as a last resort in hand to hand combat, it is not likely to have been a preferred method of waging war. In modern cases of warfare, death is typically the result of gunshot wounds, explosive injuries and blunt trauma (Aboutanos and Baker, 1997; Danic et al., 1998; Ilic et al., 1999; Taher, 1996).

Asphyxiation is seen in cases of individual violence that flare up suddenly, when no weapon is at hand. Epidemiological studies of violence and homicide reveal asphyxiation as a cause of homicidal death occurs in low frequencies around the world. In a study of 251 victims of homicide in Germany during the period 1978-1988, 29.5% died as a result of strangulation. Women were commonly killed, literally, at the hands of men with whom they were involved in relationships (Fischer et al., 1994). A similar rate of homicide resulting from asphyxiation (31.7%) was observed in a Japanese study of 63 homicidal deaths over the period 1985 to 1994 (Kominato et al., 1997). In contrast, a Swedish study spanning the years 1996-1998 shows a much lower frequency of asphyxiation homicides at only 10% (Ericsson, 2002).

VI. Drowning

Evidence of drowning is difficult to obtain. It is more a matter of eliminating other possibilities, than of proving drowning. Without a witness, evidence from the scene, evidence of bruising, or binding, it is very difficult to determine whether drowning is the result of a homicide, suicide or accident. Traditionally, the skeleton had nothing to offer toward a determination of drowning, but now diatoms are being used to demonstrate that water entered the lungs of a living person, passing through the circulatory system to become lodged in the marrow of the femur (Pollanen et al., 1997).

Drowning is also an unlikely cause of death due to warfare, unless the individuals were involved in a naval battle, or were approaching their target by water. In the former situation the remains should be found in association with a ship. In the latter case, bodies may be left in the water, or removed by relatives after the fighting is over and given a proper burial. If the archaeological evidence suggests that a water approach may have been used during an attack, it is possible that non-fatal injuries could have been sufficient to incapacitate the victim, leaving him vulnerable to drowning. Diatom analysis may help elucidate cause of death in such cases (Pollanen, 1997; Ludes et al., 1996).

3. MANNER OF DEATH

Pattern analysis is the key to determining manner of death. Certain differences exist in terms of the location, type and number of wounds associated with the manner in which an individual dies – homicide, suicide, accident, natural, or unknown. Injuries inflicted in the course of a homicide can occur anywhere on the body, but areas inaccessible to the victim are particularly suggestive. Where there is intent to kill, injuries are directed to the most vulnerable areas – the head, throat and chest. In many cases of interpersonal violence these are the only areas of the body affected (Gilthorpe et al., 1999). During homicidal beatings and kickings the head is a primary target (Murphy, 1991; Strauch et al., 2001). Multiple injuries may be sustained anywhere on the vault, but tend to be directed toward the upper regions (Galloway, 1999; Murphy, 1991).

Analysis of violence and injury patterns has led Filer (1997) to conclude infracranial fractures may, or may not be accidental, but cranial injuries are more likely to be the result of interpersonal violence. The face is a target in both fatal and non-fatal violent episodes. In cases of domestic violence the face, in particular, the mandible, is fractured more than any other part of the body (McDowell and Brogdon, 2003). Female victims tend to know their attackers (Bailey et al., 1988; Greene et al., 1999), while male victims of interpersonal violence often do not know their assailants (Hussain et al., 1994). Men who do not know their attacker suffer similar frequencies of face and hand injuries as women, while males

who incur injuries during violent encounters with other men they know show lower frequencies of face and dorsal hand trauma (Brink et al., 1998).

Torture may be one of the components of a homicide. There are numerous types and variations of physical torture, for example: amputation or crushing of digits; repeated and prolonged beatings over a period of time; crucifixtion; drawing and quartering; hamstringing; gunshot wounds that are not immediately fatal, for the purpose of causing pain and/or immobilization. Torture is less often associated with typical homicide than with punishment for criminals, treatment of enemies during warfare, and serial killers. When mutilation is incorporated into torture, there is a high risk of the victim being killed and victims subjected to torture of the trunk are more likely to die or be killed than those subjected to torture of extremities (Vogel and Brogdon, 2003).

Some victims have the opportunity and ability to fight back, resist or try to protect themselves during an attack. Defensive wounds sustained by the victim in the course of protecting him/herself, or responding to an assailant are clear evidence of homicide. They tend to occur on the hands and forearm in an attempt to ward off, deflect or prevent injury. For this reason, the palmar surfaces of the hand and wrist bones must be carefully examined for evidence of cut or puncture marks indicative of defensive wounds sustained during a stabbing. In cases where blunt trauma is the cause of death, defense wounds are more commonly observed on the forearm in the form of a parry fracture, as the victim attempts to protect his/her head from the weapon. Boxing fractures, observed on the heads and necks of metacarpals, are another form of defensive wound signifying the victim's effort to fight off an attacker (Brink, 1998; Galloway, 1999).

Studies of homicidal beatings reveal some victims are bound and rendered incapable of defensive action (Strauch et al., 2001). Thus, the absence of defensive wounds should not be considered evidence that the manner of death was something other than homicide. While bindings, blindfolds and gags are indicative of homicide, in some forensic contexts and most archaeological contexts these items are not preserved. In situ analysis of the remains by a forensic or skeletal biologist is essential to ensure that transitory evidence, such as the position of the bones of the hands, wrist, feet, ankles, and mandible indicative of binding and gagging will be recovered, and the significance of these observations interpreted correctly.

One final sign of homicide is overkill. Overkill refers to the use of excessive force or the occurrence of numerous fatal injuries. Ericsson and colleagues (2002) recommend using total number of injuries to evaluate the degree of violence, rather than the number of lethal injuries for two reasons: (1) the difficulty in determining whether overlapping areas of blunt trauma all represent individually lethal injuries and, (2) the improbability that perpetrators inflict violence on a victim intending some injuries to be lethal and others not.

In contrast to homicide injuries, suicide wounds tend to occur on accessible areas that are often bared to intensify the effect, e.g., sleeves rolled up to permit the slashing of wrists. Generally the instrument used to inflict the injury is nearby. Although slashing is common, actual stab wounds are quite rare in suicides. With the exception of suicidal gunshot wounds and hanging, where the location and angle of fractures can be used to deduce the manner of death, suicidal injuries may be difficult to observe on the skeleton and even harder to interpret correctly. Wrist slashing, overdosing, and drowning leave little evidence on the skeleton and in the latter two examples can easily be mistaken for accidents.

Accidental injuries tend to be single wounds, occurring on any part of the body. Usually, the instrument is present at the site. In the case of both accidents and homicide, Colles fractures may be present. These occur at the distal end of the radius and are the result of using the hands to break a fall. Colles fractures occur in conjunction with accidents involving falls, but may also occur when a victim attempts to escape an assailant and has the misfortune to stumble (Roberts, 1996). In the latter case, the associated trauma may occur in patterns that are inconsistent with a fall, supporting a determination of homicide.

"Warfare" is not an established category under manner of death. Deaths that occur during war may be classified as homicides, suicides, or "other", although in some countries they may be listed as casualties of war. The official manner of death will depend on which side of the conflict performs the death investigation. In Argentina during the Dirty War (1976-1983), some police forensic doctors disguised the real cause of death on death certificates as part of the governmental cover-up of the disappeared (Doretti and Snow, 2002). Allies of the deceased and international investigators, in contrast, are unequivocal in their determination of homicide where evidence warrants such a finding.

Caution must be exercised when attempting to evaluate manner of death. Unlike cause and mode of death, manner requires the interpretation of evidence relating to the injury (location, pattern, number) and context (proximity of weapon, position of body, blood spatter patterns, etc.), and is, therefore, subject to debate, deliberate falsification, and honest misinterpretation. The clearest evidence of homicide is the occurrence of trauma in association with overkill, defense wounds, binding, gagging, blindfolds and torture.

A closer examination of warfare using two civil conflicts as examples provides the basis for a framework to distinguish deaths resulting from homicide from deaths due to warfare.

4. CHARACTERISTICS OF MODERN CIVIL WARFARE: EXAMPLES FROM ARGENTINA AND RWANDA

According to Kelly (2000) warfare can be distinguished from other forms of violence on the basis of social substitutability, where one group member is substitutable for another. Violence is not personally directed, but directed toward the group. The group is responsible for inflicting injury and liable for restitution of those injuries. The proximate and ultimate causes of warfare are inexorably tied to the social context; together they determine the goal of the conflict. In some cases it is to defeat and subjugate an enemy, e.g., the disappeared of Argentina, in other cases it is to annihilate the enemy, e.g., genocides of Rwanda.

The purpose of the conflict will determine the demographic profile of the victims, the nature of the wounds, the pattern of wounds, the occurrence of torture, the types of weapons used, and the disposition of the remains. In this section, two major conflicts, Argentina's Dirty War of 1976-1983, and Rwanda's Tutsi genocide of 1994, will be compared to demonstrate the difficulty of devising an all-purpose model of human warfare.

In 1976, the military chiefs of the Argentinian army, navy and air force deposed President Isabel Peron, forming a new ruling body called the Junta. In the Dirty War that followed, the Junta's enemies were systematically kidnapped, tortured, and executed by the armed forces and the police. So-called subversives were abducted and taken to a clandestine detention centre, where they were interrogated and tortured for several weeks or months. Afterward they were released, became legal prisoners, or were executed. Almost 9,000 people were "disappeared" during the 8 years the Junta was in power (Doretti and Snow, 2003).

Although the disappeared included individuals from newborns to 70 years old, demographic analysis reveals that 70% of the disappeared were between the ages of 16-35 years at the time of disappearance, and $^2/_3$ were male (Doretti and Snow, 2003). Nearly all died violently from gunshot wounds, many execution style to the back of the head, some in the chest. Fresh or healing fractures from blunt force trauma were also seen. Others showed no signs of trauma to the skeleton, but a number of the disappeared died as the result of electrical torture (Doretti and Snow, 2003). Other forms of torture included hanging, rape, constant beatings, and near drowning (Steadman, 2003), all of which have the potential to leave marks on bone. The bodies of some of the disappeared were dumped from military aircraft while flying over the Argentine Sea. In most cases, however, the victims were buried in unmarked graves in municipal cemeteries (Doretti and Snow, 2003).

The Rwandan genocide tells a different tale of violence. During the spring and early summer of 1994, Hutu Power leaders from the military high command undertook a deliberate program of genocide against their Tutsi neighbours. In just 100 days over 800,000 people were killed (Gourevitch, 1998). In the end, some 1,250,000 Tutsis were massacred. Where the goal of war is extermination, there tends to be a long history conflict and grievances on both sides. The hatred and perceived injustices build until one side believes that the only solution to their problems is to be found in the annihilation of the other, "For those who set about systematically exterminating an entire people...have to want it so badly that they consider it a necessity" (Gourevitch, 1998:18).

In Rwanda the scope of the massacre was such that it is difficult to obtain demographic information and details about injury patterns for the entire country. Nevertheless, as the goal of the Hutu Power party, openly stated on the radio, was to exterminate all Tutsis, and as Hutus received militia training for the sole purpose of killing Tutsis (Gourevitch, 1998), detailed information from one mass grave behind the Kibuye Church is likely indicative of the events that were taking place across the country. The MNI at this site was 493. All age groups from infants to those 45 years and older were represented, but 81% were less than 35 years of age, 44% were children under the age of 15 years, 25% being less than 10 years old (Haglund, pers. comm., 2003). Of those over 15 years of age, 69% (n=156) were female, 39% (n=100) were male (Schmitt, 1998).

Blunt force trauma was the cause of death for 60% of the individuals, 12% died from sharp force trauma, 2% had both lethal sharp and blunt force wounds, 1% showed evidence of "other" injuries including gunshot and shrapnel wounds to the head, 15% demonstrated no evidence of trauma, and 10% were too fragmentary to determine cause of death (Haglund, pers. comm., 2003). Weapons of choice during the genocide were the machete and masu (a club studded with nails), supplemented by a few strategically placed grenades and burst of gunfire (Gourevitch, 1998). Some of the bodies were left where they were killed, in churches and other places of refuge, as in Kibuye. Others were thrown in the river, and still others were buried in mass graves (Gourevitch, 1998).

Both the Argentine Dirty War and the Rwandan genocide, meet Kelly's (2000) criterion of the substitutability of participants that defines warfare. In the Argentine case, the Junta initially sought out particular individuals thought to be subversives, killing them, their families and their associates, but in the end the military leaders were after sympathizers, those who remained indifferent, and the timid (Steadman, 2003). For Rwandans the message was clear from the beginning – all Tutsis must die. Both the Argentine and Rwandan conflicts were civil wars. In Argentina, the enemy was strictly political, in Rwanda political machinations were enacted through a policy of "ethnic cleansing". In these cases, the demography of the dead reflects the politics of the living. The disappeared of the Dirty War were socially, intellectually and politically active people, mostly young men between the ages of 16-35 (70% were males and females between 16-35 years). In contrast, only 37% of the victims of the Kibuye Church massacre were between 16-35 years. The demographic profile of the Tutsi dead reflects the current profile of the living for the entire country (Tutsi and Hutu). According to the CIA World Factbook for 2002, children, 0-14 years represent 41.7% of the population, individuals aged 15-64 years represent 55.4%, and the elderly, 65 years and over, comprise 2.9%.

The nature and pattern of wounds, occurrence of torture, and the instruments used to inflict injuries and pain, are also context specific. The Dirty War was a military operation, designed to eliminate political enemies by death, or intimidation. Torture and repeated beatings were used to elicit information from prisoners. Bodies with multiple fractures, some in different stages of healing, were common, but the primary mode of death was gunshot wound to the skull. During the 8 years of Junta power, over 8,000 people disappeared. The Tutsi genocide, in contrast, was brief and devastating. The weapons were "low tech", primarily machete and masu. The sheer number of perpetrators participating in the massacres resulted in extremely high body counts (estimated at 1.25 million) over a short period of time (spring and summer of 1994). Attacks were intended to be fatal, although some Tutsis managed to survive, leaving them with amputated limbs and other serious injuries (Gourevitch, 1998).

One common thread between the Argentine and Rwandan examples is the disposition of the dead. The bodies of victims were disposed of in several different ways, but in both cases mass graves were used for some of the dead. In Argentina, victims were occasionally dumped into the sea, but more often were buried in the municipal cemetery, among citizens who had died from causes unrelated to war. Some of the disappeared were buried in mass graves, others were buried individually (Doretti and Snow, 2002). In Rwanda, many of the bodies were left in place at sites of refuge, some were thrown in the river, and others were buried in mass graves (Gourevitch, 1998).

5. HOMICIDE VERSUS WARFARE IN A MODERN CONTEXT AND ITS RELEVANCE FOR ARCHAEOLOGICAL POPULATIONS

Distinguishing deaths due to homicide from those of warfare can be problematic, even in a modern context. The Argentine and Rwandan wars demonstrate the extreme variability observed in the physical parameters of warfare: the demographic profile of victims, types of weapons used, type of wounds, patterns of wounds, occurrence of torture, and disposition of remains. Because of this variability, there will be cases where the evidence of warfare is virtually indistinguishable from the patterns associated with homicide deaths. In this section, the characteristics of homicide and warfare are compared within a modern context to provide recommendations for interpreting evidence and recognizing warfare in an archaeological context.

The World Health Assembly declared violence a leading global public health problem in 1996 (Reza et al., 2001). In 1990, an estimated 1, 851, 000 people died of violence related deaths, accounting for approximately 3.7% of all deaths in the world. Suicide was the most common form of violent death (42.5%), followed by homicide (30.4%), and war-related deaths (27.1%) (Reza et al., 2001).

The estimated number of homicides for 1990 was 563, 000, with a male to female ratio of 3.4:1. Age specific homicide rates were highest for females aged 0-4 years, in contrast to males, whose age-specific homicide rates were highest for

15-29 year olds (Reza et al., 2001). An estimated 502, 000 people died as a result of war in 1990. The male to female ratio was 1.3:1. The war-related death rate for females was highest in the 0-4 year old category, with a peak in the 15-29 year and 60-69 year categories. For males, the highest death rate was seen in the 15-29 year old category, but peaks were seen in the same age categories as women, 0-4 and 60-69 years (Reza et al., 2001).

Walker's (2001) observation that the demographic profile of modern warfare parallels that of modern civilian homicides, where the victims are predominately young males in their early twenties, is an over-simplification based on limited comparative data. The sex ratio of victims of violent encounters do favour males, but the ratio decreases with the intensity and scope of the violence, from between 2.8:1 to 5:1 for nonfatal injuries (Iida et al., 2001; Sojat et al., 2001), to 3.4:1 for homicide (Reza et al., 2001) and 1.3:1 for warfare (Reza et al., 2001). In some specific cases of warfare, e.g., the Argentine Dirty War, the victims are primarily young males, but the sex ratio is much lower (2:1) than Walker (2001) argues is usually the case in modern warfare.

On a global level, the demographic profile of victims of warfare mimics the profile of the society, with a high proportion of female and juvenile deaths (Reza et al., 2001; Rojnik et al., 1995). In a review of modern wartime injuries, Aboutanos and Baker (1997) note civilians have been specifically targeted, resulting in higher casualties and fatalities among civilians than soldiers. The proportion of civilians dying in war zones has risen steadily from 10% in WWI, to 50% in WWII, and 80% in subsequent wars (Weinberg and Simmonds, 1995). Women and children account for a large number of war-related deaths, as wars have a devastating effect on the health of civilians by decreasing access to food, water, shelter, and transportation. Wars also interrupt or destroy health infrastructures that normally protect populations from adverse health conditions, or provide timely assistance in medical or health-related crises (Reza et al., 2001). Outbreaks of communicable diseases and increased levels of malnutrition are common complications of war (Toole et al., 1993; Weinberg and Simmonds, 1995); the broader the conflict, the greater the potential for all members of society to be affected by the violence.

A comparison of homicide weapons with weapons of war reveals overlap between the two. Weapons developed for warfare are used in non-combative contexts, both accidentally and intentionally, in areas where disarmament does not occur post-conflict (Meddings, 1997). Conversely, farm, garden and household tools, such as machetes and knives, have been pressed into service as weapons of war during civil conflicts in regions with limited access to technologically advanced weapons; Rwanda and Guatemala, for example (Gourevitch, 1998; Steadman, 2002).

Weapons of opportunity are used by assailants during acts of interpersonal violence, as well as by those engaged in warfare. Homicidal blunt force injuries are frequently inflicted with weapons seized by an assailant during an attack, e.g., hammers, boards, bottles etc. (Murphy, 1991). Everyday

items also become incorporated into arsenals during war. During the 1987-89 conflict between Palestinians and Israeli soldiers on the West Bank and Gaza Strip, 62% of the injuries sustained by the soldiers were the result of thrown stones (Heering et al., 1992). From a forensic or archaeological point of view, it may be necessary to infer the weapon responsible for an injury on the basis of wound characteristics, because the weapon or ammunition may not be associated with, or embedded within, the body.

Analysis of the mode of death for civilian and military deaths during the war in Croatia (1991-1992) reveals the proportion of injured civilians and soldiers with head and neck wounds was not significantly different, nor was there a notable difference in the proportion of civilians and soldiers dying from head and neck wounds. There were similarly no significant differences between civilian and soldier frequencies of wounds to the thorax, or the abdomen (Prgomet et al., 1998). Maxillofacial and associated injuries were of the same type and pattern for civilians and military personnel (Aljinovic-Ratkovic et al., 1995). Civilians and soldiers will suffer comparable types of injuries and die from those injuries at a similar rate within the context of a war.

According to Scope and colleagues (2001), mortality due to military injuries differs from civilian mortality in terms of a greater number of deaths due to penetrating trauma in the former and blunt trauma in the latter. A comparison of war-related deaths to civilian homicides in a modern context reveals this pattern is inconsistent. Fischer and colleagues (1994) report 51.4% of 251 German homicide victims from 1978-1988 died as a result of blunt trauma, 31.9% died of sharp trauma, 29.5% from strangulation, 18.7% from shooting and 4% due to assorted other causes. Combined injuries were common. In a Japanese study of 63 homicides over 10 years, 38.1% of deaths were caused by blunt force injury, 31.7% by asphyxia, 17.5% by stabbing, 9.5% by burns and only 3.2% by shooting (Kominato et al., 1997). Yet in the United States, penetrating trauma due to gunshot wounds is more common than blunt trauma, and is typically attributed to the greater availability of guns in the U.S. compared to other countries (Morrison et al, 2000). Conversely, in wars waged with less advanced weapons, blunt trauma is more common than penetrating trauma, e.g., Rwanda.

With the exception of the new non-lethal weapons, weapons devised for warfare, regardless of the culture or time period, are designed to inflict the maximum number of deaths as fast as possible preferably at a distance. Many of these produce penetrating wounds, e.g., guns in a modern context and arrows or points in the past. Weapons used in close combat can be either penetrating (swords, knives), or blunt (clubs). On an individual level it would be virtually impossible to distinguish a war death from a homicide on the basis of the weapon employed, but inferences of this type may be credible at the population level if high frequencies of weapons injuries are observed in a collection (Walker, 2001).

Combining information about the location of wounds on the body with the type of weapon used will not significantly contribute to the differentiation of deaths due to war and homicide, as both exhibit significant proportions of cranial injuries. The head and neck are the primary targets in assaults and homicides resulting from beating, kicking and gunshot wounds (Murphy, 1991; Strauch et al., 2001). Many victims exhibit injuries exclusively in these areas (Gilthorpe et al., 1999). During war, the mortality rate is higher in victims with head and neck injuries than for the thorax, or abdomen (Prgomet et al., 1998). A review of 26 conflicts since 1914 revealed a higher than expected frequency of head and neck injuries compared to the rest of the body. During the Falklands Campaign and conflicts in Northern Ireland, 3-8% of all casualties sustained fractures to the middle or lower third of the facial skeleton (Dobson et al., 1989). Of the 7,043 wounded civilians and soldiers treated at the Dr. Josip Bencevic General Hospital in Slavonski Brod during the 1991-1992 war in Croatia, 728 (10.3%) were treated for head and neck injuries.

The occurrence of torture may be an important distinction between homicide and war-related deaths. Torture frequently occurs within the context of war as part of a campaign of widespread persecution and human rights violations (Silove, 1999). The global prevalence of torture is so high that several foundations and institutions have been established for the sole purpose of identifying and treating survivors of torture (Edston, 1999; McGorry, 1995; Reid et al., 1990). At the Centre for Torture and Trauma Survivors in Stockhom, 201 subjects from 34 countries were the focus of a 5-year study to understand the physical markers of torture, for the purpose of educating physicians around the world to recognize such evidence in their own practices (Edston, 1999). Physicians have developed surveys tools, such as the Harvard Trauma Questionnaire, which have been translated into several other languages to facilitate the process of identifying victims of torture worldwide (Halepota and Wasif, 2001). Assessing the validity of these tools is an ongoing component of the medical literature (Willis and Gonzalez, 1998), as are publications dealing with the treatment of the physical and psychological effects of torture (Gray, 1998; Silove et al., 2002; Weinstein et al., 1996).

Torture is far less common within the context of homicide, the exception being the sexually sadistic serial killer. The modus operandi for 6 of 27 (22%) serial killers whose histories were examined by Promish and Lester (1999) included torture. Warren and colleagues (1996) determined that torture is a common occurrence in sexually sadistic serial killers who enjoy controlling and degrading others. In contrast, numerous large-scale analyses of violent injuries and homicide deaths expressly state trauma to the head is the sole injury inflicted on the victim (Murphy, 1991; Strauch et al., 2001), or make no mention of torture in their detailed investigation of victim wounding (Brink et al., 1998; Fischer et al., 1994; Howe and Crilly, 2002). Even studies demonstrating an increase in the intensity and frequency of violence, which specifically address the phenomenon of overkill do not report evidence of torture (Ericsson and Thiblin, 2002). A search of PubMed, an online index of worldwide medical references compiled by the National Library of Medicine, accessed April 2003, revealed no publications addressing the occurrence of torture in homicides

unrelated to serial killers. Given the low frequency of serial killings in modern society, evidence of torture may be an important indicator of warfare in the past.

The prevalence of amputated limbs in a burial context may also prove useful as an indicator of warfare. Amputation is a common surgical intervention employed on battlefields to remove infected, gangrenous limbs, or limbs torn apart by explosives (Aldea et al., 1987; Kirkup, 1995; Petri and Aguila, 2002; Wiley, 1952). Skeletal collections with high frequencies of amputees, or burial pits containing amputated limbs, suggest increased levels of violence. In a forensic context removal of limbs typically takes place shortly after the victim's death. Dismemberment is used by perpetrators trying to (1) transport/dispose of bodies, (2) conceal the identity of the victim (Rajs et al., 1998).

Amputation can be distinguished from dismemberment by the pattern of destruction to the body and the presence of healing on the retained limb. An amputation may be made at any point on the shaft, depending on the location of the fracture or necrosis, but biomechanical considerations, such as maximizing energy expenditure and facilitating prosthetic fitting, play an important role in the decision process (Hartford et al., 1994). Dismemberment, whether for transport or concealment, typically involves the removal of the victim's head. When the perpetrator has some knowledge of anatomy, e.g., butcher, physician, veterinarian, or hunter, he may disarticulate the limbs at the joints. This pattern is never seen in amputations because of biomechanical considerations, the loss of joint mobility, and the importance of providing a tissue pad to protect the truncated bone.

A final consideration in the comparison of homicide and war-related deaths is the issue of body disposal. In many cases of homicide, the body is recovered at the scene of the crime, often in the home of the victim (Kominato et al., 1997). In the West, the disposition of homicide victims' remains are treated no differently than those dying from other causes. Clandestine burials and disposition of remains by the perpetrator exhibit a completely different, distinctive pattern. Killam (1990) has conducted a study of body "dump" sites to establish patterns associated with illegal disposal of human remains. The primary concerns of an individual attempting to conceal a body are haste and secrecy, thus "dump" sites often exhibit the following features:

1. they are near a road or parking area

2. they are usually downhill or on the same level as the road

3. they are in soil that is easy to dig into (not rocky or full of tree roots)

4. they are secluded (not within sight of nearby houses)

5. they are accessible by flashlight (the dump may have taken place at night)

6. they are on land owned or familiar to the suspect

7. they are near the crime scene, particularly if done in haste

8. they may take advantage of pre-existing features, e.g., well, landfill, water (Killam, 1990:17).

The disposition of casualties of war is extremely variable, depending on the nature and intensity of the conflict, the duration of the hostilities, the number of dead, whether the war takes place domestically or in a foreign land, cultural attitudes toward war dead/heros, whether the victim was a soldier or civilian, and potentially unlimited additional factors. This variability makes it difficult to contrast disposition patterns of homicide and war-related deaths, particularly when the two contexts overlap, as in modern gang warfare. Gang warfare can be viewed as civil warfare at the most local level, where Kelly's (2000) criterion of substitutability is evident, but conflict is enacted within the framework of everyday life. The factors contributing to the development and maintenance of gang warfare may parallel those of larger conflicts, but the fatalities and combatants are treated as victims and perpetrators of homicide; victims being buried alongside other members of the community in a virtually indistinguishable manner.

Amongst the variability of wartime body disposal, the phenomenon of mass burials is distinctive from homicide-related disposition of remains. Typical cases of homicide involve a single death. In atypical cases, serial killers tend to acquire and dispose of one victim at a time, while mass murders (usually mass shooting) often turn their weapons upon themselves, or simply leave their victims where they fall (Hempel et al., 1999). Mass graves may be a key factor distinguishing war fatalities from homicide, but other variables must be considered to distinguish mass war graves from plague pits, ossuaries, sacrifices, and other forms of communal burial.

DISCUSSION AND CONCLUSIONS

The physical remnants of warfare - injury patterns, body counts, and burial context - do not produce a universal signature. Convincingly demonstrating the occurrence of warfare in past populations requires a systematic approach to the recognition of trauma, the differentiation of acts of violence from accidental injuries, and the analysis of patterns in the osteological record, the archaeological context and the bioarchaeological interface, i.e., positional evidence of binding and gagging, taphonomic changes, etc. Correctly utilizing the concepts of cause, manner and mode of death will facilitate the process of identifying, analyzing and interpreting the osteological evidence of violence.

Cause of death deals with the specific injury responsible for the fatal outcome. It involves documenting wounds with respect to vital organs and assessing the degree of damage to vital centres of the body. Although it is not feasible to evaluate the damage to vital organs in an archaeological context, it is possible to distinguish perimortem trauma from postmortem damage and assess the skeleton for evidence of injury, documenting (1) the type of lesion, (2) the number of lesions, (3) the location of injury (bone, side, aspect, surface), (4) the size of the wound, (5) the shape of the wound, (6) the presence of foreign matter, (7) the relationship of bony injury to underlying anatomical structures, and (8) evidence of healing. This information, combined with the angle of weapon/bullet entry, direction and force of blows and the patterns and timing of events, are used to establish mode of death.

Osteologists and paleopathologists have incorporated most aspects of cause and mode of death in their analyses of past populations, although the two are sometimes confused or combined into a single analysis. In an archaeological context the mode of death can be ascertained more accurately than the cause, since it is not necessary to have access to soft tissues to establish most modes of death. Having identified evidence of trauma, the next step is to interpret its nature. Pattern analysis is used to determine the manner of death. Table 1 provides an overview of key characteristics of accident, suicide, homicide and warfare.

Using these guidelines it is possible to identify specific evidence of malevolent intent, as recommended by Walker (2000). The use of this approach will help prevent researchers from underestimating the frequency of violent injury in a collection. Walker (2000) suggests limiting the identification of violence to cases in which malevolence is clear, assuming

Table 1. Manner of Death

Wound Traits	Accident	Suicide	Homicde	Warfare
Location	anywhere	accessible	head & neck	head & neck
Number	usually 1	1 fatal	multiple, fatal & nonfatal	multiple, fatal & nonfatal
Defense Wound	none	none	may occur	may occur
Offence Wound	none	none	may occur	may occur
Additional	may exhibit Colles fracture	clothing removed stabbing rare	binding, gag, blindfold	binding, gag, blindfold
Diagnostic		hesitation marks	overkill	torture

that less obvious examples of malevolence (Walker's example involves several arrows in a skeleton from a mass grave accompanied by other young men exhibiting cut marks consistent with scalping) are more likely cases of accidental injury. Nonviolence should not be the default interpretation in equivocal cases. Accidental and suicidal deaths exhibit distinctive characteristics that should be considered when attempting to differentiate violent from nonviolent injuries in the bioarchaeological record.

Homicide and warfare share several key characteristics. When examining a diachronous skeletal collection for evidence of warfare, it is important to approach the data from several perspectives and not be limited by expectations about the nature of warfare. One notion that may be impeding our recognition and interpretation of ancient conflict is the idea that warfare is inevitably lethal, and will result in large numbers of war dead. Even with modern warfare's weapons of mass destruction, the number of wounded exceeds the number of dead (Coupland and Meddings, 1999). In ancient conflicts involving low velocity weapon injuries, the number of survivors would have exceeded the number of fatalities, with the exception of massacres, which exhibit their own distinctive characteristics. In these cases, high frequencies of healed trauma in a cemetery may be more indicative of warfare than unhealed, fatal trauma.

Walker (2001) suggests the majority of injuries sustained by ancient people are not discernable in an archaeological context because soft tissue injuries exceed fractures in frequency during violent interaction. In an examination of 950 consecutive patients an urban university hospital in London, Hussain and colleagues (1994) found that the most common cause of soft tissue injury was falls, in contrast to fractures where the main cause was interpersonal violence. True, we will not be able to identify every minor injury arising from every skirmish between any two members of past cultures, but significant injuries do tend to have significant effects.

Comparative analysis of demographic profiles for victims of homicide and warfare suggests the demographic profile of war is more variable than homicide; the former depends on the nature of the conflict, while the latter consistently shows higher fatalities among young men (Panichabhongse et al., 1999; Reza et al, 2001; Seltzer, 1994). Women and children are just as vulnerable in certain types of conflicts as men, e.g., massacres, raids, civil war. If the conflict is endemic or extended, as in the case of a siege, the members of the society may suffer reduced health and begin to exhibit nontraumatic manifestations of warfare resulting from poor living conditions that affect nutrition, health care, and sanitation. If analysis of the archaeological environment indicates the physical requirements to maintain proper nutrition and sustain health were present, yet the population exhibits high levels of stress indicators, social and cultural factors, such as warfare should be considered.

Warfare may be waged by a minority and target only a small proportion of the population, e.g., gang warfare and the Argentinian Dirty War, resulting in relatively few deaths. In both examples, mass graves are not necessary to accommodate the dead. Such wartime fatalities may be treated to the same disposal practices as other members of the society, if the social structure of the community is not compromised by the fighting. The lack of universal burial practices for victims of warfare may lead to difficulties in recognizing large-scale conflict in the archaeological record, if one relies on the single parameter of body disposal. Multiple lines of evidence must be evaluated in order to convincingly demonstrate the presence of warfare in archaeological populations.

Given the variety of reasons people engage in warfare and the ends they hope to achieve, it is unrealistic to expect warfare to exhibit a single diagnostic pattern in the bioarchaeological record. Analysis of modern warfare and homicide exhibit greater variability in injury patterns and victim demography for the former compared to the latter. Body counts in modern warfare range from a few deaths to millions, depending on the reasons for the conflict. The burial context of war dead includes graves indistinguishable from others in the cemetery, to mass graves. Our potential to recognize violence, particularly warfare, in the bioarchaeological record is impaired by our assumptions concerning: (1) the nature of conflict; (2) the type and seriousness of injuries sustained; (3) the demography of war dead; (4) the number of fatalities; and (5) the burial context. Analysis of modern warfare and homicide demonstrates the potential scope of characteristics that may apply to ancient warfare, encouraging a broader perspective to the study of conflict in past populations.

Authors address

Tracy Rogers, Ph.D.
Department of Anthropology and Religion
University of Toronto at Mississauga,
3359 Mississauga Road North,
Mississauga, Ontario, Canada l5l 1C6
trogers@utm.utoronto.ca

References

ABOUTANOS, M. B., and S. P. BAKER. 1997. Wartime Civilian Injuries: Epidemiology and Intervention Strategies. *Journal of Trauma* 43(4): 719-726.

ALDEA, P. A., ALDEA, G. S., SHAW, W. W. 1987. A Historical Perspective on the Changing Methods of Management for Major Trauma of the Lower Extremity. *Surgery, Gynecology and Obstetrics* 165(6):549-562.

ALJINOVIC-RATKOVIC, N., VIRAG, M., MACAN, D., ZAJC, I., BAGATIN, M., UGLESIC, V., KNEZEVIC, G., GRGUREVIC, J., KOBLER, P., SVAJHLER, T. 1995. Maxillofacial War Injuries in Civilians and Servicemen during the Aggression Against Croatia. *Military Medicine* 160(3):121-124.

BAILEY, B. M., CARR, R. J., BERMINGHAM, D. F., SHEPHERD, R. G. 1998. A Comparative Study of Psychosocial Data on Patients with Maxillofacial Injuries in an Urban Population – a Preliminary Study. *The British Journal of Oral and Maxillofacial Surgery* 26(3):199-204.

BERRYMAN, H. E., and S. A. SYMES. 1998. "Recognizing Gunshot and Blunt Cranial Trauma Through Fracture Interpretation", in *Forensic Osteology: Advances in the Identification of Human Remains (2nd edition)*. Edited by K. J. Reichs, pp. 333-352. Springfield IL: Charles C. Thomas.

BRINK, O., VESTERBY, A., JENSEN, J. 1998. Pattern of Injuries due to Interpersonal Violence. *Injury* 29(9):705-709.

BROGDON, B. G. 1998. "Forensic Radiology". New York: CRC Press.

BYERS, S. 2002. *Introduction to Forensic Anthropology.* Boston: Allyn and Bacon.

CARMEN, J. 1997. "Appoaches to Violence", in *Material Harm*. Edited by J. Carmen, pp. 1-23. Glasgow: Cruithne Press.

COUPLAND, R. M., and MEDDINGS, D. R. 1999. Mortality Associated with Use of Weapons in Armed conflicts, Wartime Atrocities, and Civilian Mass Shootings: Literature Review. *British Medical Journal* 319:407-410.

DANIC, D., PRGOMET, D., MILICIC, D., LEOVIC, D., PUNTARIC, D. 1998. War Injuries to the Head and Neck. *Military Medicine* 163(2):117-119.

DOBSON, J. E., NEWELL, M. J., SHEPHERD, J. P. 1989. Trends in Maxillofacial Injuries in War-Time (1914-1986). *The British Journal of Oral and Maxillofacial Surgery* 27(6):441-450.

DORETTI, M., and C. C. SNOW. 2003. "Forensic Anthropology and Human Rights: The Argentine Experience", in *Hard Evidence: Case Studies in Forensic Anthropology*. Edited by D. W. Steadman, pp. 290-310. New Jersey: Prentice Hall.

EDSTON, E. 1999. [Bodily Evidence Can Reveal Torture. 5-year Experience of Torture Documentation] abstract [article in Swedish]. *Lakartidningen* 96(6):628-631.

ERICSSON, A., and I. THIBLIAN. 2002. Injuries Inflicted on Homicide Victims. A Longitudinal Victiminologic Study of Lethal Violence. *Forensic Science International* 130:133-139.

FISCHER, J., KLEEMANN, W.J., TROGER, H.D. 1994. Types of Trauma in Cases of Homicide. *Forensic Science International* 68(3):161-167.

FILER, J. M. 1997. "Ancient Egypt and Nubia as a Source of Information for Cranial Injuries", in *Material Harm*. Edited by J. Carmen, pp 47-74. Glasgow: Cruithne Press.

GALLOWAY, A. 1999. *Broken Bones*. Springfield, IL: Charles C. Thomas.

GILTHORPE, M. S., WILSON, R. C., MOLES, D. R., BEDIS, R. 1999. Variations in Admissions to Hospital for Head Injury and Assault to the Head Part 1: Age and Gender. *The British Journal of Oral and Maxillofacial Surgery* 37:294-300.

GRAY, G. 1998. Treatment of Survivors of Political Torture: Administrative and Clinical Issues. *The Journal of Ambulatory Care Management* 21(2):39-42.

GREENE, D., MAAS, C. S., CARVALHO, G., RAVEN, R. 1999. Epidemiology of Facial Injury in Female Blunt Assault Trauma Cases. *Archives of Facial Plastic Surgery* 1(4):288-291.

GOUREVITCH, P. 1998. *We Wish to Inform You that Tomorrow We Will be Killed With Our Families*. New York: Farrar Straus and Giroux.

HALEPOTA, A. A., WASIF, S. A. 2001. Harvard Trauma Questionnaire Urdu Translation: the Only Cross-Culturally validated Screening Instrument for the Assessment of Trauma and Torture and their Sequelae. *Journal of the Pakistan Medical Association* 51(8):285-290.

HARTFORD, J. M., ABDU, W. A., MAYOR, M. B. 1994. Reconstructive Amputation after Grade IIIC Open Tibial Fracture. One Method of Preserving Residual Limb Length. *Journal of Orthopedic Trauma* 8(4):354-358.

HEERING, S. L., SHOHAT, T., LERMAN, Y., DANON, Y. L. 1992. The Epidemiology of Injuries Sustained by Israeli Troops During the Unrest in the Territories Administered by Israel, 1987-89. *Israel Journal of Medical Sciences* 28(6):341-344.

HEMPEL, A. G., MELOY, J. R., RICHARDS, T. C. 1999. *The Journal of the American Academy of Psychiatry and the Law* 27(2):213-225.

HOUCK, M. C. 1998. "Skeletal Trauma and the Individualization of Knife Marks in Bones", in *Forensic Osteology: Advances in the Identification of Human Remains (2nd edition)*. Edited by K. J. Reichs, pp. 410-424. Springfield IL: Charles C. Thomas.

HOWE, A., and CRILLY, M. 2002. Violence in the Community: A Health Service View from a UK Accident and Emergency Department. *Public Health* 116:15-21.

HUMPHREY, J. H. and D. L. HUTCHINSON. 2001. Macroscopic Characteristics of Hacking Trauma. *Journal of Forensic Sciences* 46:228-233.

HUSSAIN, K., WIJETUNGE, D. B., GRUBNIC, S., JACKSON, I. T. 1994. A Comprehensive Analysis of Craniofacial Trauma. *Journal of Trauma* 36(1):34-47.

IIDA, S. KOGO, M., SUGIURA, T., MIMA, T., MATSUYA, T. 2001. Retrospecitve Analysis of 1502 Patients with Facial Fractures. *International Journal of Oral and Maxillofacial Surgery* 30(4):286-290.

ILIC, N., PETRICEVIC, A., TANFARA, S., MIMICA, Z., RADONIC, V., TRIPKOVIC, A., FRLETA ILIC, N. 1999. War Injuries to the Chest. *Acta Chriurgica Hungarica* 38(1):43-47.

KELLY, R. C. 2000. *Warless Societies and the Origin of War.* Ann Arbor: University of Michigan Press.

KILLAM, E. W. 1990. *The Detection of Human Remains.* Springfield IL: Charles C. Thomas.

KIRKUP, J. 1995. Perceptions of Amputation Before and After Gunpowder. *Vesalius* 1(2):51-58.

KOMINATO, Y., SHIMADA, I., HATA, N., TAKIZAWA, H., FUJIKURA, T. 1997. Homicide Patterns in the Toyama Prefecture, Japan. *Medicine, Science and the Law* 37(4):316-320.

LOVELL, N. C. 1997. Trauma Analysis in Paleopathology. *Yearbook of Physical Anthropology* 40:139-170.

LUDES, B., COSTE, M., TRACQUI, A., MANGIN, P. 1996. Continuous River Monitoring of the Diatoms in the Diagnosis of Drowning. *Journal of Forensic Sciences* 41(3): 425-428.

MANN, R. W., AND D. W. OWSLEY. 1992. Human Osteology: Key to the Sequence of Events in a Postmortem Shooting. *Journal of Forensic Sciences* 37(5):1386-1392.

MARGERISON, B. J., and KNÛSEL, C. J. 2002. Paleodemographic Comparison of a Catastrophic and an Attritional Death Assemblage. *American Journal of Physical Anthropology* 199:134-143.

MCDOWELL, J. D., and BROGDON, B. G. 2003. "Abuse of Intimate Partners", in *A Radiologic Atlas of Abuse, Torture, Terrorism, and Inflicted Trauma*. Edited by B.G. Brogdon, H. Vogel, J. D. McDowell, pp. 45-60. New York: CRC Press.

MCGORRY, P. 1995. Working with Survivors of Torture and Trauma: the Victorian Foundation for Survivors of Torture in Perspective. *The Australian and New Zealand Journal of Psychiatry* 29(3):463-472.

MEDDINGS, D. R. 1997. Weapons Injuries During and After Periods of Conflict: Retrospective Analysis. *British Medical Journal* 315:1417-1420.

MERBS, C. 1989. "Trauma", in *Reconstruction of Life from the Human Skeleton*. Edited by M.Y. Iscan and K. A. R. Kennedy, pp. 161-189. New York: Wiley-Liss.

MORRISON, A., STONE, D. H., 2000. Eurorisc Working Group. Trends in Injury Mortality Among Yound People in the European Union: A Report from the EURORISC Working Group. *Journal of Adolescent Health* 27:130-135.

MURPHY, G. K. 1991. "Beaten to death". An Autopsy Series of Homicidal Blunt Force Injuries. *The American Journal of Forensic Medicine Pathology* 12(2):98-101.

ORTNER, D. J., and PUTSCHAR, W. G. J. 1985. *Identification of Pathological conditions in Human Skeletal Remains.* Washington: Smithsonian Institution Press.

PANICHABHONGSE, V., SMATIVAT, V., WATANAKAJORN, T., KASANTIKUL, V. 1999. Homicide: A Report of 4,122 cases from Bangkok and Provinces. *Journal of the Medical Association of Thailand* 82(9):849-854.

PETRI, R. P., and AGUILA, E. 2002. The Military Upper Extremity Amputee. *Physical Medicine and Rehabilitation Clinics of North America* 13(1):17-43.

POLLANEN, M. S. 1997. The Diagnostic Value of the Diatom Test for Drowning, II. Validity: Analysis of Diatoms in Bone Marrow and Drowning Medium. *Journal of Forensic Sciences* 42(2):286-290.

POLLANEN, M. S., CHEUNG, C., CHIASSON, D. A. 1997. The Diagnostic Value of the Diatom Test for Drowning, I. Utility: A Retrospective Analysis of 771 Cases of Drowning in Ontario Canada. *Journal of Forensic Sciences* 42(2): 281-285.

POLLANEN, M. S. and D. A. CHIASSON. 1996. Fracture of the Hyoid Bone in Strangulation: Comparison of Fractured and Unfractured Hyoids from Victims of Strangulation. *Journal of Forensic Sciences* 41(4):110-113.

PRGOMET, D., DANIC, D., MILICIC, D., PUNTARIO, D., SOLDO-BUTKOVI, S., JELIC, J., JAKOVINA, K., LEOVIC, D. 1998. Mortality Caused by War Wounds to the Head and Neck Encountered at the Slavonski Brod Hospital During the 1991-1992 War in Croatia. *Military Medicine* 163(7):482-485.

PROMISH, D. I., and LESTER, D. 1999. Classifying Serial Killers. *Forensic Science International* 105:155-159.

QUATREHOMME, G., and M. Y. I. ISCAN. 1999. Characteristics of Gunshot Wounds in the Skull. *Journal of Forensic Sciences* 44(3):568-576.

RAJS, J., LUNDSTROM, M., BROBERG, M., LIDBERG, L., LINDQUIST, O. 1988. Criminal Mutilation of the Human Body in Sweden – a Thirty-Year Medico-Legal and Forensic Psychiatric Study. *Journal of Forensic Sciences* 43(3):563-580.

REICHS, K. J. 1998. "Postmortem Dismemberment: Recovery, analysis and Interpretation", in *Forensic Osteology: Advances in the Identification of Human Remains (2nd edition).* Edited by K. J. Reichs, pp. 353-188. Springfield IL: Charles C. Thomas.

REID, J., SILOVE, D., TARN, R. 1990. The Development of the New South Wales Service for the Treatment and Rehabilitation of Torture and Trauma Survivors (STARTTS): The First Year. *The Australian and New Zealand Journal of Psychiatry* 24(4):486-495.

REZA, A., MERCY, J. A., KRUG, E. 2001. Epidemiology of Violent Deaths in the World. *Injury Prevention* 7:104-111.

ROBERTS, C. A. 1996. "Forensic Anthropology 2: Positive Identification of the Individual; Cause and Manner of Death", in *Studies in Crime: An Introduction to Forensic Archaeology.* Edited by J. Hunter, C. Roberts, and A. Martin, pp. 122-138. London: Routledge.

ROJNIK, B., ANDOLSEK-JERAS, L., OBERSNEL-KVEDER, D. 1995. Women in difficult Circumstances: War Victims and Refugees. *International Journal of Gynecology and Obstetrics* 48:311-315.

SAUER, N. J. 1984. "Manner of Death: Skeletal Evidence of Blunt and Sharp Instrument Wounds", in *Human Identification: Case Studies in Forensic Anthropology.* Edited by T. A. Rathbun and J. E. Buikstra. Springfield IL: Charles C. Thomas.

SAUER, N. J. 1998. "The Timing of Injuries and Manner of Death: Distinguishing Among Antemortem, Perimortem and Postmortem Trauma", in *Forensic Osteology: Advances in the Identification of Human Remains (2nd edition).* Edited by K. J. Reichs, pp. 321-332. Springfield IL: Charles C. Thomas.

SCHMITT, S. 1998. Stephan Schmitt's Human Rights and Forensic Anthropology Website. http://garnet.acns.fsu.edu/~sss4407/ accessed February 2003.

SCOPE, A., FARKASH, U., LYNN, M., ABARGEL, A., ELDAD, A. 2001. Mortality Epidemiology in Low-Intensity Warfare: Israel Defense Force's Experience. *Injury* 32:1-3.

SELTZER, F. 1994. Trend in Mortality from violent Deaths: Suicide and Homicide, United States, 1960-1991. *Statistical Bulletin of Metropolitan Insurance Company* 75(2):10-18.

SILOVE, D. 1999. The Psychological Effects of Torture, Mass Human Rights Violations, and Refugee Trauma: Toward an Integrated Conceptual Framework. *The Journal of Nervous and Mental Disease* 187(4):200-207.

SILOVE, D., STEEL, Z., MCGORRY, P. MILES, V., DROBNY, J. 2002. The Impact of Torture on Post-Traumatic Stress Symptoms in War-Affected Tamil Refugees and Immigrants. *Comprehensive Psychiatry* 43(1):49-55.

STEADMAN, D. W. 2003. "Applications of Forensic Anthropology", in *Hard Evidence: Case Studies in Forensic Anthropology.* Edited by D. W. Steadman, pp. 245-255. New Jersey: Prentice Hall.

STEWART, T. D. 1979. *Essentials of Forensic Anthropology.* Springfield IL: Charles C. Thomas.

STRAUCH, H., WIRTH, I., TAYMOORIAN, U., GESERICH, G. 2001. Kicking to Death – Forensic and Criminological Aspects. *Forensic Science International* 123:165-171.

SOJAT, A. J., MEISAMI, T., SANDOR, G. K. B., CLOKIE, C. M. L. 2001. The Epidemiology of Mandibular Fractures Treated at the Toronto General Hospital: A Review of 246 Cases. *Journal of the Canadian Dental Association* 67(11): 640-644.

TAHER, A. A. 1996. Craniomaxillofacial Injuries: Experience in Tehran. *Journal of Craniofacial Surgery* 7(5):384-393.

TOOLE, M. J., GALSON, S., BRADY, W. 1993. Are War and Public Health Compatible? *Lancet* 341(8854):1193-1196.

VOGEL, H. 2003. "Electric Torture", in *A Radiologic Atlas of Abuse, Torture, Terrorism, and Inflicted Trauma.* Edited by B.G. Brogdon, H. Vogel, and J. D. McDowell, pp 119-121. New York: CRC Press.

VOGEL, H., and BROGDON, B. G. 2003 "Section II: Torture", in *A Radiologic Atlas of Abuse, Torture, Terrorism, and Inflicted Trauma.* Edited by B.G. Brogdon, H. Vogel, and J. D. McDowell, pp 105-107. New York: CRC Press.

WAKELY, J. 1997. "Identification and Analysis of Violent and Non-violent Head Injuries in Osteo-archaeological Material", in *Material Harm.* Edited by J. Carmen, pp. 24-46. Glasgow: Cruithne Press.

WALKER, P. L. 2001. A Bioarchaeological Perspective on the History of Violence. *Annual Review of Anthropology* 30:573-596.

WALSH-HANEY, H. A. 1999. Sharp-force Trauma Analysis and the forensic Anthropologist: Techniques Advocated by William R. Maples, Ph.D. *Journal of Forensic Sciences* 44(4):720-723.

WARREN J.I, HAZELWOOD R.R, DIETZ P.E. 1996. The sexual sadistic serial killer. *Journal of Forensic Sciences* 41(6):970-974.

WEINBERG, J., and S. Simmonds. 1995. Public Health, Epidemiology and War. *Social Science and Medicine* 40(12):1663-1669.

WEINSTEIN, H. M., Dansky, L., Iacopina, V. 1996. Torture and War Trauma Survivors in Primary Care Practice. *The Western Journal of Medicine* 165(3):112-118.

WENHAM, S. J. 1989. "Anatomical Interpretations of Anglo-Saxon Weapon injuries", in *Weapons and warfare in Anglo-Saxon England.* Edited by S. Chadwick Hawkes, pp. 123-139. Oxford: Oxford Committee for Archaeology Monograph No. 21.

WHITE, T. D. 1992. *Prehistoric Cannibalism.* New Jersey: Princeton University Press.

WILEY, B. I. 1952. *The life of Billy Yank. The Common Soldier of the Union.* New York: Bobbs-Merrill Publishers.

WILLIS, G. B., GONZALEZ, A. 1998. Methodological issues in the use of Survey Questionnaires to Assess the Health Effects of Torture. *The Journal of Nervous and Mental Disease* 186(5):283-289.

The World Factbook, 2002 www.odci.gov/cia/publications/factbook/index.html

OSTEOLOGICAL EVIDENCE FOR MESOLITHIC AND NEOLITHIC VIOLENCE: PROBLEMS OF INTERPRETATION

M.K. JACKES

Abstract: Initial interpretations of Mesolithic Portuguese material as evidence for violence are questioned: the alternative suggestion is of accidental trauma, especially in childhood. A situation of undoubted extreme interpersonal violence in Kenya is shown to relate to within-population conflict caused by external pressures. Intensified violence between North American groups of Northeast Woodland peoples in the seventeenth can also be related to external factors (and constraints on resources): though documented ethnohistorically, the osteological evidence for this violence is extremely limited, demonstrating that absence of evidence is not to be relied upon. A Neolithic Chinese site is examined next, as the focus of the paper, since it provides clear physical evidence of violence, despite the lack of archaeological recognition of conflict, pointing to the need to be wary of the interpretations in this sensitive area of anthropological study. The background of the Jiangzhai sample is described and it is noted that 64% of the victims were female. Meggitt's research on violence within and between groups is cited in the following discussion, and the conclusions focus around the need for care in concluding that violence has or has not occurred; the need to avoid simplistic explanations for evidence of violence and the necessity of setting that evidence within a broad context – one with chronological and social/geographical depth and breadth; and the need for sensitivity in recording and interpreting violence.

Keywords: interspersonal violence, skeletal trauma, Mesolithic Portugal, Jiangzhai Yangshao China, Iroquoian Ontario

INTRODUCTION

Accurate recognition of the presence of violence in a skeletal sample is not a straight forward matter. Interpretation of the evidence cannot be pushed very far beyond simple description, despite Walker's (2001:2) contention that osteologists have available to them evidence which is "immune to the interpretative difficulties posed by literary sources." In this paper I examine Mesolithic and Neolithic Portuguese burials and previously undescribed material from a Neolithic Chinese site, but I will use examples from ethnographic literature and from my own research on human skeletal material in different areas and from different time periods (pre-Contact Ontario, 20th century material from Kenya) to illustrate the problems of interpretation.

PORTUGAL

From 1984 to 1989 I was involved in a project to analyse and describe the human remains from the classic Mesolithic sites at Muge (Moita do Sebastião and CabeHo da Arruda) as well as a number of Neolithic sites in Portugal (Jackes *et al.* 1997; Lubell *et al.* 1994). Cranial analysis was done in collaboration with Christopher Meiklejohn, and postcranial observations on the Mesolithic material were made in collaboration with an experienced physician, also trained in osteology, Gerd Weih. We observed some, very limited, evidence that might be interpreted to have resulted from violence.

Among the skeletons from Moita do Sebastião was one (Ossada 2) where a broken bladelet is still embedded below the sustenaculum tali of a right calcaneus. While an accident, rather than violence, might be a reasonable explanation, there was the possibility of interpersonal violence because of the presence of forearm fractures in two females (see APPENDIX 1:1 for a summary of the Portuguese skeletal elements discussed here). Moita Ossada 25a had a healed fracture in the distal third of the right ulna (Figure 1a), and Moita Ossada 10 an interesting lower midshaft pseudarthrosis in the right ulna (Figure 1b). This latter individual, represented by fragmentary remains only, also had slight abnormalities of the right clavicle and proximal ulna which accorded with unusual function of the right arm over a long period. An abnormality of the left acetabulum was also noted. In addition, there was Moita Ossada 30, consisting of two individuals, incomplete and mixed, one a short and heavy male, and one a lighter built individual who was taller, and perhaps female. The distal third of a right ulna shaft had a perfectly aligned healed fracture, perhaps greenstick (a childhood injury in which a bone is not fractured across the shaft) (Figure 1c). Unusual radial morphology perhaps also indicated fracturing, but the radii were too fragmentary to reach a positive conclusion.

Trauma to the forearm, perhaps caused by an attempt to parry a blow, has long been considered a clear indication of violence – a classic "night-stick fracture" occurs in the distal third of the ulnar shaft. While midshaft and lower midshaft forearm fractures can result from a fall on the hand as well as from a direct blow on the forearm (Adams 1972:153, 158), if there was no dislocation or displacement a fall is a less likely cause than a blow. A direct blow sustained by a fairly young individual could have a reasonably well-aligned outcome, but a heavy fall would be likely to result in greater angulation. Falls onto the outstretched hand are most likely to fracture the head of the radius in young adults, or to result in a Colles'

23

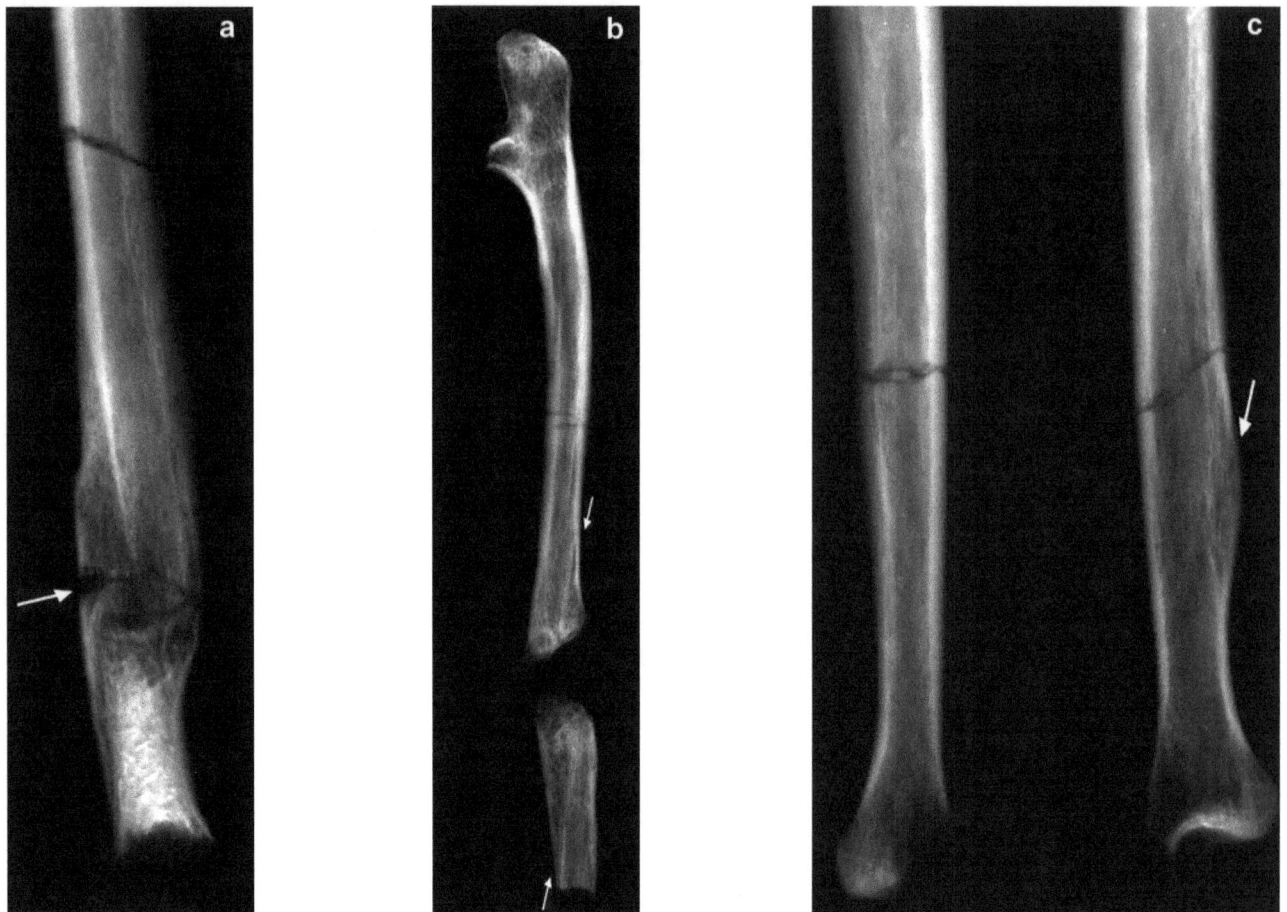

Figure 1a Moita do Sebastião Ossada 25a: healed fracture in the distal third of the right ulna
(x ray: 11 14/7/84 Santiago do CacJm).
Figure 1b Moita do Sebastião Ossada 10: right ulna with psuedarthrosis at midshaft Figure D
(x ray: 7 14/7/84 Santiago do CacJm).
Figure 1c Moita do Sebastião Ossada 30 ("1030"): both distal ulnae pictured - distal third of a right ulna
shaft with apparent greenstick fracture (x ray: 11 14/7/84 Santiago do CacJm).

fracture in those over 40 years of age. A fracture at the midshaft of a forearm long bone in a child is most likely to be the result of a childhood fall and it may heal without very severe displacement. Thus, the unknown factor of age of injury is important in the aetiology and outcome.

The radiograph of the Moita Ossada 25a ulna (Figure 1a) demonstrates some misalignment (since the extremities of the bone are damaged it is impossible to estimate the degree of functional impairment): the location and degree of misalignment may make a childhood fall the best guess for the cause, but a parry fracture could not be ruled out. Moita Ossada 10 could indeed have suffered a direct blow to the forearm. Because a false joint developed incorporating new bone following displacement (Figure 1b - note the arrows indicating the border between new bone and the original bone surfaces) and also because the olecranon joint surface was restricted, a very long-standing disability is probable. Moita Ossada 30 (Figure 1c) definitely seemed to have suffered a childhood injury.

The count of adult right ulna fragments examined for Moita in 1984 was 41, but not all of these retained a complete shaft allowing observation: the percentage of right ulnar shaft

trauma is certainly well below than 13% (3/23). However, in none of our Portuguese work did the circumstances of analysis permit systematic checking of all fragments of all individuals for reconstruction, necessary whenever there has been mixing of individuals.

In publications from the very beginning of our work in Portugal, when we were just starting to try to understand the Mesolithic (Lubell and Jackes, 1985; Lubell et al., 1989), we suggested the possibility of violence, mentioning "parry fractures", for example. Subsequently, in 1985 and 1986, we examined material from Cabeço da Arruda, a very slightly later site which we thought more likely than Moita to represent pressures resulting from increased sedentism and higher fertility levels (e.g. Jackes and Lubell, 1999a,b). Nevertheless, Arruda did not provide definite evidence of violence.

The skeleton labelled Arruda Ossada XVII was of an adolescent male, but stored with his bones was an extra right radius (skeletal elements from this site have been extensively mixed since excavation, the extra radius was probably not buried with Arruda Ossada XVII). This fragmentary radius had only the distal end present. The bone appeared to have a distal shaft fracture, but no obvious fracture was evident from the radiograph. Perhaps a greenstick fracture would explain this case. Exactly the same situation appears in the next specimen to be discussed.

Arruda Ossada XIV had two left radii, one of which might have sustained a hairline fracture with healing in perfect alignment and without callus tissue build-up, but with some wasting of the arm – while a fracture was the initial diagnosis, none is evident from the radiograph and the atrophy could have derived from causes other than bone fracture.

The left ulna radiograph of Arruda Ossada H (an elderly adult, with generally male postcranial dimensions but female sciatic notch form) shows almost perfect alignment of a lower midshaft fracture (Figure 2), and therefore is likely to have been the result of a childhood fall.

A presumably fractured right clavicle, the radiograph showing healing in reasonable alignment, is present in an unidentified individual. Arruda was excavated in the nineteenth century and in the 1980s when we were inventorying and removing the material from wooden sliding drawers for repacking and storage in special individual boxes, this clavicle was found with a number of stray bones, many of them clavicles, as "an individual" whom I nicknamed "Shiva", or Arruda SH (see Jackes and Lubell 1999 for a

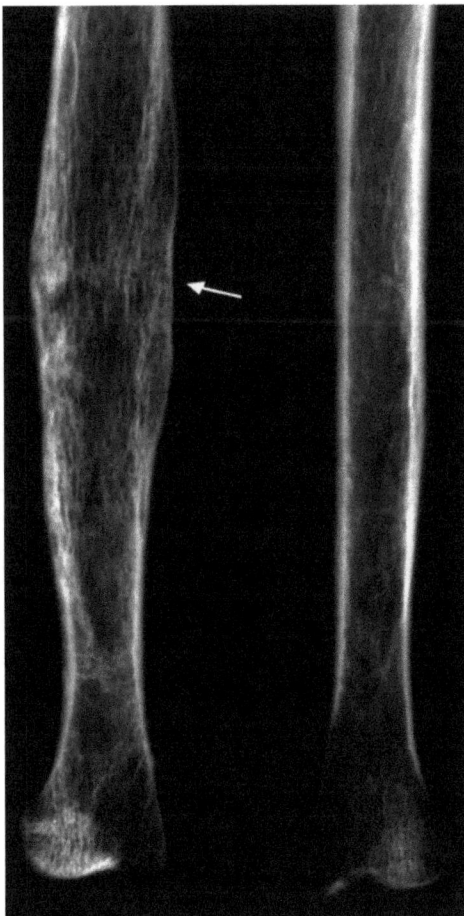

Figure 2 Cabeço da Arruda Ossada H: both ulnae, the left (on the left) with a perfectly aligned fracture (x ray: D3D 5/11/85 Sintra).

summary on the excavation and curation of the Mesolithic sites). Arruda SH also showed several fragmentary left ribs which had probably sustained trauma. The ribs of Arruda Ossada XIII, a fragmentary elderly individual, probably male, are also likely to have sustained fractures. A right ulna stored with a number of stray bones as an "individual" whom I nicknamed "Toes" or Arruda TO (because of the large number of metatarsals present) showed the abnormal curvature of the shaft, which is typical of a "greenstick" fracture.

An individual from another site, Samoqueira (fully discussed in Lubell and Jackes 1985), indicates that traumatic falls or blows to the elbow occurred in Mesolithic Portugal, added to which there were several instances of elbow abnormalities at Arruda. Arruda Ossada Q was a male with a rather unusual amount of arthritic damage for the population. He also had an apparent childhood fracturing of the left elbow (Figure 3). Arruda Ossada 29, a very large middle-aged male, had a bilateral abnormality of the coronoid process of the ulna, with marked deformity of the humeral distal articular surfaces. Once again, the best interpretation seems to be a childhood injury, prior to the complete formation of the distal epiphysis.

The only humerus present in Arruda Ossada XXV (E), the left, shows the possibility of delayed fusion of the medial epicondyle epiphysis which was completely absent, though partial fusion might have been expected in this late adolescent male (Figure 4a). The individual had an early onset of spurring of the eminence between the radial and coronoid fossae of his distal humerus. For comparison, a shorter individual, Arruda Ossada 60, roughly the same age, already had a fused medial epicondyle. Medial epicondylar epiphysis fracture in children is associated with elbow dislocation occurring by violence or more often because of a fall (Adams 1967:142), and is relatively common in young adolescent males (Green and Swiontkowski 1994:239). The possibility of an abnormality in the left elbow of Arruda Ossada XXV (E) is perhaps supported by the fact that one individual from Moita, Moita Ossada XIV, also a male, had a left medial epicondyle quite different from that on his right humerus. On the right the epicondyle extended 1.5 cm beyond the articular surface, whereas the left epicondyle was a small nubbin of bone half the height of that on the right, and extending barely .75 cm beyond the articular surface (Figure 4b).

These two individuals present very puzzling cases, in which congenital factors and/or activity patterns might be implicated An interesting suggestion comes from Ogawa and Ui (1996) that teenage boys indulging in arm-wrestling are liable to fracture-separation of the medial epicondyle. As Glencross and Stuart-Madacam (2000) have noted in presenting an archaeological case comparable with those under discussion here (see also Glencross and Stuart-Madacam 2001), little attention is paid in the anthropological literature to childhood injuries, because of the lack of certainty in the diagnosis. However it is clear that the early adolescent males are particularly vulnerable to injury: there is "an increase in muscle strength, a decrease in the shear strength per unit area of epiphyseal cartilage immediately before closure, and [a] resultant relative mechanical imbalance" (Ogawa and Ui

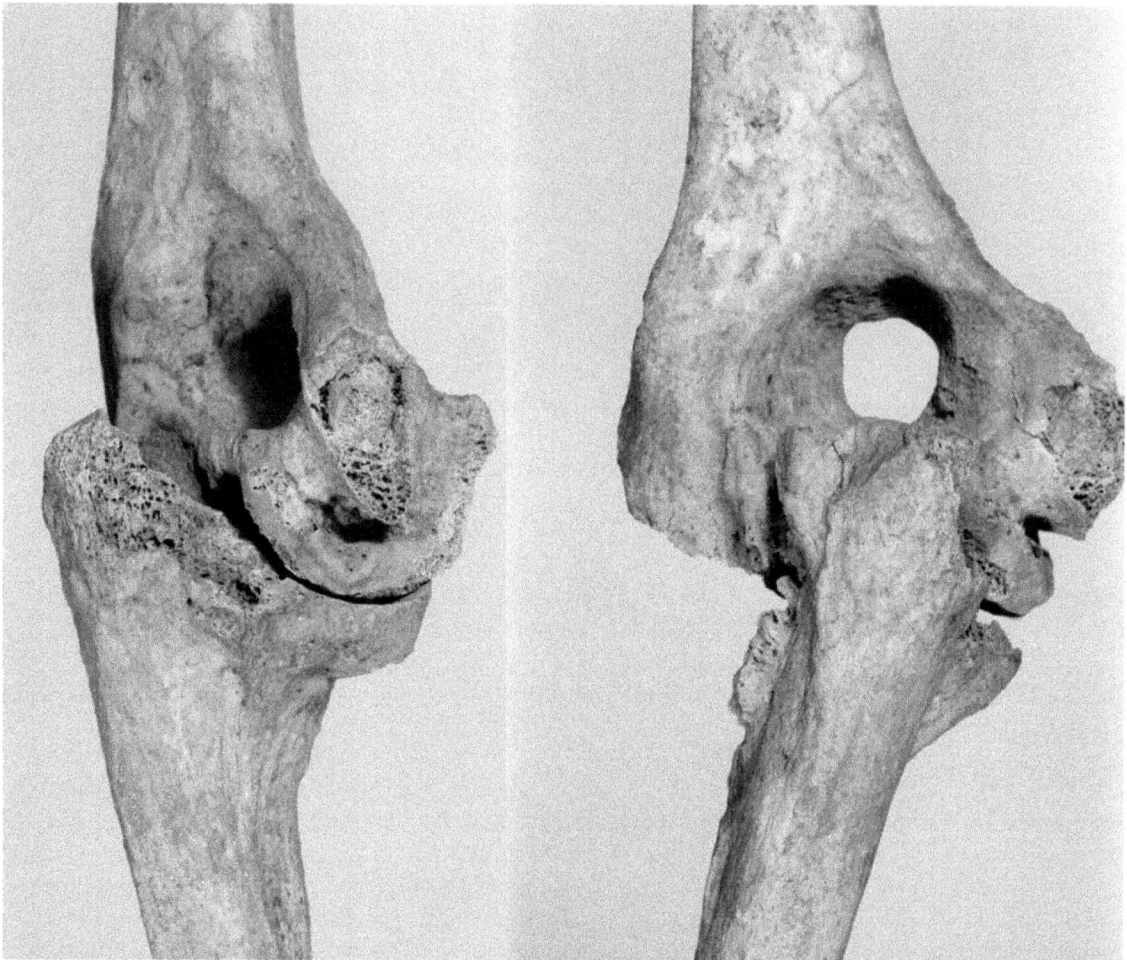

Figure 3 Cabeço da Arruda Ossada Q: medial and posterior views of the left humerus and ulna.

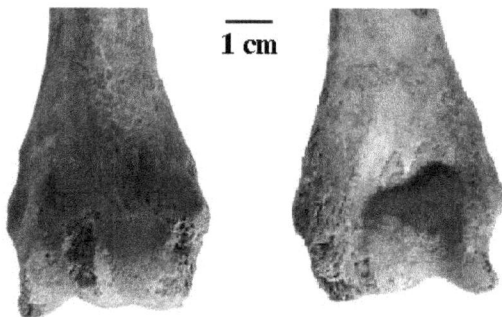

Figure 4a Cabeço da Arruda Ossada XXV (E): anterior (left) and posterior views of left humerus.

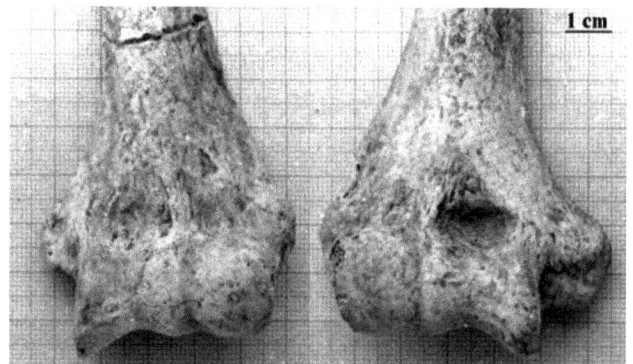

Figure 4b Moita do Sebastião Ossada XIV: anterior view of left (on the left) and right humeri.

1996:496). Medial epicondylar fractures of the humerus are likely to lead to displacement and to fibrous rather than bone reunion (see e.g., Josefsson et al. 1986 and Dias et al. 1987).

That extraordinary stresses were placed on Portuguese Mesolithic arms could be deduced from the great development of the ulna supinator crest (see Kennedy, 1983), or signs of unusual muscle activity (examples are listed in Table 1:1, e.g. for Moita Ossada 5 and Ossada 6).

The count of Arruda right ulnae in which the full shaft could be observed for fractures is more accurate than that for Moita,

because the method of recording was more detailed, but again systematic reconstruction could not be attempted. For comparison with Moita, of the 47 whole or fragmentary adult right ulnae present, 23 definitely had the full shaft length available for observation: the trauma rate for the lower middle to distal one third of the right ulna shaft would thus be only 1/23, or 4%. There were 33 observable adult left distal humeri, so the three apparently abnormal left elbows would mean a frequency of around 9%.

From this brief summary, we might validly assume that signs of violence within the Portuguese Mesolithic were not the result of intergroup aggression, but rather of anger within a domestic setting. We might more validly conclude that there is no evidence of violence, and that the trauma was accidental, and generally suffered in childhood. A further consideration here is the possibility that some activity was placing special stress on the elbows and forearms of young males. It may be that the distal growth plates of the humerus were at especial risk.

Neolithic sites, presumably displaying still further sedentism and population increase, provided no absolutely convincing proof of violence. Before the start of our project we expected to see increased dental and postcranial pathology in the Portuguese Neolithic, based on our preconceptions derived from the literature and work on North American horticulturalists. We also thought that in the Neolithic we might see signs of an immigrant population and that an increase of violence might thus be expected. Our expectations were not met in any area.

Zambujal Cave at the Neolithic site of Melides showed disruption of the distal articular surface of a left humerus, the radiograph showing that there was a complete medial epicondylar area fracture (Figure 5). A right humerus lateral epicondyle from the same site displays unusual spurring perhaps from repeated and forcible extension and rotation at the elbow. Once again, childhood falls or specific activities suggest themselves.

Nowhere did we see clear evidence of cranial/facial trauma. Meiklejohn and I, in collaborating on examining the Mesolithic skulls from Moita and Arruda, had agreed that there was no cranial trauma suggestive of real interpersonal violence. Trephination had previously been reported for the Neolithic of Portugal (Barbosa Sueiro 1933), and we examined and confirmed that attempts had been made in these cases, though a reported Mesolithic trephination seemed to us open to several interpretations. Trephination slightly

confuses the issue of the only apparent cranial trauma from Feteira, a Neolithic burial cave (see Zilhão 1984). The skulls from this excavation are in general broken and dispersed. Three small portions of cranial vault showed oval depressions, one (No.1949) definitely suggested trephination, so the fact that the other two seem also to echo the oval form of the identified trephinations in other Portuguese Neolithic sites, along with the extreme fragmentation of the skulls, makes it very difficult to positively identify the cause. Certainly, some form of scalp wounding, with involvement of the underlying bone, has occurred in one (No. 1644), and in the other two cases (Nos. 1949 and 1786) complete healing after removal of bone seems likely. The healing had created deep depressions with thin floors. Each of these three lesions is about 4.5 cm in length and just under 2 cm across.

Our examination of material from the large and important Neolithic burial cave, Casa da Moura, provided no evidence of violence: in fact most of the evidence of trauma was provided by four metacarpals and one metatarsal, which did not surprise us, since trauma and infection of the hands and feet had been evident from the Mesolithic sites as well (some examples noted APPENDIX 1:1), not unexpected since harvesting of shellfish from rocky Atlantic shores must have figured at some point in the lives of all these groups.

Our final conclusion was that we had been premature in suggesting the possibility of violence in the Portuguese Mesolithic – certainly we could not identify warfare between groups. Broadening the chronological context altered interpretation of the trauma. It seems likely that an historical approach to violence should be taken wherever that is possible, and may lead to a modification of interpretations.

KENYA

On the other hand, evidence of more extensive violence should not lead us immediately to conclude that there was warfare between groups, nor to make simplistic assumptions about the causes of violence.

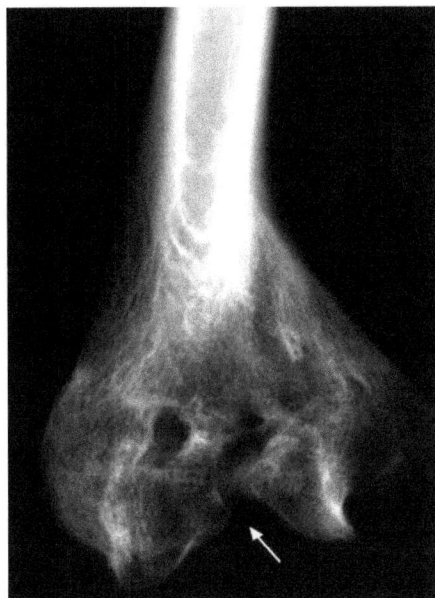

Figure 5 Melides Zambujal 15: left humerus
(x ray: 77.9 7/6/86 Sintra).

I have examined the skeletons of those who were pulled from latrine pits in Kikuyu villages after the panga murders of the Mau Mau Emergency in Kenya (Jackes 1977:29). The signs of violence were all too evident. Violent death by panga is marked by deep cuts which are almost random, not clustered at sites of muscle and ligament insertions around major joints. Land alienation following upon European settlement, coupled with population growth, led to land degradation and social and economic disruption (Throup 1987). The consequence, triggered by the deepening ecological disaster, was a self-destructive frenzy *within* Kikuyu society: the rebellion "turned inwards to consume its own supporters – to become a Kikuyu civil war" (Sorrenson 1967:100). As Carman (1997:10) discusses, internecine conflict may result from the pressures exerted by outside political forces. The historical context is important in this example, as also in the next.

CANADA

While unequivocal in the Mau Mau instance, there is the possibility that premortem use of blades cannot always be clearly differentiated from postmortem disarticulation (Havercourt and Lubell 1999, but see Jackes and Lubell, this volume). However, with regard to Eastern Woodland peoples of North America there is no doubt: evidence for postmortem disarticulation is clear in Canadian Iroquoian Huron skeletons buried in large ossuary pits such as that at Kleinburg in Ontario (Jackes 1977:9). Multiple fine "cutmarks" are very specifically located, for example on femoral necks. Among the Ontario Iroquoian Neutral Nation, in which wholesale disarticulation at burial was not practised, such cutmarks are rare (Jackes 1996). The Huron provide a situation where ethnohistorical evidence of secondary burial following disarticulation is available, and in which it is clearly possible to identify postmortem cuts to bones. Such cutmarks are illustrated by Ubelaker (1989:106).

Positive identification of violence, on the other hand, seems to be relatively rare for Ontario Iroquoian skeletons. There is little skeletal evidence of interpersonal violence, and yet this was a period of post-contact war well-documented ethnohistorically. Prior to European contact there was a period (known through large-scale archaeological excavations) during which villages of increasing size, placed in strategic locations and with multiple palisades (see e.g. Finlayson 1998:16), add weight and time depth to the ethnohistorical evidence of war between and among various Iroquoian and Algonquian groups.

There are reports of skeletal marks of violence (see Anderson 1986, Ossenberg 1969, Pfeiffer 1986: cranial or facial trauma and two instances of projectile points in bone, both in vertebrae), but in general violence is sparsely reported. For example, at the completely excavated Grimsby Neutral cemetery, in Ontario, there is major trauma, but very little of it can be definitively ascribed to violence – perhaps only two cases of cranial trauma (Jackes 1988:83 ff.). This evidence is surprisingly meagre, given the known fact that warfare was carried out on two fronts by men of the Neutral Iroquoian Nation during the period of use of the cemetery (1615 to 1650 A.D.). Ethnohistorical documents suggests that those who died by violence might not have been given normal burial (see e.g. Tooker 1967), so we would expect to see indications of well-healed or minor wounds only.

Because raiding parties of warriors travelled great distances, those who were severely wounded are unlikely to have survived the return journey. Few wounded warriors are likely to have escaped being made prisoners and killed far from home. Absence of evidence is not necessarily convincing, but the relative paucity of signs of warfare is surprising in view of the fact that every Spring and Summer during the 1630s five to six hundred young Huron men left home to raid Iroquois territory to the south (Tooker 1967: 29-30). The rarity of trauma definitely resulting from violence certainly supports the Jesuits in their contention that the Huron were not violent towards their fellows. Equally, we must take it to

support the ethnohistorical sources which record exclusion from normal burial places of those who suffered violent deaths, and we can validly suggest that not many young men who were wounded in war survived to be buried later in the ossuaries and cemeteries of Iroquoian Ontario.

Special burial places may have been reserved for the victims of violence, as has been proposed for the nine young males, buried at the Van Oordt Site in central Ontario (Molto et al. 1986). Perhaps this site is best interpreted as a special place of burial for a party of warriors ambushed close to home. The absence of burning may indicate that the warriors were not killed on a distant raid, since the Jesuits wrote of the Huron: "they are accustomed to burn the flesh of a person who dies outside their own country and, extracting the bones, to take these with them" (Thwaites 1898; XI [1636-1637]:131). The lack of burning may also indicate a lack of torture.

Iroquoian violence widely encompassed the torture of prisoners of war, described in ethnohistorical sources in too vivid detail (e.g. Thwaites 1898; XIII [1637]: 37ff). The discovery of fragmentary human remains disposed of in village middens, rather than in ossuaries and cemeteries, has been interpreted as evidence of prisoner sacrifice and cannibalism (Jamieson 1983). While a small percentage of Ontario burials occurs outside specific cemetery areas (e.g. Esler 1998), and the cut marks of disarticulation and disturbance of interments by ploughing may confuse matters, there seems to be little doubt that Jamieson (1983) is correct in his association of part of the eastern Ontario Roebuck site human skeletal material with the deaths by torture of prisoners of war.

So there is evidence in Ontario of violence, but it is sparse, and the widespread violence of Iroquoian society might not have been recognized from cemetery and ossuary studies alone, without the benefit of ethnohistorical sources of information. To repeat, at a site like Grimsby there is evidence of violence (Jackes 1988:83) but it is limited and, except in a few cases, equivocal. Yet there was disruption, disease, famine and war on several fronts, and at Grimsby the demographic evidence suggests an influx of refugees (Jackes n.d.). We know that the Grimsby cemetery covers the period of the breakdown of a society under the combined influence of the European fur trade, the introduction of European weapons, and the final incursions of Iroquois from the south to destroy the Neutral Nation.

CHINA

A background in Iroquoian studies was long considered appropriate for examination of material from northern Chinese Neolithic villages. As far back as 1921 when Andersson and Zdansky were excavating at the first Yangshao site, they were visited by the Canadian, Davidson Black, who drew their attention to publications on North American material (Andersson 1973), believed to be especially relevant because of shared multiple burial practices. More relevant to later interpretations of Yangshao material by Chinese archaeologists was the matrilineality of Iroquoian nations. This was interpeted as according well with the matriarchal clan phase of Engels' unilinear scheme adopted by Marxist archaeology (Trigger 1989), deriving from L.H. Morgan's work. Since Morgan was, himself, an adopted Seneca of the Iroquois Confederacy his work gave special emphasis to Iroquoian kinship and social organization.

Whatever interpretation was laid on the early Neolithic of North China, in setting out to examine material from the Yangshao stages at Jiangzhai, now preserved at the BanPo Museum, I did not expect to meet any more evidence of violence than I had seen in Ontario skeletal collections.

The site of Jiangzhai lies in Lintong County to the northeast of Xi'an City on a terrace of a tributary of the Wei River. It was partially excavated between 1972 and 1979, an area of about 17,084 square metres being dug of the total site area of about 30,000 square metres.

The cemeteries which provided the material to be discussed here represent the first two stages of Jiangzhai, both within the Yangshao culture. Earlier dates for the site (Chang 1992:390), shown in Figure 6 (atmospheric data), are consonant with those from the nearby site of BanPo, near Xi'an, which is equivalent to Stage I Jiangzhai. Stage II must provide the youngest date, and a representative site equivalent to Jiangzhai Stage II is Shijia, Weinan County, also in Shaanxi (for Shijia dates see Chang 1992:390; Gao and Lee, 1993).

A major difference between Jiangzhai Stage I and Stage II is the switch from primary interments to multiple secondary burials (that is, collective burials).

Shijia was a complete excavation of a cemetery of just under 250 square metres with a thickness of about 1 metre average depth. Forty three graves were excavated, and the minimum number of individuals recognized by the Anatomy Division of the Xi'an Medical Institute in 1978 amounted to 730, mostly placed in rows with skulls placed in the centre.

Individual identity seems to have been retained despite disarticulation (Gao and Lee 1993).

The arrangement contrasts with the earlier BanPo site, where the village cemetery contained 175 individuals, almost all as single adult extended burials, while 73 young children were buried in urns in the village area (Hsi-an Pan-p'o po wu kuan, 1987).

It is to be noted that these sites of the Yangshao culture do not represent the earliest phase of millet agriculture on the loess terraces near the middle reaches of Yellow River in northern China. The earlier Peiligang sites are already large settlements with varied domestic architecture and distinct cemetery areas. Nevertheless, Jiangzhai is a site of great importance, in that it uniquely, perhaps, encompasses several phases of the Yangshao culture.

Like Shijia, Jiangzhai was excavated during the 1970s. This was a period of the encouragement of extremely large-scale excavation with emphasis on archaeology by and for the peasant/worker/soldier (Chang 1977). As Chang points out (Ferrie 1995:315), the first scholarly publications restored after the Cultural Revolution were in archaeology, and the political context for the emphasis on Yangshao sites is clear (Tong 1995; see also Trigger 1989:177). With a change of emphasis, the interest is still high (Li 1999:602 referring to the BanPo Yangshao burial pattern demonstrating "a non-hierarchical social organization, where ancestor cult was probably conducted on behalf of and for the common interests of the entire community").

As described in Jackes and Gao (at the 1995 Jomon to Star Carr conference, in press) and Fu (1994), nearly 3,000 skeletons were excavated from the cemeteries at Jiangzhai. The Stage I cemetery areas lay beyond the village, separated from the village area by ditches. The cemeteries were not completely excavated (see Figure 7), but yielded 174 burial pits, generally single primary extended burials of adults and adolescents. The remains of infants were contained in 206 urns which were found, for the most part, among the houses. Stage II burials were mostly excavated from a cemetery which

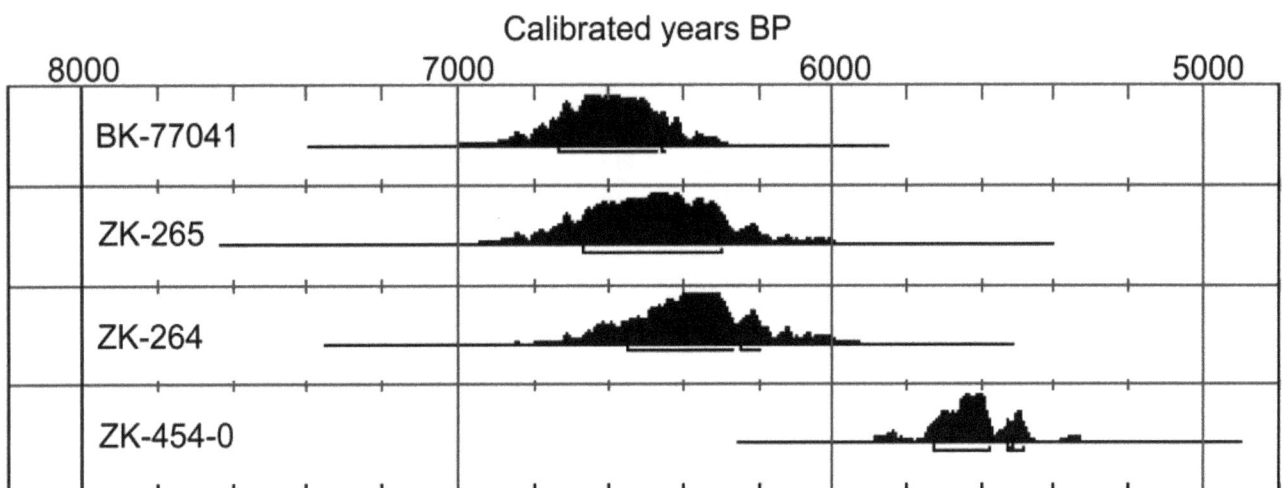

Figure 6 Calibrated dates for Jiangzhai using OxCal v3.5 (Bronk Ramsey, 2000).

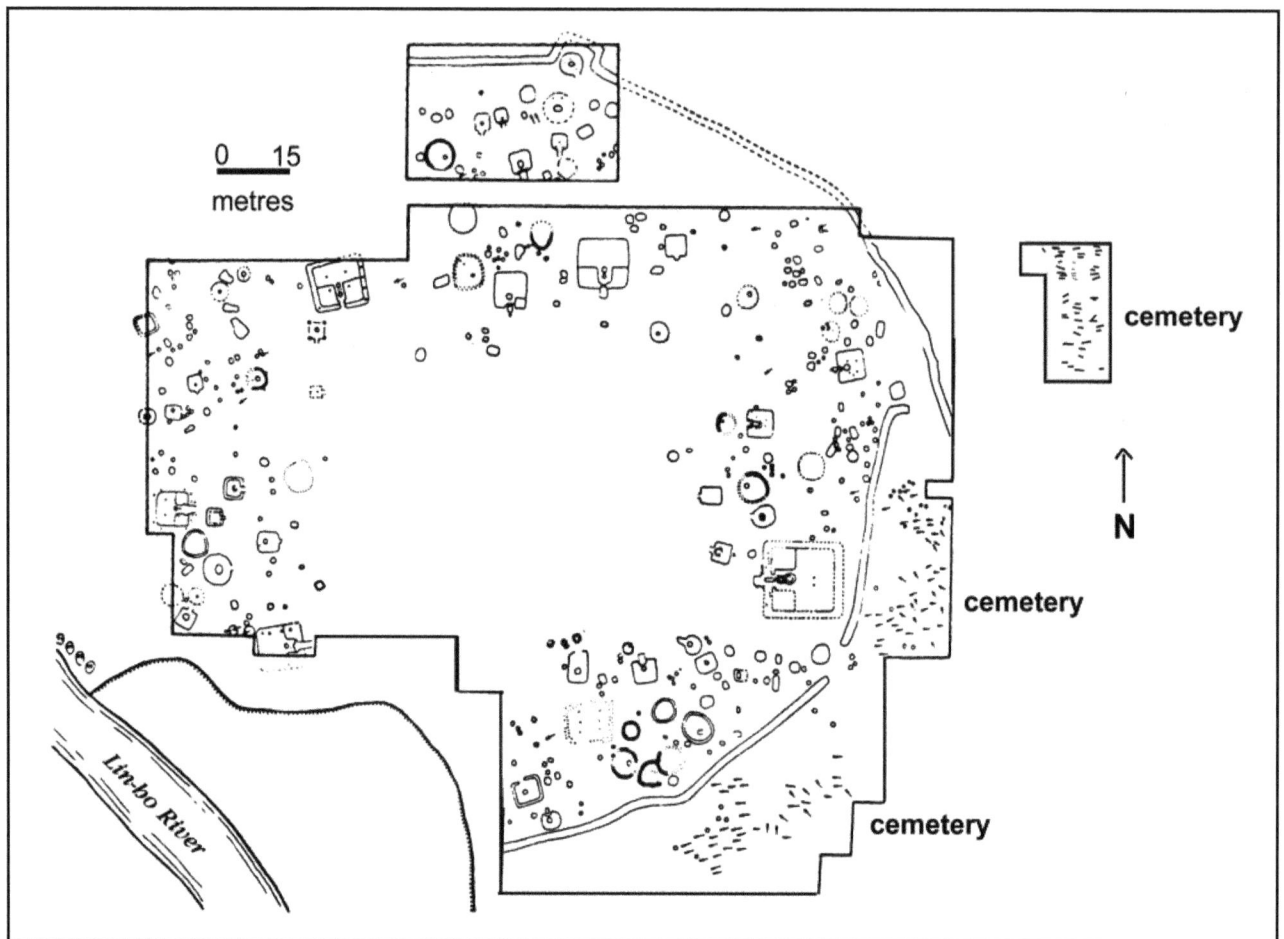

Figure 7 Map of Stage I Jiangzhai (after Gong, 1988) showing location of excavation of cemeteries.

was located in the centre of the Stage I village. The Stage II cemetery itself contained around 2,200 individuals, mostly in collective secondary burials of about 20 people. The bones were for the most part carefully arranged within large burial pits, square or rectangular, with vertical sides. Funeral urns again contained the skeletons of children, though occasionally adults were identified in urns.

The skeletons were examined on site, and an anatomist (Xia Yuan-Ming) who lived in Shanghai was very occasionally present (Gao, pers. comm. 1993). Eventually all but parts of a very few individuals were reburied, and it was disappointing to be able to identify no more than 54 individuals retained in 1993 at the BanPo Museum, Xi'an, 24 of them belonging to Stage I. Interviews with Gao, who had been present at the excavations and was assistant curator on the BanPo Museum staff, and Gong of the Shaanxi Provincial Archaeological Institute who was responsible for the excavation and publication of Jiangzhai (1988), made it clear that perhaps half of the skeletons were reburied immediately and that the selection of skeletons for reburial was completely random (Gong pers. comm., 1.vi.1993). Sometime in the late 1980s the majority of these retained skeletons were placed in a pit in the grounds of the BanPo Museum, because of lack of storage facilities. This operation would have been supervised by Gao, who informed me upon several occasions, in response to different types of questions, that there was no pattern of choice regarding the retained material.

The initial choice immediately following excavation was certainly quite random since no one with osteological expertise was involved in deciding which skeletons were to be retained. Gao, himself, at the time of the excavation was a late adolescent sent north from Guangdong during the Cultural Revolution, and I understood that none of the excavators was trained. I also infer the lack of osteological expertise from facts such as the following examples. M155 is described in the literature (1988) as a single individual, a 30 year old male. The individual in fact consists of the skull of a 13-15 year old female and the postcranials of an elderly male, an individual with a severe lumbar compression fracture. M159 is a 5 year old child, not a 9 year old, as described. M54 is described as a 15 year old female, but is, in fact, a 5 year old child. It appears that not even skeletons recognized as important by the excavators were retained in the museum by the time of my visit in 1993. While M54, just discussed above, was noteworthy for being buried with 2,052 bone beads, the individual (M7) frequently mentioned in the literature (e.g. Chang 1986:119, also Fig. 73) as having impressive grave goods (8,577 bone beads, 12 stone beads and funerary vessels) was not retained.

The random nature of the choice, and the lack of knowledge of the effects of trauma on bone, is important. Since the material available for study is a tiny percentage of the original, it is important to ask whether it is in anyway representative of the whole. I was not able to determine that anyone who had seen the bones had recognised trauma. (Criticism is not implied by this; it is merely a statement of fact. The difficulty faced by the excavators of these sites is acknowledged, see Howells and Jones Tsuchitani 1977).

The retained material from Jiangzhai presents an extraordinarily large assortment of trauma that could be attributed to violence. Smith (1996:85) has stated that the presence of "parry" fractures is not sufficient in and of itself: "A violent aetiology for mid-shaft fractures becomes more tenable when potentially corroborative craniofacial injury data are considered". By this standard, Jiangzhai is a persuasive example of interpersonal violence. Added to this, Jiangzhai is a sample of skeletons in which the lower limbs give NO indication of trauma, or of infection following upon superficial trauma: this does not suggest high rates of accidental trauma. At Jiangzhai the lower limb bones provide no evidence of trauma sustained during cultivation or falls resulting from difficult terrain. This can be compared with Grimsby where tibial periostitis typical of Iroquoian horticulturalists' skeletons (Jackes1988:63) is coupled with clear evidence of accidental lower limb fracturing (ibid. 85).

Fractures of the clavicle are not necessarily the result of violence. However, the M238 clavicle represents 50% of the entire collection of retained clavicles of same sex, stage and side. The M112 clavicle represents 100% and may well be the same individual as a female with a fractured nose. This suggests (but can not confirm) that clavicular fracturing was not rare.

Similarly, two apparent parry fractures at Jiangzhai may be unimpressive, but together the two constitute 33% of all Stage I left male ulnae. In fact, a third left ulna of a young male from Stage I (M275) had necrotic bone at the mid-shaft, suggesting a wound in the overlying soft tissue of the forearm — in fact, a third parry wound.

An additional consideration is the 100% representation of the left side in fractures of the arm (see Table 1) allowing the reasonable speculation that fighting was undertaken with a weapon held in the right hand. The use of weapons is confirmed by the presence of a depressed fracture of an unusual circular form (Figure 8), which is exactly in accordance with the numerous bola stones on display in the BanPo Museum.

Why does Table 1 record a preponderance of cranial trauma in Stage II? The retained material from that stage is, in general, of isolated skulls: for example, there are 10 observable adult male left malars from Stage II, but only one male left clavicle and one male left humerus. Bias in burial, collection and retention must always be taken into account when comparing frequencies of features between single and multiple burial sites (e.g. Jackes and Lubell 1996).

Despite the poor and probably unrepresentative sample, we begin to get a picture of a society in which there was a great deal of violence. For example, there were seven observable sets of adolescent and adult female nasal bones from Stage II at Jiangzhai, and three of those women had had their noses broken: one can only assume that this indicates violence

Table 1:

Indiv.	Cultural Stage	Sex	Age (see note)	Bone	Side	Percent of observable elements, same side, sex and stage
M238	II	male	a3	clavicle	right	50
M112	II	female	a3?	clavicle	right	100
M75.2 Figure 8	I	female	a1	frontal depressed fracture		12.5
M112:13 Figure 9	II	male	a3?	left malar fracture		10
M84:10	II	female	a3	symphysis mentis, teeth, TMJ fracturing		11
M84:10 Figure 10	II	female	a3	nasals		14
M112:10	II	female	a2?	nasals		14
M216:11	II	female	a2?	nasals		14
M162	I	female	a1	distal humerus	left	17
M151	I	male	a4	distal humerus	left	20
M150	I	male	a3	ulna (also ribs)	left	17
M275	I	male	a1	ulna	left	17

Note: The age estimates in Table 1 are derived initially from dental crown heights, periodontal disease and dental attrition, with extrapolations, since not all individuals were complete: the youngest are a1, who are adolescents; the oldest, a4, are individuals with great wear, dental pathology, extensive suture fusion, arthritic changes to the bones, osteoporosis and thinning of bones.

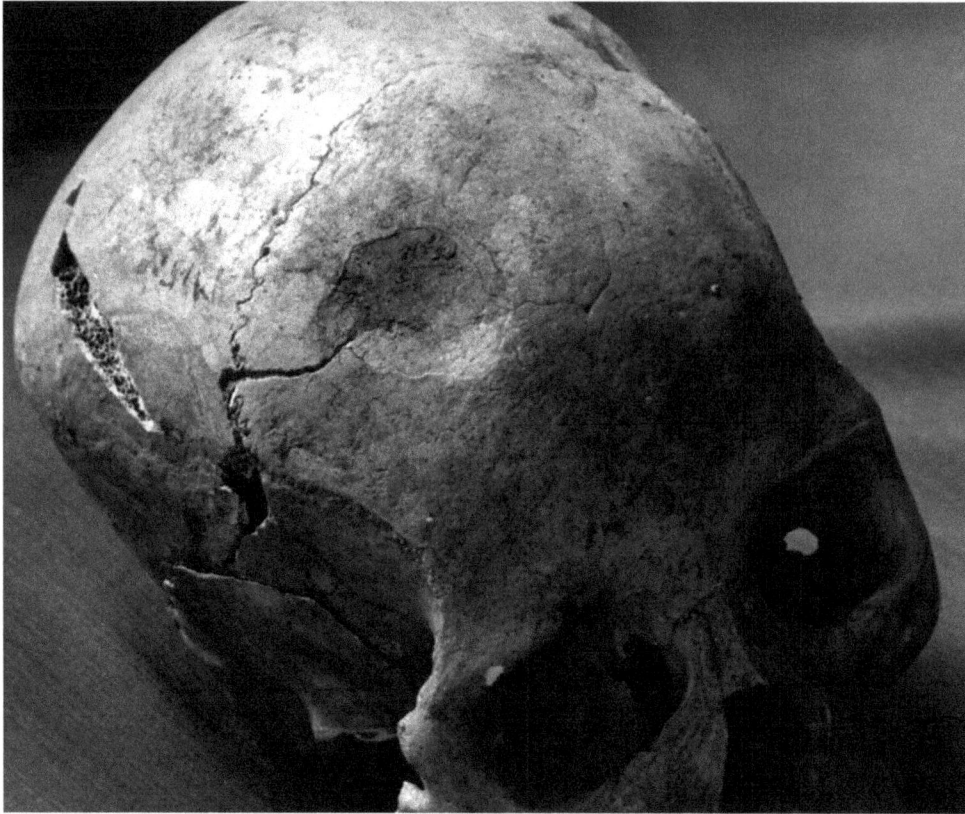

Figure 8 Depressed fracture which may have been caused by a bola stone (M75.2). The cut on the parietal is considered to be excavation trauma (the author observed large-scale excavation in similar loess sites being undertaken with hoes by village women).

against around 40% of women – excluding from consideration those without hard tissue damage, and those dying without bone healing. What are the chances that, from among the over 2,000 individuals excavated from the Stage II cemetery, a random selection of females would give such a high percentage of healed nasal fractures? In the context, Walker's comments (2001:10) regarding facial injuries in women are pertinent.

In official publications until recently (for example in the China Internet Information web material dated 1999) and in the work of Chinese archaeologists in the past (as summarized by Gao and Lee 1993), Yangshao society was seen as dependent upon the agricultural work of women, with women having high social status because of this important work. Yangshao, according to this interpretation, was egalitarian and cohesive, based on endogamous matrilineal and matrilocal clans. Matriarchy was specifically referred to (An 1988, and is still mentioned by China Internet Information 2001: "the matriarchal society at Banpo Village near Xi'an"), and was no doubt invoked on the basis of an incomplete understanding of Iroquoian parallels or problems in translation (Pearson 1988 has reviewed Chinese interpretations of Neolithic burials). The Iroquoian parallels could be drawn because both societies had collective burials, and great emphasis was laid on the importance of collective secondary burials as a reflection of basic social organization (Wang 1985-1987 has written critically on this matter, specifically in relation to Yangshao burial practices; see also Jackes 1996).

We can support the Chinese archaeological hypothesis that the females worked hard, based on activity-dependent trauma in young females (for detailed discussions of the interpretation

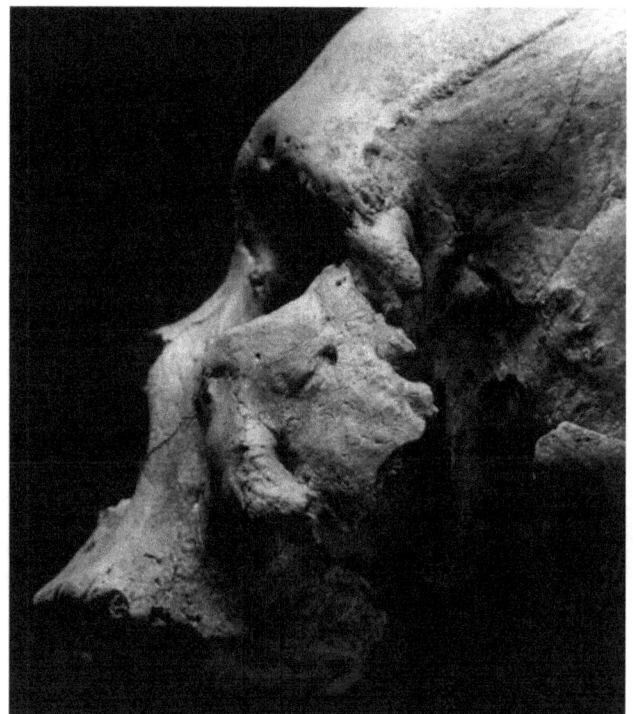

Figure 9 Healed fracture of the cheek bone (M112:13). Note the fracture and deflection backwards of the frontosphenoidal process of the zygomatic bone.

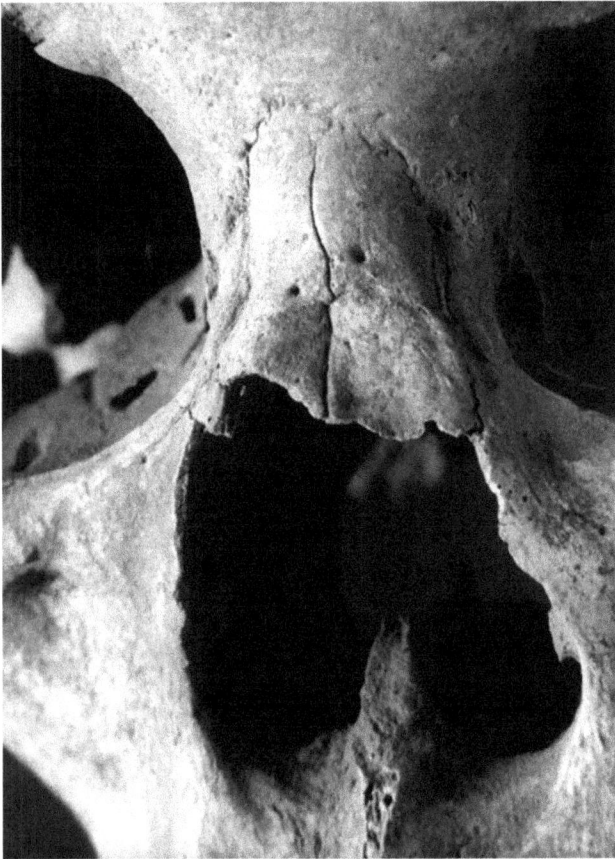

Figure 10 Healed fracture of the nasals (M84:10). The left side of the nose is depressed and distorted.

of this type of evidence of activity levels see Jackes 1977, 1988). Female vertebrae seem to have been subjected to constant stress of the type that suggests sustained labour in the fields. M181 and M161 were two Stage I females, both young, one still adolescent. Both women had extensive disruption of the vertebral body endplates, with severe intervertebral disc rupturing in the region of the thoraco-lumbar junction. In males, by contrast, there is no comparable vertebral trauma. M155 was mentioned above as the postcranials only (no skull) of a male with a lumbar compression fracture. This is the only example of major vertebral trauma in a male, and it has a different aetiology. Minor vertebral trauma is seen as small lumbar vertebral end plate defects in three elderly males from Stage I (M149, 150 and 151).

DISCUSSION

The suggestion that Yangshao women did agricultural work is maintained by the present findings, while the identification of young girls' burials with rich grave goods which is often mentioned in the literature on Yangshao sites (Pearson 1988) is questioned (see also Gao and Lee 1993). The idea propounded in the Chinese literature that women had high status is not well-supported by the osteological evidence of violence against females. One might argue that women were victims during an attack by outsiders, but that certainly would not accord with the general Iroquoian pattern (see discussion

below) which were appealed to in the initial interpretations of Yangshao society.

Underhill (1989) has pointed out that evidence for warfare in Yangshao sites is very poor (see also Pearson 1988:12). Thus we might conclude that the evidence of aggression indicates violence internal to villages, and that the society could not be described as "cohesive", contrary to the Chinese initial archaeological interpretation of Yangshao society (Pearson 1988 provides a useful summary of the rather complex history of interpretations). The problem is, of course, that the term "cohesive" may say little. We can assume that Chinese scholars were using it to refer to a close interdependency of individuals within a group, without status differentiation, and with a degree of gender equality. Such cohesion may depend upon ecological and economic circumstances, and whether the group finds greater definition in opposition to external forces (when internal divisions threaten your society, proclaim an enemy). As we will see below, the mutual interdependence of the members of a small group within a harsh environment does not always preclude interpersonal violence.

Jackes and Gao (prepared in 1995, in press) discuss the evidence for population heterogeneity in Neolithic northern China, noting that this evidence is based on meagre samples, and pointing to the urgent need for full studies of large samples in order to clarify the situation. The possibility of fortified villages, usually referred to only in the context of the later Longshan settlements, is also mentioned: this is based on the fact that even at Jiangzhai I the cemetery areas are placed beyond a series of ditches which the excavators considered to have been joined by palisade fences. We can certainly not exclude the possibility that Jiangzhai provides an example of inter-group violence.

Could we distinguish intra- and inter-group violence?

In Iroquoian society the violence was externally directed. The French administrators and missionaries who worked among the Montagnais and Huron in the first half of the 17th century were horrified by the wars among the Iroquoian and Algonquian peoples, and especially by the institution of prisoner torture. But they also commented on the rarity of internal strife, noting that it was ascribed to gambling (Thwaites 1898; X [1636]:81), and writing "It is strange what enemies the Savages are of anger, and how this sin shocks them" (Thwaites 1898; XX [1640-41]:197). The Jesuits recognized that there was public gift giving to prevent vengeance (Thwaites 1898; XXVIII [1645-6]:51) and that the system worked so well that "we find without comparison much less disorder than there is in France, though here the mere shame of having committed the crime is the offender's punishment" (Thwaites 1898; XXVIII [1645-6]:63). The more thoughtful among the priests found it salutary to contemplate the acceptance in France of harsh punishment of children, of the disturbed and the disruptive, and some of the priests came to realise that the Hurons and Montagnais viewed such French-style punishment as barbaric.

In fact, we cannot be simplistic in our approach to Iroquoian violence, based on what is known about war among the

Iroquois of the Five Nations (see Richter 1992). The wars were "mourning-wars" designed to provide war captives in order to assuage the grief of female relatives who were in mourning. Such raids into enemy territory were not designed to lead to deaths, but rather to the taking of a few prisoners, to be given to women in mourning who could choose adoption or (generally for adult males only) death for the captives. A warrior was judged by his success not in killing the enemy, but in bringing home captives. To die in battle was not glorious. War was based on premises that had nothing to do with seeking power and acquiring land; indeed peace was prized above war. We may therefore understand that the scale and frequency of the early seventeenth century prisoner torture, death and consumption, the aspect of Iroquoian life which Europeans found so offensive, was a response to the demographic crisis of the period. The demographic crisis, brought about largely by the European search for furs, led to the deaths of many: the grief for those deaths had to be assuaged by "mourning wars" and by the deaths of captives, a continuing cycle, until the Iroquoian nations in Canada were quite destroyed.

Iroquoian peoples were not violent towards females: the nation known as "Neutral", because they avoided war against other Iroquoian peoples, was exceptional in this, in that females could be tortured (Jackes 1988:32). Evidence for violence against males alone may well be a mark of societies with institutionalized inter-group aggression, such as that among the Iroquoians, and in the well-known "great fights" of Highland New Guinea (Meggitt 1977). This is not the appropriate context for a discussion of what may constitute inter-group versus intra-group aggression within the shifting focus of human conglomerates, but the referents of "us" and "them" are fluid, and this is as true in small scale societies like the Mae Enga and the inhabitants of the northeastern woodlands of North America, as among societies with populations numbering in the millions, in which defined groups may range from football team supporters to affiliates of world religions or inhabitants of whole continents.

Highland New Guinea "proxy warfare" between groups of males over access to resources may be contrasted with Warlpiri (Walbiri) violence, described in another study by Meggitt (1962) — the use of examples studied by the same anthropologist is deliberate, since the interpretation of social facts may be coloured by the personal viewpoint of the observer. Meggitt clearly found warfare to be of great importance among the Mae Enga (Meggitt 1977), whereas Warlpiri fighting was "restricted" (Meggitt 1962:49,246). Warlpiri violence was overwhelmingly intra-group. Enforcement of Warlpiri social norms might entail physical punishment (ibid. 252, 258), and physical violence towards women was common (ibid. 88, 92, 100), and viewed as punishment. Violence occurred even among women (ibid. 94, 111) and there are multiple references to women beating their adult daughters for misbehaviour (e.g. ibid. 96).

The Warlpiri may not be typical of Central Australians, and behaviour in the 1950s must already have been influenced by European encroachments (ibid. 335), so no general conclusions should be drawn from this one example of desert dwellers (but see a discussion on adult females as victims and perpetrators of violence in Australia in Larsen 1997:140-142, and on the almost uniquely high incidence of cranial trauma in Australia, Jurmain 1999:199). However, the message of Meggitt's work is that the stability of the marital relationship is central to Warlpiri society (ibid. 103) and that social cohesiveness is of prime importance. Violence against women was interpreted as an expression of cohesiveness. Noone can doubt the importance of cohesiveness to a small, egalitarian, kin-based socio-economic unit in a harsh environment.

The Mae Enga and Warlpiri are non-hierarchical societies in very different environments, one society horticultural, the other without permanent settlements, with very different relationships to the land and its resources. Iroquoians had a slightly more hierarchical system. For at least 500 years they had practised shifting agriculture across a wide sweep of the Eastern Woodlands (Hart 2001), and we might see in that movement across the land the root cause of the emphasis on shifting alliances and wars with various Algonquian and Iroquoian neighbours. Each of the three societies discussed here had a different pattern of violence, internal and external, yet none lacked social cohesion. In light of this, it seems unlikely that we could deduce a lack of cohesion from skeletal evidence of violence; indeed, we may not even be able to deduce whether a society is under great stress. The people at Grimsby were suffering extreme crisis, and were literally facing the extinction of their nation, yet it is difficult to provide direct evidence of this; we know of it from the ethnohistorical documentation. Mau Mau may well be seen as an expression of the breakdown of social cohesion among the Kikuyu as a reaction to an incipient major ecological disaster: without historical documentation, the village latrine pit skeletons would no doubt be taken as evidence of a massacre by outsiders during a war.

CONCLUSION

In summary, the recognition of violence in human skeletal remains, and its interpretation, is difficult for a number of reasons.

Evidence from the classic Portuguese Mesolithic sites must be considered equivocal, and this can be highlighted by comparison with other sites – a good archaeological contrast could be made with a late Pleistocene site in which the evidence for violence is not in dispute. Site 117 near Jebel Sahaba in Nubia (Anderson 1968; Wendorf 1968) where a number of skeletons have embedded artifacts, chips embedded in pelves and vertebral centra and neural arches, is a good example. Coupled with rather random cut marks, and many ulnar and radial fractures, the points add up to a clear picture of violence.

Firstly, since most sites lack evidence as convincing as that from Site 117, there needs to be a patterning of trauma in order to recognise violence accurately. The pattern must allow us clearly to distinguish violence from accident, and the trauma must not simply be consistent with specific activities and settings. We must be able to exclude factors like hoe trauma to the shins of agriculturalists as in Ontario, broken foot bones among those living on rocky ground as in Mesolithic Portugal, breakage consistent with falls among those living near cliffs and escarpments as in Portugal and Ontario, or hunting accidents (Portugal?).

The classic "parry" fracture, when found in conjunction with cranial trauma, may provide a good indication of interpersonal violence. But the absence of such signs of violence does not mean a non-violent society. From the human skeletal material in ossuaries and cemeteries, it would not be possible to know that the Ontario Iroquoian societies, Huron and Neutral, during the early seventeenth century were actively engaged in war on several fronts, and were on the verge of total collapse. The other side of the coin is that one cannot assume from the abundant Jiangzhai evidence of violence that the society was warlike. Information from the Mae Enga and from Iroquoian nations tells us that warfare may be institutionalized in such a way as to limit bloodshed. On the other hand, warfare was of little importance in Warlpiri society: there was a great deal of inter-personal violence, focussing especially upon polygynous marital relationships.

Violence in society may be directed inwards, or outwards. Among the Huron, internal violence was rejected - especially violence towards women (even women prisoners of war were unlikely to be harmed, Tooker 1967:31). Coupled with this, however, was a ritualized ferocity towards a broad spectrum of those outsiders with whom one's nation happened to be at war at any particular moment. The rarity of trauma definitely resulting from violence in the ossuaries and cemeteries of Ontario Iroquoian nations arises from an exclusion of those who died from violence. It also suggests that few warriors on spring and summer raiding trips survived to return with wounds that would show up in hard tissue.

Chinese archaeologists have based interpretations about Neolithic society on that stage of Yangshao culture in which there were collective burials, and cohesiveness of the society was deduced from the burial practice. However, the differences in Huron ossuary burial and Neutral multiple and single burial cemeteries cannot be used to interpret one society as more cohesive than the other, and the differences between the two nations, Huron and Neutral, demonstrate that one cannot extrapolate from mortuary practices to make broad statements about the nature of society.

Similarly, the switch from single to collective burials at Jiangzhai does not appear to have resulted in a more "cohesive" society, in the sense of a reduction of violence. With regard to the violence at this one particular Yangshao site, the most economical explanation is internal village violence, perhaps with increasing violence towards females (it must be made clear that the sample size is too small to test this statistically). But in Jackes and Gao (prepared in 1995, in press), I suggested that an important next step in Yangshao osteology was to search for the possibility of people coming into the Wei Valley area from outside, based upon the limited evidence from cranial metrical and non-metrical and dental

non-metrical data. The evidence is as yet minimal, but it is clearly worth pursuing (and the methodology is established, see Jackes et al. 2001).

It is obvious that one can reach no firm conclusions, even when provided with unequivocal evidence of violence. We have seen that societies in which there is internal violence, perhaps especially those in which women suffer violence, may be "cohesive" and not warlike. We have also seen that societies in which women generally escape violence may be equally "cohesive", but warlike to varying degrees, the violence among close neighbours perhaps being limited by ritualization of warfare. We have seen that even societies under extreme stress may display little evidence of internal or external violence, while a situation that seems to demonstrate massacre by outsiders actually shows the results of internal dissension under ecological and political pressure (and civil wars are generally accepted to entail particular ferocity).

It is worthwhile being extraordinarily careful when making broad statements regarding violence in a society, for the simple reason that there are political and judgmental overtones additional to osteological interpretations – we must be sure that we are being strictly neutral when we identify violence. In two instances discussed here, the First Nations of Canada, and the interpretation of the nature of Chinese society, whether according to the tenets of Maoism of the 1970's or the changed perspective of more recent China, the identification of violence is a loaded issue. The origin and ethnohistory of scalping and the treatment of prisoners became a political issue in the 1970s in North America, and the cohesiveness of Yangshao society and the high status of women were important political tenets of the late Maoist period.

We began by quoting the suggestion that osteologists have available to them a truthful record of violence, unadorned by biased reportage that could confuse historians (Walker, 2001:2). Certainly, "...there could never be any logic to ... human violence without the distance of time" (Ondaatje, 2000:55) – a distanced understanding of the roots of violence in competition for resources, oil, water, kangaroos, arable land, gold or coconuts, set within the context of what went before and what came after. But osteologists working on ancient remains have only the sad results of trauma. Their conclusions, for the most part, must be acknowledged for what they are – speculation. The accurate recognition of interpersonal violence, and – above all – the accurate interpretation of such violence, is a difficult matter which can not be separated from a deep, interdisciplinary and cautious study of the context of that violence.

Acknowledgements

Partial funding for the research in China reported here was provided by a special grant from the Central Research Fund, University of Alberta to MJ and D. Lubell. Invaluable assistance in China was provided by Fu Yong and his family. I am grateful to the authorities of the BanPo Museum, especially Director Wang and Director Wei, for permission to work there, to Gao Qiang for his help, and to his colleagues for generously allowing use of their research space. The BanPo Museum photographer is especially thanked for his kindness. My observations on Kikuyu skeletons were made possible through the support of a post-graduate scholarship from the National Research Council of Canada (1972-1975), and I am grateful to workers at the National Museum of Kenya, Nairobi, for their kindness to me. Portuguese research was funded by grants 410-840030 and 410-86-2017 from the Social Sciences and Humanities Research Council of Canada to David Lubell, Christopher Meiklejohn and MJ, and we thank Dr. M.M. Ramalho (Serviços Geológicos de Portugal) and Dr. J. Zilhão (Instituto Português de Arqueologia) for allowing us to study the collections in their care. I am grateful to Mirjana Roksandiæ for inviting my contribution, to anonymous internal reviewers for useful comments on a first draft, to Tim Curtin (National Centre for Development Studies, Australian National University), and especially to David Lubell for his help and advice on many aspects of this paper.

Author address

M.K. Jackes
Department of Anthropology
University of Alberta
Edmonton, AB T6G 2H4
Canada

References

ADAMS, J.C. 1972. *Outline of Fractures Including Joint Injuries* 6th ed. Churchill Livingstone, Edinburgh.

AN, Zhimin 1988. Archaeological research on Neolithic China. *Current Anthropology* 29(5): 753-759.

ANDERSON, J.E. 1968. Late Paleolithic skeletal remains from Nubia. In, F. Wendorf (ed.), *The Prehistory of Nubia*, V. II, pp. 996-1040. Southern Methodist University Press, Dallas.

ANDERSSON, J.G. 1973. *Children of the Yellow Earth: Studies in Prehistoric China*. MIT Press, Cambridge.

BARBOSA SUEIRO, M.B. 1933. La trépanation cranienne chez l'homme néolithique des stations portugaises. *Communicações dos Serviços Geológicos de Portugal* XIX: 41-51 (plus plates).

CARMAN, J. 1997 *Material Harm, archaeological studies of war and violence*. Glasgow: Cruithne Press.

CHANG, K.-C. 1977. *The Archaeology of Ancient China, Third Edition*. Yale University Press, New Haven.

CHANG, K.-C. 1986. *The Archaeology of Ancient China, Fourth Edition*. Yale University Press, New Haven.

CHANG, K.-C. 1992. China. In, R.W. Ehrich (ed.), *Chronologies in Old World Archaeology, 3rd Ed.*, pp. I: 409-415, II: 385-404. University of Chicago Press, Chicago.

China Internet Information Center 2001. *Formation of the Chinese Civilization* online, December 2002 at http://www.china.org.cn/e-gudai/2.htm

DIAS, J.J., G.V. JOHNSON, J. HOSKINSON, K. SULAIMAN 1987. Management of severely displaced medial epicondyle fractures. *Journal of Orthopaedic Trauma* 1:59-62.

ESLER, J. 1998. Burials and isolated human bone fragments from sites in the Crawford Lake area. In, W.D. Finlayson (ed.), *Iroquoian Peoples of the Land of Rocks and Water, A.D. 1000-1650: A Study in Settlement Archaeology, V. 1.*, pp. 156-176. London Museum of Archaeology, University of Western Ontario.

FERRIE, H. 1995. A conversation with KC Chang. *Current Anthropology* 36:307-325.

FINLAYSON, W.D. (editor) 1998. *Iroquoian Peoples of the Land of Rocks and Water, A.D. 1000-1650: a study in settlement archaeology* Volume I London Museum of Archaeology Special Publication 1, London, Ontario.

GAO, Qiang & Yun Kuen LEE 1993. A biological perspective on Yangshao kinship. *Journal of Anthropological Archaeology* 12:266-298.

GLENCROSS, B. & P. STUART-MACADAM 2000. Childhood trauma in the archaeological record. *International Journal of Osteoarchaeology* 10:198-209.

GLENCROSS, B. & P. STUART-MACADAM 2001. Radiographic clues to fractures of distal humerus in archaeological remains. *International Journal of Osteoarchaeology* 11:298-310.

GONG, Qi Ming 1988. *Jiangzhai: Report on the Excavation of the Neolithic Site at Jiangzhai*. Beijing: Cultural Relics Publishing House (in Chinese).

GREEN, N. E. & M. F. SWIONTKOWSKI (editors) 1994. *Skeletal Trauma in Children* v. 3 Philadelphia: W.B. Saunders.

HART, J.P. 2001. Maize, matrilocality, migration, and northern Iroquoian evolution. *Journal of Archaeological Method and Theory* 8:151-182.

HAVERKORT, C.M. & LUBELL, D. 1999. Cutmarks on Capsian human remains: implications for Maghreb Holocene social organization and palaeoeconomy. *International Journal of Osteoarchaeology* 9(3): 147-169.

HOWELLS, W.W. & P. JONES TSUCHITANI (eds.) 1977. *Paleoanthropology in the People's Republic of China : a trip report of the American Paleoanthropology Delegation: submitted to the Committee on Scholarly Communication with the People's Republic of China* National Academy of Sciences, Washington.

Hsi-an Pan-p'o po wu kuan 1987. Pan-p'o i chih : i ko pao ts'un wan cheng ti hsin shih ch'i shih tai ts'un lo i chih (*Banpo Site – a Well-preserved Site of a Neolithic Village*). Hsi-an : Shan-hsi jen min mei shu ch'u pan she : Shan-hsi sheng hsin hua shu tien fa hsing.

JACKES, M. 1977. *The Huron Spine: a study based on the Kleinburg ossuary vertebrae*. PhD Thesis, Department of Anthropology, University of Toronto.

JACKES, M. 1988. *The Osteology of the Grimsby Site*. Department of Anthropology, University of Alberta.

JACKES, M. 1996. Complexity in seventeenth century southern Ontario burial practices. In, D. A. Meyer, P. C. Dawson and D.T. Hanna (eds.), *Debating Complexity: Proceedings of the 26th Annual Chacmool Conference*, pp. 127-140. Calgary: Archaeological Association, University of Calgary.

JACKES, M.K. n.d. The demography of crisis. MS in preparation.

JACKES, M. & GAO, Q. Jiangzhai and BanPo (Shaanxi, PRC): new ideas from old bones. In, L. Janik, S. Kaner, A. Matsui & P. Rowley-Conwy (eds.), From The Jomon to Star Carr. submitted for publication October 1996 forthcoming 2003 International Series of British Archaeological Reports (BAR). BAR Publishing, Oxford, England

JACKES, M., D. LUBELL & C. MEIKLEJOHN 1997. Healthy but mortal: human biology and the first farmers of Western Europe. *ANTIQUITY* 71 (273): 639-658 (supplementary material published electronically at http://intarch.ac.uk/antiquity).

JACKES, M., A.M. SILVA & J. IRISH 2001. Dental morphology: a valuable contribution to our understanding of prehistory. *Journal of Iberian Archaeology.* 3: 97-119.

JACKES, M. & D. LUBELL 1996. Dental pathology and diet: second thoughts. In, M. Otte (ed.), *Nature et Culture: Actes du Colloque International de Liège, 13-17 decembre 1993.* Etudes et Recherches Archéologiques de L'Université de Liège, no 68, pp. 457-480.

JACKES, M. & D. LUBELL 1999a. Human skeletal biology and the Mesolithic-Neolithic transition in Portugal. In, A. Thévenin (ed.), dir. scientifique P. Bintz, *Europe des derniers chasseurs Épipaléolithique et Mésolithique: actes du 5ᵉ colloque international UISPP, commission XII, Grenoble, 18-23 septembre 1995*, pp. 59-64. Éditions du CTHS, Paris.

JACKES, M. & D. LUBELL 1999b. Human biological variability in the Portuguese Mesolithic. *Arqueologia* 24: 25-42.

JAMIESON, B. 1983. An examination of prisoner-sacrifice and cannibalism at the St. Lawrence Iroquoian Roebuck Site. *Canadian Journal of Archaeology* 7:159-175.

JOSEFSSON, P.O. & L.G. DANIELSSON 1986. Epicondylar elbow fracture in children: 35-year follow-up of 56 unreduced cases. *Acta Orthopaedica Scandinavica* 57:313-315.

JURMAIN, R. 1999. Stories from the Skeleton: Behavioral Reconstruction in Human Osteology Amsterdam: Gordon and Breach.

KENNEDY, K.A.R. 1983. Morphological variations in ulnar supinator crests and fossae as identifying markers of occupational stress. *Journal of Forensic Science* 28:871-876.

LARSEN, C.S. 1997 *Bioarchaeology: interpreting behavior from the human skeleton.* Cambridge University Press.

LI Liu 1999. Who were the ancestors? — The origins of Chinese ancestral cult and racial myths. *Antiquity* 73:602-613.

LUBELL, D., M. JACKES, H. SCHWARCZ, M. KNYF & C. MEIKLEJOHN 1994. The Mesolithic-Neolithic transition in Portugal: Isotopic and dental evidence of diet. *Journal of Archaeological Science* 21(2): 201-216.

LUBELL, D. & M. JACKES 1985. Mesolithic-Neolithic continuity: evidence from chronology and human biology. In, M. Ramos (ed.), *Actas, I Renunião do Quaternário Iberico, Lisboa, 1985*, pp. 113-133.

LUBELL, D., M. JACKES & C. MEIKLEJOHN 1989. Archaeology and human biology of the Mesolithic-Neolithic transition in southern Portugal: a preliminary report. In, C. Bonsall (ed.), *The Mesolithic in Europe: Papers Presented at the Third International Symposium, Edinburgh 1985*, pp. 632-640. John Donald. Edinburgh.

MEGGITT, M.J. 1962. *Desert People: A Study of the Walbiri of Central Australia.* Angus and Robertson, Sydney.

MEGGITT, M.J. 1977. Blood is Their Argument: Warfare among the Mae Enga Tribesmen of the New Guinea Highlands. Mayfield, Palo Alto.

MOLTO, J.E., M.W. SPENCE & W. A. FOX 1986. The Van Oordt Site; a case study in salvage osteology. *Canadian Review of Physical Anthropology* 49-61.

OGAWA K. & M. UI 1996. Fracture-separation of the medial humeral epicondyle caused by arm wrestling. *Journal of Trauma* 41:494-497.

ONDAATJE, M., 2000 *Anil's Ghost.* McClelland and Stewart, Toronto.

OSSENBERG, N.S. 1969. *Osteology of the Miller Site.* Royal Ontario Museum Art and Archaeology Occasional Paper 18, ROM, Toronto.

PEARSON, R. 1988. Chinese Neolithic burial patterns: problems of method and interpretation. *Early China* 13:1-45.

PFEIFFER, S. 1986. Morbidity and mortality in the Uxbridge Ossuary. *Canadian Review of Physical Anthropology* 23-31

RICHTER, D.K. 1992. *The Ordeal of the Longhouse: The Peoples of the Iroquois League in the Era of European Colonization.* The University of North Carolina Press, Chapel Hill.

SMITH M.O. 1996. Parry fractures and female-directed interpersonal violence: implications from the Late Archaic period of West Tennessee. *International Journal of Osteoarchaeology* 6:84-91.

SORRENSON, M.P.K. 1967. *Land Reform in the Kikuyu Country: A study in government policy.* East African Institute of Social Research, Oxford University Press Nairobi.

THROUP, D. 1987. *Economic and Social Origins of Mau Mau 1945-1953.* East African Studies James Currey Ltd., London.

THWAITES R.G. 1898. *The Jesuit Relations and Allied Documents: travels and explorations of the Jesuit missionaries in New France 1610-1791* volumes X;XI;XIII;XX;XXVIII Burrows, Cleveland, Ohio.

TONG, E. 1995. Thirty Years of Chinese Archaeology (1949-1979). In P. L. Kohl and C. Fawcett (eds.), *Nationalism, Politics, and the Practice of Archaeology*, , pp. 177-197. Cambridge University Press, Cambridge.

TOOKER, E. 1967. *An Ethnography of the Huron Indians 1615-1649* published by the Huronia Historical Development Council, Midland and the Ontario Department of Education through the cooperation of the Smithsonian Institution, Washington D.C.

TRIGGER, B.G. 1989. *A History of Archaeological Thought* Cambridge University Press.

UBELAKER, D.H. 1989. *Human Skeletal Remains: Excavation, Analysis, Interpretation.* 2nd Ed. Taraxacum, Washington, DC.

UNDERHILL, A. P. 1989. Warfare During the Chinese Neolithic Period: A Review of the Evidence. In, D. C. Tkaczuk and B. C. Vivian (eds.), *Cultures in Conflict: Current Archaeological Perspectives.* Edited by Proceedings of the Twentieth Annual Chacmool Conference, pp. 229-240. The Archaeological Association of the University of Calgary, Calgary.

WALKER, P.L. 2001. A bioarchaeological perspective on the history of violence. *Annual Reviews in Anthropology* 30:573-596.

WANG Ningsheng 1985-1987. Yangshao burial customs and social organization: a comment on the theory of Yangshao matrilineal society and its methodology. *Early China* 11-12:6-31.

WENDORF, F. 1968. Site 117: A Nubian Final Paleolithic graveyard near Jebel Sahaba, Sudan. In, F. Wendorf (ed.), *The Prehistory of Nubia*, V. II, pages 954-995 Southern Methodist University Press, Dallas.

ZILHÃO, J. 1984. *A Gruta da Feteira (Lourinhã): Escavação de salvamento de uma necrópole neolítica.* Trabalhos de Arqueologia 1, Ministério da Cultura, Instituto Português do Patrimonio Cultural, Lisboa.

APPENDIX 1:1
Portuguese skeletal remains mentioned in text

1. Material from Mesolithic shell middens stored in the Serviços Geológicos de Portugal in Lisbon.

Moita do Sebastião Ossada 2: A heavy male with unusually strongly marked muscle attachments. A broken bladelet is still embedded below the sustenaculum tali of the right calcaneus. Reactive bone surrounds the bladelet in the form of a spur. The individual had a variety of arthritic changes and there are areas of hyperostosis. The pronator quadratus ridge on the distal ulna shaft very well developed (strong pronation of the forearm) and also, just above, the distal end of the flexor digitorum profundis origin (strong flexing of the hand, as with pressure flaking in and down, is indicated).

Moita do Sebastião Ossada 5: Mixed "individual" - on the male, pectoralis muscle insertion on left humerus certainly, and on the damaged right humerus probably, indicates great muscle development, action is of drawing arm in and rotating it in and down, as with hammering.

Moita do Sebastião Ossada 6: Male. Forceful extension of the elbow and supination (i.e. in the anatomical position with the palm up or facing forwards) deduced from the ulna supinator crest development and extension of olecranon facet onto the olecranon process. Also abnormal right metatarsal II.

Moita do Sebastião Ossada 10: Fragmentary ?female. Figure 1b Lower midshaft pseudarthrosis in the right ulna and right olecranon joint surface was restricted. Abnormality of the left acetabulum also noted; slight abnormality of the right clavicle,. Association with Craneo xvii - adult attrition level 5 (see note below).

Moita do Sebastião Ossada 14: A large male. Figure 4b Left humerus: the medial epicondyle is reduced almost to absence, while on the lateral epicondyle there is a build-up of bone at the posterior medial border. The ulnae are equivalent in length but the distal portion of flexor digitorum profundis origin produces a marked ridge on the right ulna only: the distal right ulna articular surface is larger than the left and has slight arthritic lipping at the radial articular surface. The left radius is ca. 3 mm longer than the right. The first metacarpals and the clavicles differ from each other in robusticity. There would have been difficulty in pronating the left hand (i.e. turning the palm down to the ground or facing backwards) and flexing the fingers - fine control would have been compromised. Association with Craneo xxi - adult attrition level 5 (see note below).

Moita do Sebastião Ossada 25a: Very fragmentary ?female. Figure 1a Healed fracture in the distal third of the right ulna. The right radius was not available for examination. Possibly associated with Craneo xxx (adult attrition level 6). On a phalanx manus (distal, unsided), the proximal articular surface and adjacent shaft has pathology from inflamation inflammatory reaction to infection and cut marks.

Moita do Sebastião Ossada 30 ("1030"): Probably male, but mixed "individual" . Figure 1c Apparent greenstick fracture to distal third of right ulna shaft. Right clavicle with unusually strongly developed deltoideus attachment. The radii have very broad necks and strongly angled radial tuberosities.

Moita do Sebastião Ossada CT: Male with arthritis of right elbow: Ph II manus Digit V spurring at insertion of flexor superficialis (without infection).

Cabeço da Arruda Ossada XIII: A fragmentary elderly individual, probably male, fractured ribs.

Cabeço da Arruda Ossada XIV: Had two left radii, one of which might have sustained a hairline fracture.

Cabeço da Arruda Ossada XVII: Unknown individual. Extra right radius considered to have parry fracture, but radiograph show no clear break. Childhood injury.

Cabeço da Arruda Ossada XXV (E): The only humerus present, the left, shows the possibility of delayed fusion of the medial epicondyle epiphysis which was completely absent, though partial fusion might have been expected in this late adolescent male. There is a completely normal humerotangential angle (HTA), with the medial angle 94 and the lateral 86 (see Glencross and Stuart-Macadam, 2001).

Cabeço da Arruda Ossada 29: A very large middle-aged male, had a bilateral abnormality of the coronoid process of the ulnae. Marked deformity of the left humeral distal articular surfaces with arthritic changes. Right radius head particularly abnormal, but both radial heads broad and sharply angled down.

Cabeço da Arruda Ossada H: Figure 2 A fragmentary elderly ?female with osteoporosis and arthritis, mandibular dentition indicates attrition level 11, one of the 2 or 3 very oldest people studied. Left ulna fractured, and left distal humerus arthritic.

Cabeço da Arruda Ossada (900)F: Lateral spurring on clavicle.

Cabeço da Arruda Q: Figure 3 The left humerus and ulna of an arthritic male with long-standing (childhood?) fracturing of the left elbow. Apparent fracture of olecranon and through the medial distal humerus. More arthritis on the humerus than is usual for the population.

Cabeço da Arruda "SH": A mixed "individual" — fractured right clavicle, arthritis on five left ribs (bone growth unrelated to either of the facets for vertebrae), one rib appears to have a false joint, humerus with marked cortical thinning. A right ulna has abnormal supinator crest morphology.

Cabeço da Arruda "TO": A mixed "individual" left MC IV and right MC V strongly curved –broken in childhood? A slightly arthritic right ulna with flattened shaft and abnormal curvature.

Note: Mesolithic individuals from the above two sites are not complete, especially for Cabeço da Arruda. Moita do Sebastião skulls had been removed for display and numbered separately, and therefore associations are uncertain: during our research, Jackes and Meiklejohn drew up an inventory attempting to reconcile drawer contents with previous records made by Ferembach and Meiklejohn. For attrition level explanation see Lubell *et al.* 1989.

2. Samoqueira 1: Broken humerus (see Lubell and Jackes 1985 for details). Humerotangential angle (HTA) (see Glencross and Stuart-Macadam, 2001): medial angle 64, lateral angle 116, showing the extent to which the distal portion of the humerus has deviated medially. Also has broken metatarsal.

3. Neolithic ossuaries: isolated skeletal elements only

Melides Zambujal 15: (Figure 5) Left humerus in which a break at the trochlea has resulted in the medial articular surface being driven up so that it lies precisely 1 cm above (proximal to) the capitulum. The medial angle with the long axis of the humeral shaft of the line drawn from the trochlea to the capitulum is 74 degrees, and the lateral is 106 degrees - this can be compared with the expected lateral angle of slightly under 90 degrees and the expected medial angle correspondingly slightly above 90. The normal angle is therefore reversed and exaggerated. So we can understand that this is a proximal displacement of the medial epiphyseal potion of the distal humerus, which is most likely to have occurred prior to the age of fusion, and was the result of compressive forces upward on the ulna. In other words, a childhood fall.

ABOUT VIOLENT INTERACTIONS IN THE MESOLITHIC:
THE ABSENCE OF EVIDENCE FROM THE PORTUGUESE SHELL MIDDENS

Eugénia CUNHA, Cláudia UMBELINO, Francisca CARDOSO

Abstract: The Portuguese Mesolithic is well known for its large number of skeletons dated approximately from 7500 BP to 5500 BP. The paleobiological analysis of nearly 400 skeletons coming from both the Muge and the Sado shell middens provides a good framework for the study of daily life of late semi sedentary hunter gatherers in Europe. The series is characterised by a low prevalence of pathological lesions in general, and traumatic in particular.

In the present paper we examine the prevalence of traumatic injuries in these populations. This type of pathology is almost absent in sub adults, and very low in adults. Evidently, the state of preservation of the human skeleton remains a limiting factor in pathological analysis, which might consequently result in an underestimation. We present here all the identified cases and offer an overall interpretation based on type and frequency of trauma that is pertinent to the daily life of this ancient population. The majority of the injuries found could result from daily activities, which were not as demanding as has been previously assumed. Overall, there is no indication that these communities witnessed substantial interpersonal violence.

Keywords: interpersonal violence, Sado shell middens, Muge shell middens, skeletal trauma, Mesolithic Portugal

INTRODUCTION

The Muge river shell middens are important in understanding the lifestyle of the Mesolithic communities in Europe. Located on the Tagus old terraces, these shell middens have already a long research history that began in 1863 with Carlos Ribeiro and still continues, 138 years later (Cunha and Cardoso, 2002/3). The osteological series comes from four sites: Cabeço da Amoreira, Cabeço da Arruda, Moita do Sebastião and Cova da Onça. A large number of radiocarbon dates exist for the sites (Lubell *et al.*, 1986; Lubell and Jackes, 1994; Cunha e Cardoso, 2002/3). All of the four sites under examination were settled at around 7000 BP and when all the available dates are taken into account, it is possible to say that these Mesolithic communities stayed in Muge for at least a 1000 years.

Less known are the Sado shell middens located on the lower course of the Sado river, some 100 km south from Muge. Eleven sites were reported (Arnaud, 1989), six of which have yielded human skeletal remains (Cunha and Umbelino, 1995/7; Cunha *et al.*, 2003.). Several radiocarbon dates (Cunha *et al.*, 2003) confirm their contemporaneity with the Muge shell middens.

The Sado anthropological series is stored at the National Museum of Archaeology in Lisbon. Part of Muge material is housed at the Oporto Museum of Natural History (N= 109); another at the Museum of Anthropology at Coimbra University (five individuals), and the Museu dos Serviços Geológicos de Portugal in Lisbon houses another important part (N=96). In the present article we did not include some of the material housed in Lisbon, which has not yet been analysed by our team.

The examined portion of the two series totals 298 analysed individuals, differently represented from complete skeletons to single bones. The frequencies provided here are based on the total of human skeletal remains exhumed from the Sado shell middens (N= 112), and a significant part of the Muge osteological series, namely 196 individuals (around 65 % of the total)[1].

Why accurate prevalence of traumatic events cannot be assessed?

As noted, there is a considerable heterogeneity in the state of preservation of these skeletal remains. While there are individuals represented by a single bone, others are quite complete, with even small bones of hand and feet present. In addition, some skeletons were exhumed in blocks of sediments, some were treated by paraffin (Sado), whereas others remain embedded in a dense calcified matrix. Nevertheless, there is a significant portion of intact bones allowing all types of observations.

Despite the large amount of human skeletal remains, we do not consider it reasonable to present specific figures for the prevalence of traumatic episodes within the Portuguese Mesolithic because of important taphonomic alterations, which we will briefly describe.

In terms of taphonomy, we can discern two main types of extrinsic factors: one is human activity and the other includes several environmental agents. For the first, the way the skeletons were recovered and preserved seems to be the most important one. This can be partially justified by the field

---

[1] In the present article we do not include a part of the material housed in Lisbon, which has not yet been analysed by our team.

methods prevalent at the time of excavation (from the end of the 19th century to the middle 20th). In addition, paraffin was used in order to preserve the original inhumation position in several cases at Sado shell middens. Later attempts to remove the paraffin were not entirely successful and left some further damage on the bone surfaces.

Among the environmental agents, which have precluded a more detailed anthropological analysis, the most important is the dense calcified matrix embedding the bones. In effect, calcite not only covered the bone surface but also filled the medullary cavities of long bones inhibiting any kind of radiographic analysis. Other important factors include damage by plant roots, macro and micro fauna actions, particularly gnawing, which left distinctive marks on the bone surfaces. Further, in some cases, the sediment over the bones collapsed, leading to a flattened and crushed appearance of, skulls and mandibles, in particular.

Not all the above-mentioned postmortem alterations, can always be easily distinguished from antemortem lesions. Careful observation, however, allows discerning between the truly pathological cases from the pseudopathology, providing an essential first step to perform in any kind of analysis of the prevalence of diseases. In this article we analyse traumatic injuries, and have to distinguish another important postmortem alteration – the postmortem fracture – which, at first sight, may be mistaken for antemortem lesions.

Thus, having considered all the taphonomic alterations referred to, we present here all traumatic lesions encountered during our analysis of this Mesolithic series. Owing to the aforementioned problems of preservation, however, these cannot be accurately quantified.

THE TRAUMATIC CASES:

Muge

Case 1.

A healed fracture on the distal medial end of the left ulna of an adult female from Cabeço da Arruda (skeleton 1 housed at Porto Museum). The adjacent radius does not show any evidence of trauma while the tissue around the lesion does not present signs of infectious reaction. As can be seen in fig.1, there is a net bone enlargement due to osseous callus formation. X-ray does confirm the existence of an oblique fracture with lamellar bone across the fracture site. The healing process did not involve overlapping of the fractured bones, nor any kind of shortening. When comparing the length of left and right ulnas, no asymmetry is perceptible.

This fracture could have been caused either by a fall or happened during an act of deffence, the so-called Parry fracture, defined as the fracture to distal ulna inflicted to an individual defending one's face. It is the only pathological event on the entire skeleton of this individual, a fact which tends to support the second hypothesis (Parry fracture).

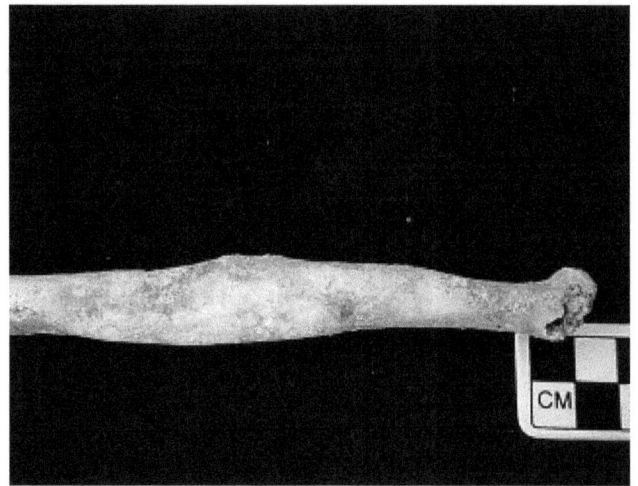

Figure 1 – Deformed ulna from Skeleton 1 from Cabeço da Arruda (housed at Porto Museum), due to osseous callus formation.

Case 2.

This case is from Cabeço da Arruda as well. A fracture on the left forearm of a sub-adult individual, around 14-16 years of age at the time of death (according to the epiphyseal fusion). Both radius and ulna were affected, presenting an unusually curve shaft, namely a medial rotational deformity (fig. 2). Trauma could be confirmed only by means of X-ray analysis. Furthermore, the absence of the *osseous callus* formation indicates that we are dealing with a well-healed ancient fracture, with complete resorption of the fracture line. In addition, no overlapping was detected. The remaining skeleton displays no pathological evidence, which points to a localised traumatic injury.

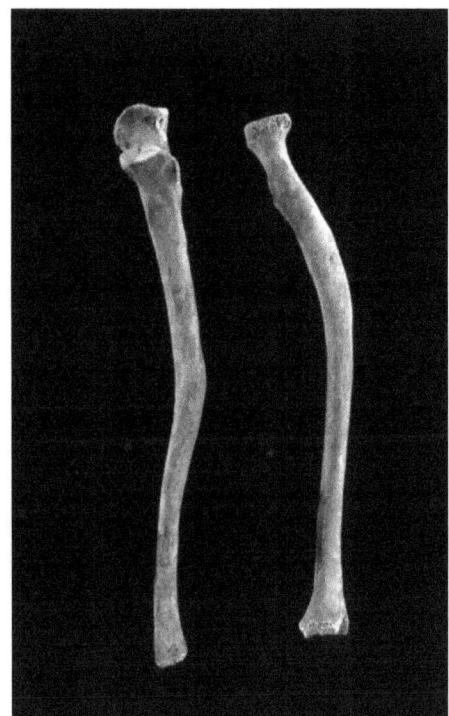

Figure 2 – One of the macroscopically most evident cases of a fracture. Non-adult from Cabeço da Arruda (M.S.G.).

Case 3.

A partial trephination can be observed on the frontal bone of a male individual (XLI), over 30 years old, from Moita do Sebastião, housed at the Museum of Serviços Geológicos in Lisbon. On the right antero-lateral portion of the frontal bone, there is an irregular area with a conic healed depression, with 13.5 mm diameter and of 6 mm depth (fig. 3). Although the skull had been varnished, it is possible to observe that the bone surface is completely remodelled, with traces of periosteal reaction, which was not active at the time of death. It does not seem that the lesion penetrated into the inner part of the skull. The hole had been performed by drilling and might have been subsequent to a traumatic injury because of the irregularity of the surface which seemed to have been scrapped before drilling (Crubézy et al., 2001). This case is particularly important because it is one of the few examples of trephination known so far from Mesolithic sites.

Until now, no post-cranial remains have been assigned to this particular skull.

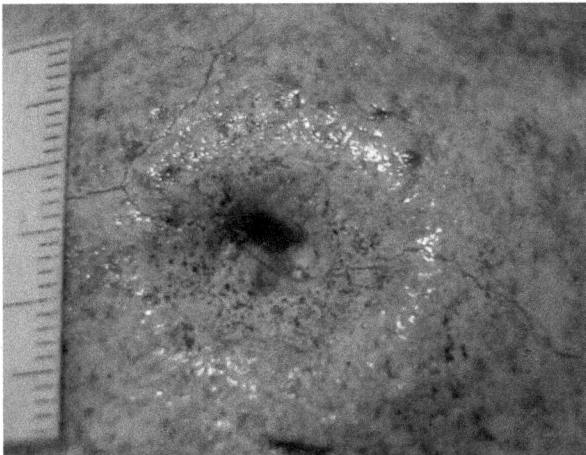

Figure 3 – Detail of the partial trephination on the Moita do Sebastião (skeleton XLI) skull.

Case 4.

On the left parietal of an isolated skull from Moita de Sebastiao (skeleton 3), an elliptical depression was detected. The form of this depression clearly suggests that it was a blunt impact injury caused antemortem. The cranium belonged to a male individual who seemed to be a young adult (20-30 years old).

Case 5.

Again, a circular depression was found on the middle of the right parietal whose characteristics point to a blunt impact injury caused antemortem. The individual is most probably a female who died in her thirties.

Case 6.

This third case of depressed fracture on the skull was found on another adult skull from Moita de Sebastião (skeleton 20).

It belongs to a male individual who might have died at an older age (according to antemortem tooth loss). This time the antemortem injury affects the frontal bone on its left part, near the temporal line. The depressed sulcus, which displays some microporosity, could have been caused by a blunt impact.

Case 7.

On an adult calvarium from Arruda (skeleton. 2), with female characteristics, a depression was detected exactly on the right parietal fossa. Again, the osseous regeneration points to an antemortem injury.

Case 8.

This case of cranial injury is more doubtful. It is a small hole detected on the left parietal of an adult skull from Arruda, housed in the Museum of Serviços Geológicos. While its endocranial view suggests an eventual postmortem etiology, its exocranial aspect, where the lesion's margins have indicators of an osteogenic response (smooth edges), points to an antemortem lesion caused by a cutting object. However, the possibility that the smooth appearance was caused by postmortem alterations cannot be completely excluded.

Case 9.

This specimen comes from Cova da Onça shell midden, the least known of the Muge valley sites (Cunha and Cardoso, 2002/3). Since the 32 individuals from this site were analysed as an ossuary, we can not assign the affected bone to an individual, a fact that precludes further inferences. It is a proximal half of a left ulna, of an adult individual. A bone enlargement just above the broken extremity indicated a traumatic event (fig. 4). The X-Ray image, confirms this by showing a transverse fracture line precisely on the affected area. This transversal fracture is healed, well aligned, with no evidence of bone reaction.

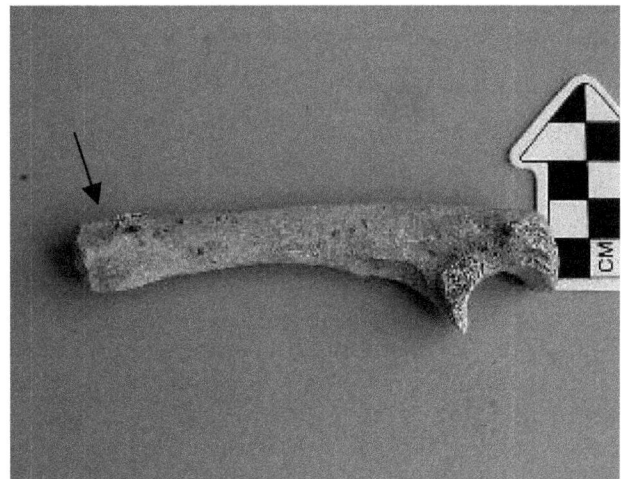

Figure 4 – Proximal half of the left ulna with a traumatic injury on its distal end (see arrow).

Case 10.

This last case of cranial trauma from the Muge valley sites, comes from Arruda. It is a severe dislocation of the left temporo-mandibular joint (TMJ). The individual is an adult male, over 50 years old. There is a loss of contact between the left mandibular condyle and the glenoid fossa on the temporal bone, with the formation a secondary articulation. Subsequently, severe osteoarthritic lesions (fig. 5) on both surfaces involved in the TMJ articulation arose. In addition this individual presented severe oral pathologies, such as caries and abscesses.

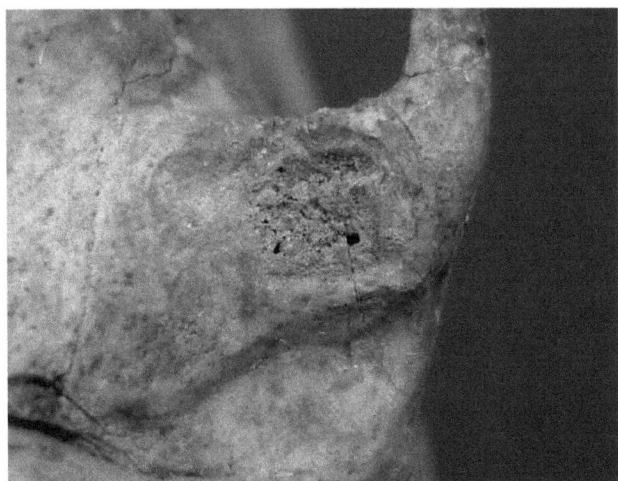

Figure 5 – Severe osteoarthrithic lesion on the secondary articular facet in a male individual from Arruda (Skeleton 3).

Case 11.

An adult male individual from Moita do Sebastião (skeleton 34) presents on the third left metatarsal bone a clear enlargement just above the lateral articular surface. The lesion is mostly visible from the plantar view, but shows no periosteal reaction. The X-ray analysis, nevertheless, was not conclusive, partly due to the incorporation of calcite into medullary channel of the shaft. There is always the possibility of this anomaly being a morphological trait, since other foot bones belonging to different individuals present it, such as the skeleton from Amoreira (see case 12).

Case 12.

From the Amoreira site there is a male individual, over 30 years old, who had a fracture on the distal shaft of the right radius. Macroscopically, looking at the anterior view, we see an overlap between the shaft and the distal end of the radius, resulting from an oblique fracture, with a distinctive callus formation. Despite the morphological changes observed, it is a healed fracture with no bone reaction. On the X-ray the aforementioned overlap between the bone parts is quite clear (Cunha e Cardoso, 2002/3).

These are the only cases with discernible traumatic aetiology from the Muge region.

Sado

The accurate number of traumatic cases from the Sado river shell midden, is even lower: only two cases were identified. Nevertheless, we have to keep in mind that for some of these shell middens, such as Poças de S. Bento, the great fragmentation of human bones did not allow a reliable analysis.

Case 1.

A fracture was found on the distal portion of the 3rd metatarsal bone, belonging to a female individual, over 40 years old at the site of Arapouco. Macroscopically we could only observe a small *osseous callus* formation. Nevertheless, a distinctive longitudinal fracture line is visible on the X-ray picture (fig. 6). The most probable cause for this event may have been an accidental trauma.

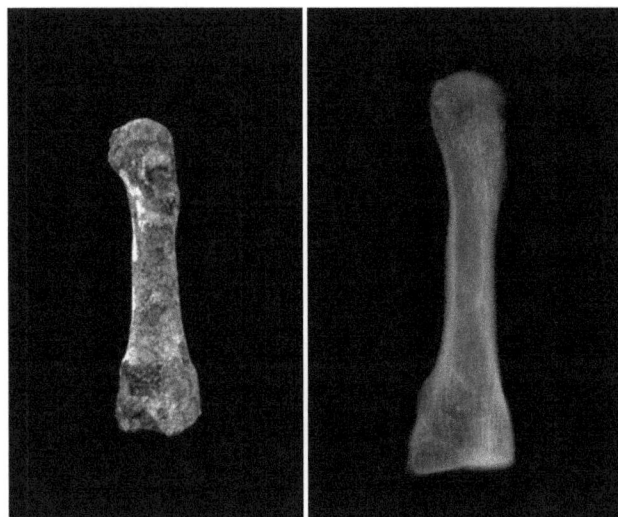

Figure 6 – Third metatarsal from an adult female from Arapouco showing a healed fracture (macroscopic and radiographic images).

Case 2.

A healed fracture with callus formation in the mid-shaft of the right fibula was identified in a male individual (skeleton 14A) who died during his 40s from the same site. Once again, the X-ray showed a radiolucent line indicating the fracture line without appositional overlap (fig. 7). The same individual shows evidence of vertebral compression fracture in the vertebral bodies as a result of a trauma with a yet undefined underlying pathology.

At least two other individuals in the Sado anthropological series, displayed signs of vertebral compression and loss of height, corresponding to a process of decalcification. That is, there are two probable cases of osteoporosis underlying a vertebral compression. These cases will not be referred to in detail because, despite being traumatic events, their aetiology is beyond the scope of the present article

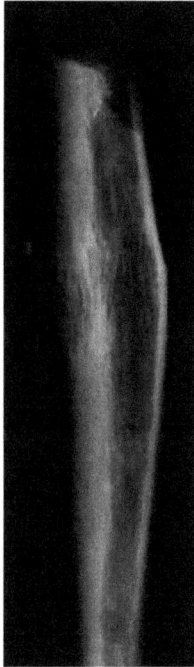

Figure 7 – X-ray picture of a fibula from an adult male from Sado (Arapouco), showing different densities of bone.

DISCUSSION AND CONCLUSIONS

Several authors (Rathbun 1984, among others) have stressed that the identification of trauma is complicated by the difficulty of discerning whether it is the result of an accident or hostility, and whether it is related to habitat and terrain or to types of physical activity (Rathbun 1984, 155).

In addition, we have to keep in mind that trauma may affect only the soft tissues and, in that case, is not necessarily observable in the skeleton (Roberts, 2000). Therefore the real incidence of traumatic events can not be ascertained solely on the basis of the skeleton. Nevertheless, trauma inferred from human bones can elucidate the lifestyle of the afflicted individuals (Roberts and Manchester, 1995), contributing to the knowledge of the behavioural aspects of past populations.

On the one hand, interpersonal violence may reflect increased sedentism, competition for resources, social inequality and complexity as well as increased trade and contact; on the other hand, domestic accidents, may reflect physical environment such as climate (Roberts, 2000, 338). Furthermore, the occurrence and patterning of trauma can clarify, among others, the subsistence strategy of foraging *versus* farming.

In all, fourteen cases in these two series could be reported as truly traumatic events. This figure was derived after a detailed work where the pseudopathological lesions, due to taphonomic alterations, were excluded. Six of the injuries affect the skull and seem to be a consequence of head or frontal confrontations. These six lesions perform half of the traumatic cases in Muge and 43% of the total incidences if we take into account Sado as well. The depressed fracture

on the frontal bone with clear signs of trephination, can be interpreted as a case of interpersonal violence. This inference can also be applied to the other depressed lesions on adult crania, which seem to result from blunt impacts. According to Larsen (1997), these kinds of injuries seem to imply the intention of the aggressor to injure rather than kill the targeted victim

In opposition, of the post-cranial traumatic events reported here, seven, seem to have derived mainly from occupational accidents rather than inter-personal violence. Even the case of forearm fracture, both the Parry fracture (case 1, Muge) and the case affecting a sub-adult do not necessarily mean interpersonal violence in and of themselves, as they may have been caused by falls (Roberts, 2000). Four of the postcranial injuries affect the forearm bones, while two were detected in metatarsal bones and one in a fibula. The remaining cases can be clearly considered a dislocation (case 10, Muge). When the ages of death of the affected individuals are taken into account, only one subadult is affected (case 2, Muge).. In what sex-ratio is concerned, among the 13 adults with traumas, four seem to be females, seven males, with the remaining two affected individuals undetermined.

Discussing now the prevalence of traumatic lesions by sites, once again, no particular cluster is found. In effect, in Muge all four sites, Arruda, Moita, Amoreira and Cova da Onça, have at least one case. In the Sado shell middens, although the two recognized cases came from the same site, Arapouco, the bone preservation at the other sites does not permit us to be categorical about their absence. That is, the absence of evidence is not necessarily the same as evidence for absence. Even though none of the individuals discussed here has been directly dated, the chronological distribution of the observed lesions, on the basis of dates[2] available from several sites and the three most effected ones – Moita do Sebastião, Arruda and Arapouco – have very similar dates around 6800 to 7240 BC (Cunha and Cardoso, 2002/3).

With regard to both their etilogy and their low frequency, several factors should be taken into account. First, more than one interpretation may be advanced. Furthermore, simple compatibility does not constitute proof unless all alternative hypotheses are incompatible with the data. This kind of approach should be considered in all types of data interpretation (Relethford, 1999).

Because of postmortem modifications in most of the osteological material in both the Sado and Muge shell middens, the identification and description of the nature of bone anomalies was not easy. The aetiologies of stains and other alterations to the bone proved troublesome. In the majority of cases, they could be interpreted as reflection of damage that occurred during deposition, related to soil and water. This implies that the examination of the margins of the lesion to get an understanding of antemortem bone response was also difficult. Of the cases presented here, the most obvious ones in terms of traumatic events were those where callus formation was evident.

---

[2] None of the individuals analysed here have been dated.

As expected, distinguishing between antemortem, perimortem and postmortem injuries although paramount (Sauer, 1998) was problematic. In addition, perimortem reactions went undetected because this type of reaction is less straightforward to identify than antemortem trauma, mainly in ancient bones.

According to Berryman and Symes (1998), the basics nature of fracture formation must be thoroughly understood in order to interpret blunt trauma. Patterned fracture characteristics depend upon various external factors such as magnitude, area, and duration of the blow as well as intrinsic factors such as bone elasticity and density. All the observed depressed skull traumas seem to have been the result of moderate aggression.

Thus, within the Mesolithic context, it has been assumed that traumatic events would occur frequently both as the result of interpersonal aggression and the lifestyle of hunter-gatherers - their unsettled way of life and the way they exploited wild resources. Hunting was based on a greater diversity of animal species and on larger animals which suggests more risks needed to be taken where traumatic injuries could take place. In view of the fact that, in fact, very few such injuries were found at these sites however, it seems that these suppositions are not supported by the osteological samples analysed here, samples which comprise about 75% of all the Portuguese Mesolithic series. Thus, of the 308 individuals examine so far, only 14 events related to trauma have been observed, corresponding to an incidence of around 4.5 %.

Meiklejohn et al., (1984), has suggested that the Mesolithic economy sees the appearance of semi-permanent settlements and increase in the density of more evenly spaced sites. This seems to have been the case with both the Muge and Sado communities. Some authors have argued in favour of a continuum of aggression positively connected with population density. However, this does not seem to have been the case with either the Muge or Sado communities.

All in all, traumatic lesions detected primarily see to represent accidental injury rather than result from group conflict.

Acknowledgements

This paper was partially funded by a Praxis grant, from Fundação da Ciência e Tecnologia, namely PCNA/BIA/114/96.

Dr. J. Brandão, from Serviços Geológicos de Portugal, and Dr. Luís Raposo, from Museu Nacional de Arqueologia, facilitated this research in many ways. Dr. Huet Bacelar, from Museu de História Natural do Porto, has also helped us a lot.

We thank Dr. Mirjana Roksandic for the invitation to participate in the present volume and for her comments and paper editing.

Authors address

Eugénia Cunha, Cláudia Umbelino, Francisca Cardoso
Departamento de Antropologia
Universidade de Coimbra
3000-056 Coimbra, Portugal

References

ARNAUD, J. M. 1989. The Mesolithic communities of the Sado valley, Portugal, in their ecological setting. In: (C. Bonsall, Ed.) The Mesolithic in Europe: Papers Presented at the third International Symposium, Edinburgh 1985. Edinburgh: John Donald, pp. 614-631.

BERRYMAN, H. E., SYMES, S. A. 1998. Recognizing gunshot and blunt trauma though fracture interpretation. In: Reichs, K. (ed.). Forensic osteology. NY. Charles C. Thomas: 333-352.

CUNHA, E., UMBELINO, C. 1995/7. Abordagem antropológica das comunidades Mesolíticas dos Concheiros do Sado. O Arqueólogo Português, série IV, 13/15, p. 161-179.

CUNHA, E., CARDOSO, F. 2002/3. New data on Muge shell middens: a contribution to more accurate numbers and dates. Muge Estudos Arqueológicos. Vol I.: 171-184.

CUNHA, E., CARDOSO, F., UMBELINO, C. 2003. Inferences about Mesolithic life style on the basis of anthropological data. The case of the Portuguese shell middens. In: Larsson, L.; Kindgren, H.; Knutsson, K.; Loeffler, D.; Akerlund, A. (ed.). Mesolithic on the Move. Oxford. Oxbow books: 184-188.

CRUBÉZY, E., BRUZEK, J., GUILAINE, J., CUNHA, E., ROUGÉ, D., JELINEK, J. 2001. The antiquity of cranial surgery in Europe and in the Mediterranean Basin. Comptes Rendue de l'Academie des Sciences Paris. Sciences de la Terre et des planètes. 332(2001) 417-423.

LARSEN, C.S. 1997. Bioarchaeology. Interpreting behavior from the human skeleton. Cambridge. Cambridge University Press.

LUBELL, D., JACKES,M., SCHWARCZ, H., MEIKLEJOHN, C. 1986. New radiocarbon dates for Moita do Sebastião. Arqueologia. 14:34-36.

LUBELL, D., JACKES, M., SCHWARCZ, H., KNYF, M., MEIKLEJOHN, C. 1994. The Mesolithic-Neolithic transition in Portugal: Isotopic and dental evidence of diet. Journal of Archaeological Science. 21, 201-216.

MEIKLEJOHN, C., SCHENTAG, C., VENEMA, A., KEY, P. 1984. Socioeconomic change and patterns of Pathology and variation in the Mesolithic and Neolithic of Western Europe: some suggestions. In: Cohen, M. N.; Armelagos, G. J. (ed.), Paleopathology at the Origins of Agriculture. Orlando, Academic Press: 75-100.

RATHBUN, T. A. 1984. Skeletal pathology from the Paleolithic through the Metal Ages in Iran and Iraq. In: Cohen, M. N.; Armelagos, G. J. (ed.), Paleopathology at the Origins of Agriculture. Orlando,. Academic Press: 137-168.

RELETHFORD, J. H. 1999. Models, predictions and the fossil record of modern human origins. Evolutionary Anthropology. 8.1:7-10.

ROBERTS, C. 2000. Trauma in biocultural perspective: past, present and future work in Britain. In: Cox, M.; Mays, S. (ed.), Human osteology in Archaeology and Forensic Science. London. Greenwich Medical Media Ltd.: 337-356.

ROBERTS, C., MACHESTER, K. 1995. The Archaeology of Disease. 2nd edition. Ithaca, NY. Cornell University Press.

SAUER, N. J. 1998. The timing ojf injuries and manner of death: distinguishing among antemortem, perimortem and postmortem trauma. In: Reich, K. (ed.),. Forensic osteology. NY. Charles C. Thomas: 321- 332.

L'ÉBIRAUMAURUSIEN ET LA VIOLENCE: CAS DES SITES DE TAFORALT ET D'IFRI N'AMMAR

A. BEN-NCER

Key-words: Sépulture, violence, Ibéromaurusien, Ifri n'Ammar, Rif oriental, Maroc.

Il va sans dire que des conditions de vie, manifestement difficiles, ont du imposer aux Femmes et aux Hommes paléolithiques une lutte acharnée d'abord en quête de gibiers de tous gabarits, mais également une lutte de pouvoir entre eux et ce, dans une perspective de faire régner ce pouvoir à l'échelle d'une aire géographique déterminée. C'est dire que la violence devait être de rigueur dans ces situations. Mais, notre propos ici est d'aborder la violence dans une échelle largement plus réduite à savoir celle qui aurait pu toucher un des éventuels membres d'une même famille ou du même groupe par les autres membres de la première ou du second. Dans ce cas de figure, on peut placer les supplices qui se seraient abattus sur d'impuissants personnages tels que des enfants démunis. C'est ce qui a du se produire pour un enfant en bas âge dont la sépulture fut mise au jour à Ifri n'Ammar (province de Nador, Maroc, cf. fig. 1 et fig. 2), et laquelle n'appelle aucun équivoque pour attester la pratique de la violence. Celle-ci pourrait être également avancée dans le cadre d'un autre exemple correspondant en revanche à 3 sujets adultes, dont les restes ont été découverts dans le site de Taforalt (province de Berkane, Maroc, cf. fig. 1 et fig. 3)

et dont le squelette cérébral laisse entrevoir les séquelles d'évidents traumatismes. Un concours de circonstances a fait que et ces adultes et l'enfant d'Ifri n'Ammar appartiennent à la même séquence «culturelle» à savoir l'Ibéromaurusien.

L'IBÉROMAURUSIEN

L'Ibéromaurusien (terme forgé par Paul Pallary au vu des similitudes culturelles qui existaient de part et d'autre du détroit de Gibraltar) est une culture qui allait se répandre au Maghreb, à partir du 22ème millénaire BP (J. Roche, 1976) pour y durer jusqu'au 10ème millénaire BP au maximum. On la retrouve dans les zones du Tell et du littoral, elle atteint également le voisinage des hautes plaines et même des zones pré sahariennes. Elle est étroitement associée aux populations de Mechta-el-Arbi (D. Ferembach, 1986). Des études récentes ont démontré que ces populations possédaient la même stature que l'Homme actuel et qu'elles étaient robustes.

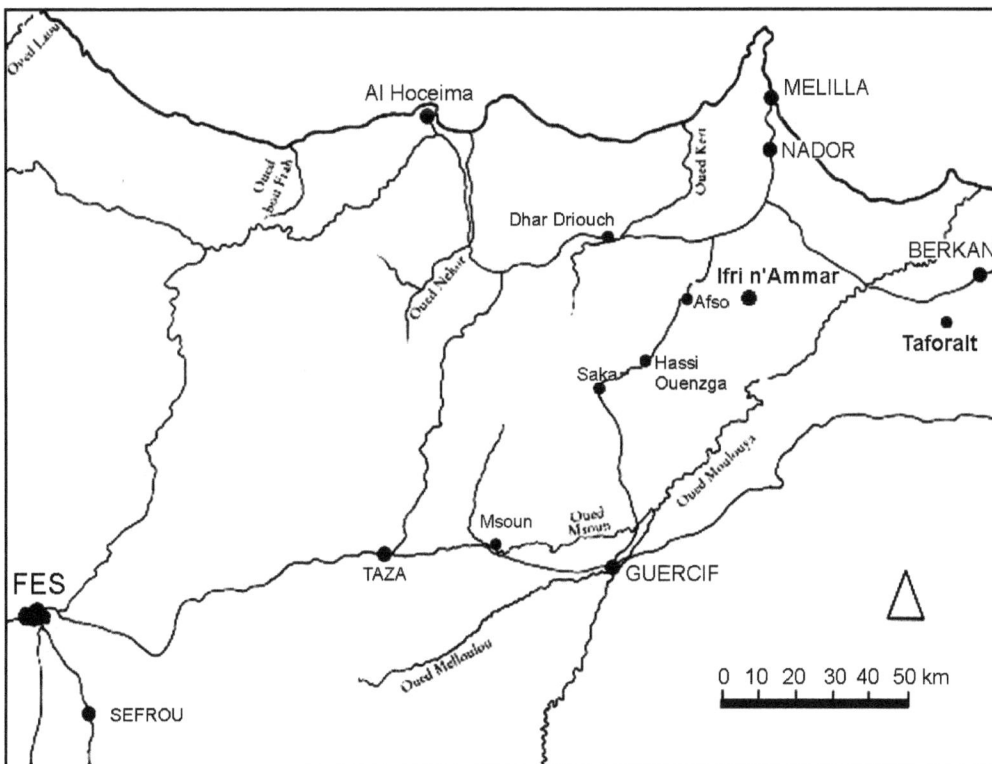

Figure 1: carte du Maroc oriental montrant les sites de Taforalt et d'Ifri n'Ammar.

Figure 2: site d'Ifri n'Ammar (photo. J Eiwanger, 2002).

Figure 3: site de Taforalt (photo. D. Ferembach, 1977).

A l'échelle du Maroc, les restes humains découverts dans la nécropole de Taforalt confirment ces résultats. Le sujet adulte de sexe féminin, dont les restes ont été mis au jour dans la grotte d'Ifri El-Baroud, ou les autres sujets, que ce soit l'adulte de sexe masculin ou les enfants, dont les restes ont été découverts dans le site d'Ifri n'Ammar, s'inscrivent tous dans cette tendance. Signalons juste au passage que, sur le plan morphologique, les Hommes ibéromaurusiens, par leurs caractères, évoquent les Cromagnons européens. A l'instar de leurs prédécesseurs, Moustériens et Atériens, les Ibéromaurusiens n'hésitaient pas à s'attaquer aux gros mammifères dangereux, dont on retrouve les ossements dans les sites d'habitat. Ils chassaient également les gazelles, les antilopes et les mouflons. Les petits carnivores n'étaient pas en reste: chacals, renards, chats sauvages, mangoustes... Les mollusques et les escargots, collectés probablement par les femmes et les enfants, entraient, en grande partie, dans leur alimentation quotidienne.

SITE DE TAFORALT

Présentation

L'existence de la grotte des Pigeons à Taforalt (cf. figure 3) (communément dit site de Taforalt), fut signalée en 1908 par le Dr Pinchon. La prospection qui y fut menée par Ruhlmann, entre 1944 et 1947, permit d'établir que cette grotte est dotée des conditions particulièrement favorables à même de permettre un habitat humain prolongé (hauteur de la voûte de la grotte, aération suffisante et lumière abondante, proximité de l'eau, existence probable de gibier en abondance, etc...). L'abbé J. Roche allait engager les premières fouilles archéologiques qui eurent lieu dans ce site, de 1950 à 1954 (Marcel Couvert et Jean Roche, 1978). Il put ainsi mettre au jour une des plus grandes nécropoles préhistoriques du Maroc, laquelle allait alors créer l'événement et révéler un tournant dans l'histoire et l'évolution de l'homme au Maroc. Les niveaux archéologiques d'où émane cette nécropole sont attribuables à l'Ibéromaurusien et ce, au vu de l'industrie lithique et osseuse qu'ils ont livrés.

L'analyse anthropologique, entreprise quelques années plus tard par D. Ferembach, montra que cette nécropole présente la composition suivante : environ 80 adultes, 6 adolescents et 98 enfants dont presque la moitié n'a pas plus d'un an (D. Ferembach *et al.*, 1962). Le Dr. J. Dastugue qui fut chargé de l'approche paléopathologique de cette série put mettre en évidence l'existence de plusieurs cas pathologiques dont essentiellement de curieux cas de traumatismes.

Cas des crânes à séquelles de fractures

Jean Dastugue qui se chargea de l'étude paléopathologique de la série de Taforalt (*in* D. Ferembach et *al.*, 1962) eut le mérite d'évoquer le traumatisme induit par «choc d'un objet contendant». En effet, selon l'auteur :

- le crâne XII C1 porte au niveau du frontal un enfoncement mesurant 13 mm de diamètre et dont le contour est abrupt. Cet enfoncement se traduit au niveau de l'endocrâne par une légère saillie qui se trouve limitée par «des traits de fracture à bords nets» (figure 4). Aucune trace de cicatrisation ou de consolidation n'est visible, ce qui laisse supposer que le coup ayant entraîné cet endommagement fut fatal pour le sujet en question. Ainsi, il va de soi qu'il s'agit là d'un acte de violence incontestable ;

- le crâne XII C2 montre au niveau du pariétal droit un petit enfoncement de «contour presque quadrangulaire, mesurant 10/12 mm» et limité vers l'avant par «un trait de fracture linéaire long de 17 mm» (page 138). Dans ce cas, également il n'y a aucune trace de consolidation, ce qui laisse admettre que le sujet en question n'a pas survécu à sa blessure ;

- le crâne XXVI, quant-à lui, porte aussi au niveau du pariétal droit un enfoncement de forme circulaire, mesurant 31 mm de diamètre. L'empreinte de cet enfoncement au niveau de l'endocrâne laisse entrevoir un léger renflement au contour abrupt. Toutefois, l'existence d'une probable amorce de

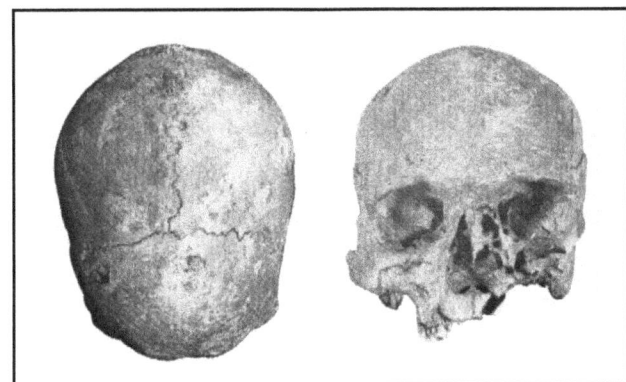

Figure 4 : le crâne XII montrant l'enfoncement existant sur le frontal, à droite (photo. Ferembach et *al.*, 1962)

consolidation laisse supposer que le choc asséné au sujet en question n'a pas été suivi de mort rapide.

Mais quoi qu'il en soit, l'on pourrait admettre, que les 3 enfoncements sont induits par des chocs peut-être accidentels ou par des coups assénés de la manière la plus violente au point d'être en mesure d'entraîner la mort, ce qui fut, *a priori*, le cas des sujets dont les crânes (XII C2 et XXVI) montrent des lésions sans la moindre trace de soudure.

Par ailleurs, il existe, au niveau du squelette post-crânien, d'autres fractures, qui ont pour la plupart réussi leur consolidation. Cela veut dire que ces fractures, quel que soit l'endroit où elles se trouvent n'ont pas été fatales. La question qui se pose maintenant est de savoir si ces fractures ont été induites par accident, une chute par exemple, ou sont le résultat d'une action agressive préméditée ou d'un violence relative ? Apparemment rien ne permet de trancher. Toujours est-il que si on se met dans la perspective de la violence, celle-ci n'a pas été exercée jusqu'au bout. Bien au contraire, les sujets ayant subi ces dommages ont du être l'objet, à la suite de ces derniers, d'une attention toute particulière consistant à les soutenir et à prendre soins d'eux. C'est *a priori*, ce qui a du se produire pour le sujet féminin dont les deux os de l'avant bras gauche qui laissent voir, quoique par des cals vicieux et exubérants, une consolidation rendant le soutient démonstratif.

SITE D'IFRI N'AMMAR

Présentation

Le site d'Ifri n'Ammar (cf. figure 2) (province de Nador, Nord-Est du Maroc) fut découvert en 1996, dans le cadre d'un programme de coopération en matière de prospections et de fouilles archéologiques entre l'Institut National des Sciences de l'Archéologie et du Patrimoine (INSAP) (Rabat, Maroc) et l'Institut d'Archéologie allemand (KAVA) (Bonn, RFA). D'emblée, l'on a estimé qu'il s'agissait là d'un site qui pourrait s'avérer extrêmement important. Les sondages engagés en 1997, sont venu confirmer cette importance. La stratigraphie est l'une des plus importantes de l'Ibéromaurusien (A. Mikdad et J. Eiwanger, 2000). Elle se distingue par le fait qu'elle nous livre, dans ses secrets les plus profonds, davantage de révélations sur une culture aussi spéciale qu'est la culture ibéromaurusienne.

Les fouilles entreprises dans ce site, ces dernières années, on permis la mise au jour d'une très riche stratigraphie avec des niveaux archéologiques à même d'affiner nos connaissances sur la civilisation ibéromaurusienne.

Des analyses au ^{14}C et à l'AMS créditent la partie supérieure de cette stratigraphie d'une datation qui s'intercale entre les 15ème et 13ème millénaires avant J.-C.. C'est dans cette partie qu'a eu lieu la mise au jour de quatre squelettes d'enfants tous en bas âge. Pour trois d'entre eux, des sépultures, en bonne et due forme avaient été aménagées. C'est dire d'emblée que leurs aînés les avaient entourés d'une attention toute particulière, au point qu'il serait permis d'admettre, qu'ils les avaient bien chéris. Toutefois, un sort différent semblait avoir été réservé au quatrième sujet. C'est bien sur celui-ci qui aurait subi des supplices.

Sujet ayant subi des supplices

En charge du volet paléoanthropologique, ma satisfaction fut totale lors de la mise au jour, durant la même campagne de fouilles archéologiques, de quatre sépultures d'enfants dans les niveaux ibéromaurusiens du site d'Ifri n'Ammar. Tout semblait être normal: il s'agissait des sépultures en bonne et due forme, d'enfants décédés en bas âge, l'une d'elles a crée la surprise en livrant des restes bizarrement agencés. Il s'agit de la sépulture IV, dont l'agencement des os est révélateur d'un comportement malveillant voire de la pratique d'une certaine forme de violence à l'égard du défunt en bas age (environ 2 ans).

En effet, lors du décapage progressif de cette sépulture, les premiers os, ou plutôt fragments osseux, qui commençaient à affleurer furent ceux de la calotte crânienne restée curieusement en parfaite connexion avec la mandibule. Ceux-ci reposaient directement sur un amas d'os longs, pratiquement regroupés en faisceaux. Le démontage du crâne permit de voir plus clair. L'amas en question était essentiellement composé des os longs des membres inférieurs tels que le fémur gauche, en parfaite connexion avec les tibia et fibula gauches, ou les tibia et fibula droits. Ces derniers sont en parfaite connexion entre-eux et se superposent aux tibia et fibula gauches. Toutefois, je m'attarderai ici sur les agencements anatomiques, à mon sens très explicites et à même de révéler la pratique de la violence. Cela concernera, la région céphalique et le fémur gauche et les tibias et fibulas des 2 membres.

D'abord, pour la région céphalique, il convient de souligner les faits remarquables suivants : la crâne se présentait par la face inférieure ; la connexion maxillo-mandibulaire est restée intacte, en dépit du déséquilibre qui l'animait ; on note l'absence de toute autre connexion adjacente au crâne. Tout se passe comme si l'on était venu, lors de l'inhumation, déposer la tête à l'envers (cuir chevelu ou «face supérieure» en bas et mandibule ou «face inférieure» en haut) par dessus le reste du cadavre (cf. figure 5). Une telle position implique que la tête a du rejoindre, à l'état frais, le reste du cadavre et que l'inhumation a du se produire tout de suite après. Nous avons, dans ce cas de figure, une décomposition qui a lieu dans un milieu à colmatage progressif, soit un milieu où le volume initialement occupé par les parties molles est progressivement remplacé, lors de la décomposition du cadavre, par le sédiment ambiant (H. Duday *et al.*, 1990). Il serait ainsi possible d'admettre que l'on avait, dans un premier temps, décapité cet individu pour ensuite, dans un second temps, enterrer sa tête avec le restant de son cadavre. Si cet acte de décapitation a bien eu lieu, il a pu se produire du vivant du sujet. Auquel cas, il serait ainsi possible de considérer que cela fut le coup fatal qui aurait occasionné la mort du sujet. Mais l'acte de décapitation, aurait pu aussi être mené après le décès du sujet. Dans un cas comme dans l'autre, le maintien en connexion des crâne et mandibule plaide en faveur de l'inhumation de cette partie anatomique à l'état frais et ce, avec le restant du cadavre (voir infra).

Mais hélas, ce scénario semble ne pas correspondre tout à fait, ne serait-ce que dans la quantification des supplices subis par cet individu, à la réalité des événements. En effet, des supplices, nous allions nous en apercevoir, ont porté sur d'autres parties du corps, en l'occurrence la moitié inférieure de celui-ci. C'est du moins ce qui s'est dégagé de l'observation effectuée au fur et à mesure du décapage de la sépulture en question.

Ainsi, tout en progressant dans le décapage, les os des membres inférieurs à savoir les fémur, tibia et fibula gauches et les tibia et fibula droits se montrent en partie en stricte

Figure 5: photo de la sépulture 4 montrant la mandibule à l'envers (face inférieure)
(photo. J. Moser, 2002).

connexion entre-eux. En revanche, leur disposition donne l'image de deux membres isolés que l'on a délibérément superposés à l'état frais. Les os adjacents : les os du bassin, d'une part, et les os des extrémités, d'autre part, censés tenir la position qui leur revient, ne sont pas là. Tout prête à croire qu'il s'agit de deux ensembles, en l'occurrence 2 membres isolés, que l'on aurait dissociés du tronc et que l'on aurait superposés l'un à l'autre à l'état cadavérique. Le maintien en connexion des os de ces membres en est la preuve patente.

Ainsi, il est établi que, non seulement le sujet a été l'objet d'une décapitation, mais qu'au vu de la position dans la sépulture des os des membres inférieurs, ou du moins de ce qui en reste, le sujet aurait également fait l'objet de démembrement, celui-ci ne concernant que les membres inférieurs.

Toutefois, je n'irai pas jusqu'à conclure à un découpage qui aurait touché la région du bassin du sujet en question. Toutefois, l'investigation au niveau des os n'étant qu'à ses débuts, il est donc difficile à présent d'être catégorique et de se prononcer pour l'hypothèse du découpage. La même réserve fait force de loi en ce qui concerne l'éventualité de la décapitation, si décapitation il y a, par le même biais, à savoir le découpage. Dès lors, par mesure de prudence, une réserve fondamentale est à faire valoir pour admettre la pratique d'un éventuel découpage du cadavre. Une telle pratique, même si elle est suggérée par la disposition des os dans la sépulture, mérite d'être étayée par un examen tracéologique desdits os.

Mais, quoi qu'il en soit tous les faits s'accordent pour signifier que des supplices ont dû manifestement s'abattre sur un enfant, d'environ 2 ans, soit de son vivant ou après la mort. A ce propos, plusieurs hypothèses peuvent être avancées comme explications. La première, consiste à dire que des supplices auraient été menés sur cet enfant en guise de punition et que celle-ci se serait involontairement et malheureusement soldée par le décès de l'enfant, lequel aurait succombé à ses blessures.

L'on peut aussi supposer, c'est la deuxième hypothèse, que les supplices qui se sont abattus sur le sujet en question ont été menés de son vivant en guise de torture et de châtiments et ce, en vue d'aboutir au décès (une sorte de mort préméditée).

Mais, alors comment expliquer, par rapport à ces deux hypothèses, la suite des évènements à savoir le traitement qui a été réservé au cadavre de l'individu ?

Dans les deux cas, on aurait enterré ce sujet sans autre modification de son cadavre. Cela ne fut pas le cas.

L'on est ainsi conduit à supposer, c'est la troisième hypothèse, que des supplices auraient bel et bien pu exister, mais ne se

seraient abattus que sur le cadavre de cet enfant. Ce dernier aurait, ainsi, fait l'objet d'un découpage et aurait été aussitôt enseveli, sans *a priori* faire l'objet au préalable d'un quelconque éventuel traitement d'extraction de moelle ou autre. Cela nous donne, ce qu'on pourrait qualifier de traitement *post-mortem* particulier du cadavre.

Mais enfin, rien n'exclue la possibilité de la pratique de supplices avant et après la mort de cet enfant. C'est à dire à avancer l'hypothèse d'une violence *ante-mortem* qui aurait été suivie d'une autre *post-mortem*. Quoi qu'il en soit, et quelle que soit la volonté qui aurait prévalu ou qui aurait motivé l'une et/ou l'autre des hypothèses, rien ne permet de réserver un sort pareil à un enfant : la pratique d'un éventuel «découpage» de son cadavre en plusieurs morceaux, pour que ces derniers fassent ensuite l'objet d'un dépôt concomitant, avec bien entendu la tête en dernier.

Author address

A. Ben-Ncer
Enseignant-Chercheur, INSAP,
Rabat, Maroc.

Bibliographie

BEN-NCER A., 2002. Les sépultures d'enfants d'Ifri n'Ammar *in Beiträge zur Allgemein und Vergleichenden Archäologie*, Band 22, 2002, Verlag Philipp von Zabern, Mainz, pp. 1-20

COUVERT M. et ROCHE J., 1978. L'environnement de la grotte de Taforalt durant la fin du Paléolithique et l'Epipaléolithique. Le tapis végétal et son interprétation climatique. *Bulletin d'Archéologie Marocaine*, Tome XI, pp. 1-2.

DASTUGUE J., 1962. Paléopathologie *in la nécropole épipaléolithique de Taforalt (Maroc oriental). Etude des squelettes humains.* Avec la collaboration de D. Ferembach et M. J. Poitrat-Targowla. Edita Casablanca, pp. 138-139.

DUDAY H. *et al.*, 1990. L'anthropologie «de terrain» : Reconnaissance et interprétation des gestes funéraires. *Bull. Et Mém. De la Soc. D'Anthrop. De Paris*, n. s., t.2, n° 3-4, pp. 36-39.

FEREMBACH D., 1986. *Homo sapiens sapiens* en Afrique du Nord et du Sahara. *In l'homme son évolution sa diversité, manuel d'anthropologie physique*, D. Ferembach *et al.* éd., Paris, CNRS, pp. 245-247.

MIKDAD A., EIWANGER J. *et al.* 2000. Recherches préhistoriques et protohistoriques dans le Rif oriental (Maroc), Rapport préliminaire. *Beiträge zur Allemeinen und Vergleichenden archäologie*, Band 20, pp. 109-158

ROCHE J., 1976. Cadre chronologique de l'Epipaléolithique marocain, *IXème congrès de l'U.I.S.P.* ; Nice, colloque II, pp. 153-167 du pré tirage, 4 planches au trait, 1 planche photo.

PINCHON (Dr), 1908. Quelques recherches préhistoriques sur la frontière algéro-marocaine. *L'Anthropologie*, t. XIX, pp. 425-435.

CONTEXTUALIZING THE EVIDENCE OF VIOLENT DEATH IN THE MESOLITHIC: BURIALS ASSOCIATED WITH VICTIMS OF VIOLENCE IN THE IRON GATES GORGE

Mirjana ROKSANDIC

Abstract: Interactions of foragers and farmers are at the center of debate on the Lepenski Vir Mesolithic of the Iron Gates Gorge (Serbia-Romania). While typology played a major role in determining Lepenski Vir culture as Epipaleolithic (Boroneanṭ, 1973), Mesolithic (Srejović, 1972) or Neolithic (Jovanović, 1984b), it is currently understood that foraging economy and semi-sedentism characterize the sites even after the contact with the farming communities in the region becomes evident, in the second half of the 7th millennium B.C. (Radovanović, 1996b; Roksandić, 2000a). To date, violent interactions in the region have been discussed only briefly, and in the context of possible conflict between foragers and farmers at the left bank site of Schela Cladovei (Boroneanṭ et al., 1999). Here I examine the evidence for violent interactions on the right bank of the Danube, and associated burial practices, in an attempt to distinguish individual acts of interpersonal violence from possible warfare. The data are further contrasted with evicence from the site of Schela Cladovei located in the flood plane on the left bank of the Danube, downstream from the Gorges.

Key words: Lepenski Vir, violent trauma, interpersonal violence, burial ritual, Mesolithic/Neolithic transition, Iron Gates Mesolithic.

1. INTRODUCTION

Violence in any society has to be examined in the context of local history (Simons, 1999). While it is inevitable in archaeology to look for broader patterns and explanatory mechanism on a larger scale, we must not assume a violent or a non-violent pattern of behaviour to be "typical" of prehistoric hunter gatherers (see Roksandic, this volume). Societies – or types of economies and social structures – do not have a "natural propensity" for violence or otherwise. In any specific group, all interactions within a community, including violence, are sanctioned by learning and socialisation (Ember and Ember, 1997). We have to remember that these interactions, both within a group and with other groups, change over time. As prehistorians, we work with long stretches of time collapsed into a single "cultural" unit or its phase; everyday dealings of individuals, even when observable, have to be interpreted on a larger scale. Short-term changes in behavioural pattern remain unrecognized, and specific incidences of violence are interpreted as a pattern of behaviour applicable to the society as a whole, or – even more broadly – to an entire period. Based on sporadic evidence for violence in Mesolithic series, the period itself is portrayed as the beginning of organised inter-group violence and warfare (Frayer, 1997; Keeley, 1997; Thorpe, 2000; Vencl, 1999). This has been accepted as fact even outside the field (De Pauw, 1998). As pointed out by Dennell (1985), contact of colonizing Europeans with indigenous peoples was used as a model for early contact between European Mesolithic peoples and farmers. For these reasons, it is not surprising that the sporadic evidence of violence in the Mesolithic/Neolithic contact period is often regarded as indicative of endemic warfare (e.g. Boroneanṭ et al., 1995). While it is not necessarily incorrect to interpret this violence as evidence of warfare, we must not jump to conclusions, especially when defence structures and differentiated implements for hunting *versus* warfare are lacking. In fact, what we need is a more solid understanding of how warfare can be identified in the osteological and archaeological records.

Given the lack of archaeological data representing defence structures and armament, we have to rely on bio-archaeological data derived from skeletal lesions associated with violent trauma and warfare (Walker, 2001). I have already discussed difficulties in inferring warfare, including feuding, (as defined by Kelly, 2000) from skeletal evidence in the Introduction to this volume. Tracy Rogers' (this volume: 9-22) forensic perspective on the problem further points out the difficulties in building a plausible model for determining warfare, while Mary Jackes has brought forward archaeological and ethno-archaeological examples that illustrate this difficulty (this volume: 23-40). While not always conclusive, I suggest that the most promising approach is provided by rigorous interpretation of mortuary behaviour associated with victims of violence. In such a way, for example, synchronicity of burials that are presumably derived from a massacre (as claimed for Ofnet by Frayer, 1997) can be confirmed or refuted. Furthermore, a more thorough understanding of the social persona, an understanding that goes beyond age and sex to examine individual's role or position in the society – to the extent it can be inferred from the totality of burial data – can potentially elucidate the problem and give supporting evidence to skeletal information.

In this paper, evidence of violent trauma in the Iron Gates Gorge Mesolithic (IGM), a relatively restricted regional manifestation, is discussed in light of the accompanying burial data. Detailed examination of burial context associated with the individuals who engaged in violent behaviour is proposed as a source of information on their status and on the acceptability of such behaviours, provided we can 1) positively identify these individuals from their skeletal remains, 2) ascertain that special burial and ancestral rituals were associated with them. While it may be difficult to meet these two requirements, the attempt is worthwhile since combining these two lines of evidence has a potential to provide plausible explanations for at least some of the instances of violent death.

2. DISCERNING TRAUMA AND VIOLENCE IN THE SKELETAL RECORD

Violence can be traced in skeletal remains from archaeological sites if it involves skeletal trauma. Trauma "occurs as a result of violent encounters with environmental hazards, inter and intra-species conflict, and in rare instances, self-mutilation and suicide." (Merbs, 1989: 161). In order to assess traumatic injuries correctly we have to be able to distinguish between premortem, postmortem and perimortem conditions. The premortem trauma could be caused by accident or violence. Postmortem effects may obscure trauma, as we can not always distinguish between pre-and postmortem damage to the bone. Berryman and Haun (1996: 2) suggest that perimortem trauma is underreported in the archaeological context primarily due to lack of familiarity with forensic evidence and a lack of understanding of bone breakage patterns. While forensic methodology is no doubt very important in our understanding of traumatic injury, reporting perimortem trauma does not provide an immediate measure of the frequency of violent trauma. In the *Encyclopaedia of Human Paleopathology,* Aufderheide and Rodriguez-Martin (1998: 23) suggest that evidence of healing is the most useful indicator of premortem fracture. However, for the fracture to show signs of healing at least two weeks of survival are required between the traumatic accident and death (Mann and Murphy, 1990). Furthermore, the differences between premortem trauma and postmortem damage are obscured by the fact that bone does not lose its elasticity immediately. Bone is still somewhat plastic up to two months after death, and we could consider "perimortem" fractures as those occurring at any time between two weeks before death and two months after (Aufderheide and Rodriguez-Martin, 1998: 23). For this reason, evidence of "perimortem" fracturing is rather ineffective in helping us reach an interpretation of bone breakage.

Postmortem trauma can occur at the time of burial, either accidentally or with a ritual purpose. After burial, animal or human activities can result in further damage, as can movement of the sediments. Further damage can occur during excavation or during cleaning, curating, analysis and storage. While postmortem trauma is often easy to recognise (fresh breakage or cutting), the perimortem traumatic changes are the most problematic. For example, the blunt force impact on skull resulting in depressed fractures could easily be the cause of death and therefore a premortem trauma, or a postmortem intentional or ritual breakage of the skull or even rough handling of the body after death (Walker 2001:77). Along the same lines, the accidental

breakage of the long bone shafts soon after death (due to sediment collapsing within the grave or similar causes) can be misinterpreted as premortem trauma. Careful excavation and recording of the exact position of every bone fragment can clarify the issue in many cases (Duday, 1987; Roksandic, 2002), but where such documentation does not exist, it is necessary to rely on circumstantial evidence, positioning of the trauma, type of fracture, or experience (Maples 1986). In many cases we have to admit our inability to provide one definitive explanation and a list of possible causes has to be considered. Moving further into identifying trauma as evidence for violence gives more grounds for uncertainty in identification.

In this paper an attempt is made to use all available evidence to demonstrate the level of violent interactions in the Iron Gates Gorge and identify possible changes in the prevalence of violence. In identifying changes through time, we will follow the archaeological classification of the sites into three periods: Pre-contact or Mesolithic proper, Contact or Mesolithic/Neolithic period, and Neolithic period (for definition of these periods see Roksandic, 2000a: 24).

3. THE REGIONAL PICTURE OF THE IRON GATES GORGE

The sites from the Iron Gates Gorge Mesolithic and Early Neolithic period examined here include Padina, Lepenski Vir, Vlasac, Hajdučka Vodenica, Ajmana and Velesnica. All of them are situated on the right bank of the Danube: the first three in the Upper Gorge, one in the Lower Gorge (Hajdučka Vodenica) and the remaining two downstream from the Ključ region in the plain beyond the gorges (Figure 1). All of the sites are characterised by a relatively large number of burials and – with the exception of Ajmana and Velesnica – with houses of the Mesolithic Lepenski Vir type. The four sites in the Gorges were excavated in a rescue operation prompted by the building of the Hydroelectric dam 'Djerdap I' in the late 60s and early 70s. The excavations were undertaken by Dragoslav Srejović (1966; 1968; 1969; 1971; 1972) and Borislav Jovanović (1972; 1974; 1984a; 1984b; 1984c; 1987). The two sites downstream from Ključ were dug in salvage excavations prompted by the building of the dam 'Djerdap II' in the 80s: Ajmana was excavated by Blaženka Stalio (1986) and Velesnica by Rastko Vasić (1986). Previous anthropological research on the sites has been mostly oriented towards understanding individual sites (Nemeskeri, 1978; Nemeskeri and Lengyel, 1978a; 1978b; Nemeskeri and Szathmary, 1978a; 1978b; 1978c; 1978d; 1978e; Radosavljević-Krunić, 1986; Živanović, 1975a; 1975b; 1975c; 1976a; 1976b; 1976c; 1979a; 1979b; 1986; 1988). The first comprehensive study of all sites was provided only recently and concerns only two aspects of population biology (Roksandic 1999, 2000). As palaeopathological analyses are underway, here I will present only the traumatic lesions that could be interpreted as evidence of violence. An attempt is made to integrate this information into the overall picture of the archaeology of the Mesolithic/Neolithic period in the Iron Gates Gorge.

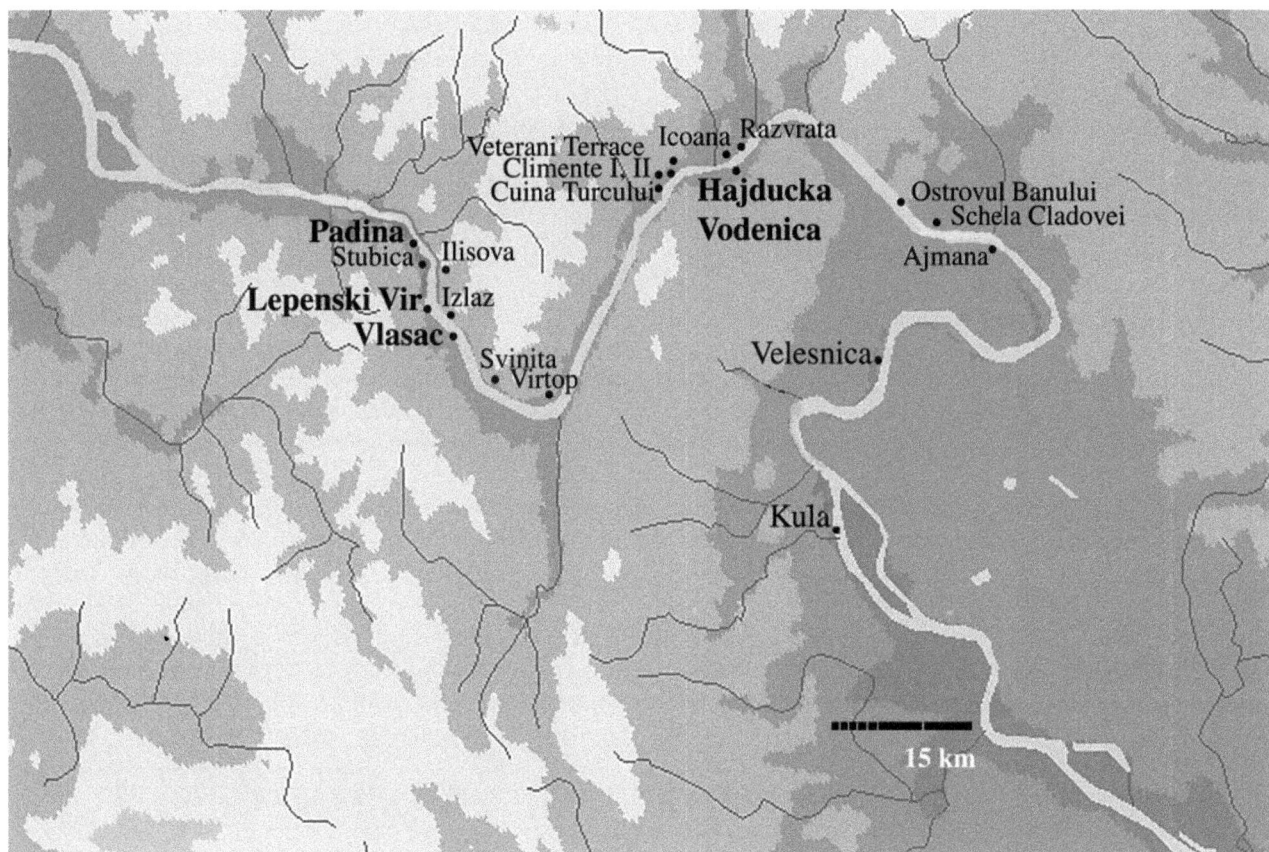

Figure 1. Iron Gates Gorge Mesolithic/Early Neolithic sites

3a. Basic demographinc data

The burial practices of Mesolithic peoples are characterised by great variability, which is certainly true for the IGG Mesolithic: the encountered practices embrace cremation, primary inhumation, secondary interment, including removal and re-organisation of body parts, with re-burial of skulls and fragmentary remains. Ubelaker (2002: 332) suggests that commingling is a relatively common occurrence in the archaeological record, even when it can not be ascertained due to the lack of recognisable doubling of elements. It is inherently problematic to assume that the number of burials excavated is representative of the number of individuals originally buried in the cemetery, even in cultures where single primary interments predominate; it is obviously impossible in cases of multiple or group burials, or complex burials such as we are witnessing in the Lepenski Vir culture.

The speed of the initial excavation of the sites, and the fact that re-analysis of the excavation documentation is incomplete, means that there are problematic features which cannot yet be elucidated. The most straightforward approach was to rely on the archaeological determination of the burials as separate entities, and to determine the minimal number of individuals (MNI) for each of these burial units.[1] Within any single burial, the assessment of the MNI followed the common procedures of establishing recognisable osteological elements that were doubled, as well as those that presented incompatibility of age and sex markers. Pairing of bones on the basis of age and general robusticity was accepted only in cases of good preservation and obvious similarities. For Lepenski Vir, assessment was limited by the fact that the field documentation was not available, for Vlasac, I could rely on published drawings (Srejović and Letica 1978) and for Padina and Hajdučka Vodenica on unpublished documentation provided by Borislav Jovanović. Since the MNI in any single burial unit did not exceed eight individuals, it was not necessary to use the procedures appropriate for ossuaries.

While "extra individuals" within any of the burials could be regarded as resulting from the inclusion of the earth from disturbed burials, these "extra bones" are so common in IGM that their patterning requires more meaningful explanation. Therefore they were incorporated into MNI of individual graves.

A further set of problems results from the "scattered human remains," or fragments of human bone found in the archaeological deposits without any evidence of burial, a circumstance noted as a common occurrence in the Mesolithic. The situation is especially complex for Lepenski Vir where the quantity of bones "from the layer" can sometimes exceed the quantity of bones present in a recognised "grave." Since theoretically, such scattered bones could belong to any of the buried individuals, they were not counted as separate individuals.

[1] More satisfactory answers to these questions may come from my current study of burial practices, planned to include detailed consideration of taphonomic information derived from bones and archaeological documentation.

Sex determination was based on the pelvic bones whenever possible and followed standard procedures (Buikstra and Ubelaker, 1994; Phenice, 1969; Workshop of European Anthropologists, 1980). Noteworthy is the fact that the preauricular sulcus was present in almost all of the examined pelves which showed female morphology. As discussed earlier (Roksandic 1999, 2000a), the degree of sexual dimorphism is remarkable and the secondary skeletal markers of sex on postcranial bones could be used with great reliability where the pelvic remains were missing. A different pattern is observed with skull remains, which could account for discrepancies between present determinations and those of Nemeskeri (1978d), Zoffmann (1983), and Živanović (1975a).[2]

Age determination presented more problems. In order to avoid point age estimates in adults, which are highly dependent on the reference population (Bocquet-Appel and Masset, 1982) and unreliable in building mortality profiles (Love and Müller, 2002), adult ages were assigned to four large categories, namely, "young adult" (YA), "full adult" (FA), "mature adult" (MA), and "senile adult" (SA). This approach was deemed optimal since restricting age assessment to a set of pre-selected criteria would have greatly reduced the number of possible observations (Roksandic and Love 2000). The problem created by individuals represented by a single bone or a bone fragment could be only partially circumvented in this way, so they were, except in rare cases when they preserved specific age markers, assigned to a non-specified "adult" (A) group.

Age determination for children up to 12 years of age was based on observation of tooth formation and eruption and when available, long bone epiphyseal union. Age was assigned by reference to tables in Buikstra and Ubelaker (1994). In other cases, the general aspect of bones was used to establish that the skeleton belonged to any of the subadult groups: "neonatal" (n), "small child" (sc), "pre-pubertal child" (ppc), and "pubertal child" (pc). The precision with which the age in the subadults was assessed depended on preservation and the representation of different body parts, therefore some of the individuals were assigned to quite a large age range.

The skeletal series examined consists of 501 records. These include individuals in closed burial context as well as individuals or fragments of individuals in different "disturbed contexts." As discussed above, and in keeping with previous publications (Roksandic, 1999; 2000a), all the burials are treated as discrete units and every individual discerned *within the burial* is recorded as an individual, regardless of the state of preservation and the amount of bone by which it was represented. Thus the MNI was calculated for each of the closed burial contexts. Since it is possible that the individuals outside specific burial contexts could have belonged to any of the individuals in the burial context, they are excluded from further consideration. By adding the MNIs from burial contexts, we have calculated a MNI of 418 individuals for all sites.

Of these 418 individuals, 155 are represented by immature remains. The only immature skeleton with a macroscopically identifiable traumatic condition is the "Velesnica 2C" individual, a pre-pubertal child approximately 9 years old, with a circular depression on the occipital bone, slightly above and to the right of the exoinion, approximately 25 mm in diameter (Roksandic, 2000b). Galloway states that the depressed fractures of the skull are 3.5 times more common in children than in adults (1999: 68 and quoted literature) and can cause both infection and brain damage. Due to the generally thinner and more flexible bones of the cranial vault in young children, these lesions are often limited to a depression, and may not involve actual fracturing of the bone. In the Velesnica 2C specimen, the pitting observed on the floor of the lesion and in its immediate surrounding indicates a post-traumatic infection. Although it is not possible to exclude violence as an aetiology, given its position, the age of the individual, and the fact that the lesion is healed, the fracture is more consistent with accident. Immature remains will not be further considered in this analysis.

While out of the 263 adult individuals examined, a total of 16 adults (or 6 %) show evidence of trauma, only 2.7 % can be assigned to violence as *the most probable* cause of the pathological condition. Here I present all the cases of potential violent trauma in the series.[3] A brief description of the trauma (folowing Roksandic *et al.* submitted) is followed by a detailed examination of the biological data and archaeological documentation for each of the burials containing elements with traumatic lesions.

4. CRANIAL INJURIES: BLUNT FORCE TRAUMA

In distinguishing blunt force trauma, or healed depressed fractures of the cranial vault, it is very important to exclude lesions of infectious origin (Walker, 1989: 313 and Fig. 2). In addition, trauma can be accompanied by a post-traumatic infection (as seen above with Velesnica 2C). While healed fractures present difficulties in identification because of potential similarities with the lesions of infectious origin, a much greater ambiguity arises when there is no evidence of healing. Ascertaining trauma in those cases becomes far more complicated, if not impossible. Lepenski vir 69 (see below, Figure 4) illustrates this well. Several conditions can be observed: a) evidence of partial excavation or cleaning damage at the b) site of the perimortem traumatic injury and c) and d) two healed and therefore premortem fractures.

In order to distinguish violent trauma from other possible causes we have examined all available material and particular

---

[2]   For example, cranial and mandibular robusticity, on which the sex determination by Nemeskery and Szatmary was based, discriminates poorly among sexes in this population. Nemeskeri J, and Szathmary L (1978c) Individual Data on the Vlasac Anthropological Series. In Z Letica (ed.): Vlasac. Mezolitsko naselje u Djerdapu. Beograd: SANU, pp. 285-426.

---

[3]   No elements outside the burial context, or the "scattered human remains," have any evidence of trauma.

Table 1. Blunt force trauma in the IGG skeletal sample.

Site	grave no	period	MNI	#	sex	age	Blunt impact
Vlasac	82a	M	5	4	m	MA/SA	Frontal
Lvir	69	M	1	1	m?	MA	Frontal, repeated
Vlasac	69	M/N	4	1	m?	MA	Frontal, perimortem
Lvir	20	M/N?-N?	1	1	m?	MA	Frontal, deep

Period: M=Mesolithic, M/N=Mesolithic in contact with Neolithic, N=Neolithic. MNI in the burial = minimal number of individuals for the burial from which the skeleton is issued, #of the individual = sequential number assigned to the individual within the burial, sex: m = male assigned based on pelvic remains, m?=male assigned based on postcranial robusticity; age: MA=mature adult, SA=senile adult.

sites of injury both macroscopically and radiographically. Detailed descriptions and procedures can be found elsewhere (Roksandic *et al.* submitted). Here only a very brief discussion on the location of the trauma and evidence corroborating violence, together with a photo of the condition, are presented for each individual. All of the cases resulting from *possible* violence are discussed.

All instances of healed blunt force trauma in the sample are provided in Table 1. All of the skeletons can be determined as male on the basis of either their pelvic morphology or postcranial robusticity (a good indicator of sex in this population, Roksandic 2000a:). All of them are mature adults, while one (Vlasac 82) shows some evidence of senile pitting on the posterior cranial vault, in addition to the blunt force trauma on the frontal bone. All of the injuries are on the frontal bone. A total of four healed and two perimortem traumas are observed on the four frontal bones. Given their limited number we cannot talk about a trend towards either an increase or a decrease of this condition in different chronological periods; the distribution seems uniform.

Vlasac 82a: (Figures 2 and 3; table 2)

Description of the injury: on the right side of the frontal bone, between the coronary suture and the tuberosity, there is an ellipsoid area depressed inwards. The dimensions of the injury are 45 mm x 25 mm. The bottom of the lesion is rough,

but without evidence of changes in the bone structure, and the medial margin is prominent. The inner table of the skull vault in the affected area has no visible changes (Roksandic *et al.* submitted). Some portions of the skull were found commingled with the extra bones assigned by archaeologists to Vlasac 82.

Skeletal data from the burial context: The burial is described as a secondary burial of the skulls and long bones of four adult men (Srejović and Letica 1978: 65). During the 1997 /1998 analysis five left coxal bones were identified in the burial, raising the MNI to five. Three of the coxae were sufficiently preserved to allow sex determination and one of them exhibited female morphology. According to the postcranial robusticity, one of the two remaining skeletons was male and the other female. Thus we have a burial of five adults of different ages: three fully adult individuals, one mature, and another mature or senile adult. Three of these were males and two females (Table 2.).

Noteworthy is that out of the five individuals in the burial, three (82, 82a, and 82c) have a discrete trait known as the 'acetabular mark' (Saunders, 1978: 67, plate 10, p. 501) or '*fossae faciei lunatae*' (Czarnetzki et al., 1985), while the remaining other two coxae were not sufficiently preserved to allow observation of this trait. Even though raw discrete data cannot be used to argue kinship (Sjøvold, 1984), the fact that the same discrete trait appears in three out of three possible observations (100%) in one grave could be interpreted as indicative of a family unit. While frequencies range from 20% to 40% in North American samples (Saunders, 1978), the situation in the Iron Gates Gorge is different: the frequency in the series as a whole is much lower at 8% (five positive out of 40 possible observations, sides combined) and restricted to the burial 82 and an additional case in burial 48 at Vlasac, and burial 17 from Hajdučka vodenica, (Roksandic 1999: Appendix 1). Both Vlasac 82 (multiple burial of 5 individuals) and Vlasac 48 (single female) are located in the Western Sector of the site, and according to Srejović and Letica (1978: 57 and 63), there is an important chronological difference between them. Radovanović (1996: 204-207) places both Vlasac 82 and 48 into the same chronological unit, her group of 'Later type of formal disposal area,' which is synchronous with the multiple burial of Hajdučka Vodenica 17.

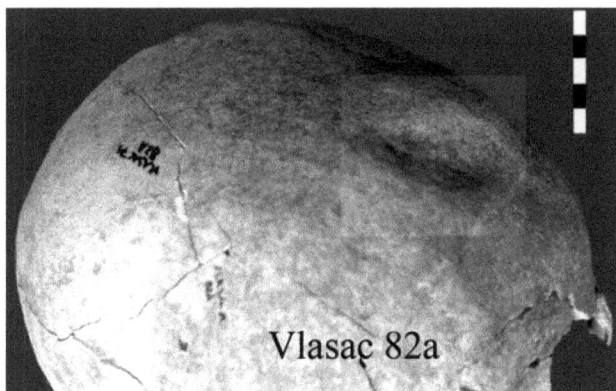

Figure 2. Vlasac 82a. Highlighted square indicates the position of the blunt impact.

Table 2. All of the individuals in association with the burial 82a.

Site	burial no	CHRO	MNI	#	sex	age	notes
Vlasac	82(82abc/1234)	M	5	1	m	FA	fossa facies lunatae (left)
Vlasac	82(1)+82b	M	5	2	m?	MA	
Vlasac	82(2)+82c	M	5	3	f	FA	fossa facies lunatae (left)
Vlasac	82(4)+82a	M	5	4	m	MA/SA	fossa facies lunatae (left)
Vlasac	82(3)	M	5	5	f?	FA	

Period: M=Mesolithic, M/N=Mesolithic in contact with Neolithic, N=Neolithic. MNI in the burial = minimal number of individuals for the burial from which the skeleton is issued, #of the individual = sequential number assigned to the individual within the burial, sex: m or f = male or female assigned based on pelvic remains, m?/f? male or female assigned based on postcranial robusticity; age: YA=young adult, FA=fully adult, MA=mature adult, SA=senile adult.

Burial data and interpretation: The field drawing (Srejović and Letica 1978 , Fig. 97; Radovanović 1996: 206-8, Fig. 4.13) shows a number of skull fragments separated into four distinct crania, while the photo (Figure 3) shows only two skulls – calottes that look well preserved and complete. According to Srejović and Letica (1978:65) the additional two skulls were found a little bit to the east of this group of bones. The collected fragments of the cranial vaults belong to only two skulls (82 and 82a). In addition there are three relatively complete mandibles (82a, 82b and 82c) and one incomplete mandible (82). Since the collection of bones at Vlasac was thorough, the two additional skulls (82b and 82c) could have been misplaced or lost due to inadequate storage. The complete lack of vertebral and rib fragments, together with the rearrangement of long bones "above and blow the skulls, placed in a rather orderly way" (Srejović and Letica 1978: 65, my translation) conform to a secondary burial, while the presence of foot bones could provide a counter argument.

Figure 3. Vlasac 82 burial – Photo courtesy of Institute of Archaeology in Belgrade.

Alternatively, the burial could be interpreted as representing a rearrangement of the primary burial(s) with removal of a number of bones from each individual. One could also envisage a combination of primary and secondary burials with bone rearrangements and removal. Without detailed plotting of every single bone fragment in 1:5 ratio (Duday, 1978; Duday, 1987; Roksandic, 2002), it is impossible to speculate further. Available documentation and skeletal parts preservation do not allow us to reach a more definite conclusion.

To summarize, individual Vlasac 82a, represented by a skull of a mature or senile male with a healed frontal depressed fracture, was found within a kin burial of five adults of both sexes. This multiple burial is most probably a secondary burial, although a primary burial with bone rearrangement and removal cannot be excluded on available evidence.

Lepenski Vir 69. (Figures 4 and 5, table 3)

Description of the injury: Lepenski vir 69 shows evidence of postdepositional damage caused during or after excavation on the posterior margin of the perimortem traumatic injury (Figure 4a). The postdepositional damage is easily recognized by difference in colouring. The perimortem injury is an ellipsoid defect in the region of the coronary suture, of the right parietal and right frontal bone, 35 mm x 12 mm in diameter, 12 mm from the median plane. It lacks the characteristic concentric fracture and beveling typical of fresh bone fracture (Berryman and Haun, 1996: 5) and was more likely damage to the dry bone because of the irregular and sinuous aspect of some of the issuing cracks (Botella et al., 2000: 93). However, since the actual site of breakage is missing, it is not possible to treat it as a certain postmortem damage.

In addition, there are two healed depressed fractures: one on the left frontal near bregma, (Figure 4b) and the other on the right side near the frontal protuberance (Figure 4c). The first one, on the frontal squama approximately 15 mm below bregma, is an oval depression, 35 mm x 24 mm in diameter. The walls of depression are smooth, with rounded edges. The depth of injury is about 7 mm. The other is a shallow

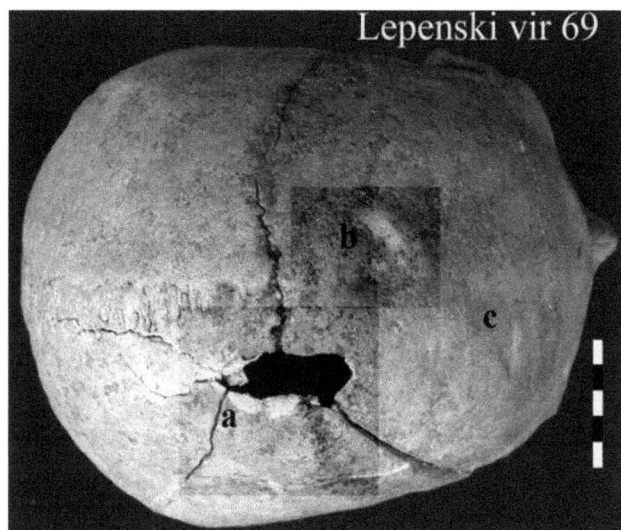

Figure 4. Several instances of blunt force on the skull Lepesnki Vir 69: a) represents a perimortem fracture exemplified by an open wound with post-excavational damage on the lateral margin b) and c) represent healed blunt impact injuries. (Roksandic et al., in prep).

depression, located in the region of right frontal protuberance, irregular in shape, 14 mm x 7 mm in diameter. Repeated trauma has often been regarded as indicative of violent interactions, since repeated accidents would be far less likely to occur (but see Walker, 2001). Judd (2002: 92) proposed that in samples where multiple injuries are common, particularly lesions indicative of non lethal interpersonal violence (cranial and direct force isolated ulna fractures) or accidental falls, the panorama of injuries displayed by a person may be the result of repeated injury, rather than a single traumatic episode.

Skeletal data: While field documentation reveals a particularly well preserved and complete skeleton, only the skull and two femora could be found during my 1998 analysis.[4] Based on the postcranial robusticity the individual was male, of mature adult age indicated by the general aspect of the preserved elements and advanced dental attrition. There are no other observable pathologies on the preserved bones.

Burial data and interpretation: From the field photographs it is possible to ascertain that Lepenski Vir 69 was a particularly well preserved and excavated burial (Radovanović, 1996a: 172, Fig. 4.2; Srejović, 1969: 161, Fig. 64). Even though only skull and femora were preserved, field photographs allow a more detailed explanation of the burial position.

It is doubtless a primary burial with all the bones in articulation and no post-depositional movement outside the

volume of the body. According to Radovanović (1996:177) the individual is buried between the houses, in a stone enclosure, perpendicular to the course of the river, with head towards the rear of the site, arms alongside the body and legs crossed. There are no grave goods. The deceased person was described as buried in a 'seated' position, sometimes also referred to as 'position *à la turque*,' a conventional way of describing the person lying on its back with legs crossed at ankles, and with knees at 90° to the axis of the body (Figure 5). While stone construction is obvious above the burial, the pictures do not reveal the exact architecture.

Certain additional observations can be made on the basis of the position of the bones. On the right side of the body there is an indication of architecture at the level of the thorax (Figure 5a): 'the effect of the wall' constricts the expected movement of the scapula and humerus towards the ground. The lateral aspect of both the right scapula and humerus can be seen, apparently in an unstable position. Ribs have not splayed to the sides; they are contained in the volume of the architectural space. On the other hand, the left side of the body presents the opposite picture: the anterior (or ventral side) of the scapula and the anterior side of the humerus are visible, as expected in dorsal decubitus, and the ribs are splayed both towards the pelvis and laterally (Figure 5c). Furthermore, the sternum has migrated towards the left rib cage. No movement is observed in the pelvic region and the leg articulations are all in place, including the left patella (Figure 5-b), which is still in its anatomical position and has not rolled over (as would be expected without architectural support). The legs are flexed at the knees perpendicular to the axis of the skeleton. The feet were crossed at the ankles and retained perfect anatomical connection, the bones of the right foot showing their medial and plantar aspect. The most obvious post-depositional movement was that of the left forearm that has induced further movement of the left hand (Figure 5d). It is likely that the left hand was on the left thigh and that the decomposition of the thigh has entailed the separation of the distal radius and ulna. The skull was most probably propped up by a perishable support at the time of the disposal of the body. Srejović explains the position of the skull by interment into a shallow burial pit that follows the contours of the body. The "shallow burial pit has approximately the same form as the house-floors of Lepenski Vir I and follows the same orientation as the houses in the settlement." (Srejović 1969: 133, my translation[5]). While this explanation is plausible, it is important to note that the decomposition of the soft tissue often produces the change in coloration around the skeleton that is, in turn, commonly interpreted as a shallow burial pit. The 'effects of the wall' on the right side of the thorax counters Srejović's explanation of a triangular shape of the pit and argues for the burial on flat ground with architectural elements (stone construction in this case) supporting the body in its observed position. While the "shallow burial pit" is disputable, the observation of the proportions remains valid. The burial was used by Srejović and Babović to explain the house-floor proportions and outlines (1983: 45, Fig 18).

---

[4]   The most plausible explanation is that the rest of the postcranial bones were not collected during the excavations. According to Professor Z. Mikić, who participated in the excavations as a student, the collection of bones was not standardized in the first season of the excavations. This mistake was later redressed at the site of Vlasac where the collection was systematic. (Z. Mikić, personal communication: 20/07/1998). Alternatively, the postcranial bones could have been lost due to inadequate storage in the early 1990s.

---

[5]   Unless stated otherwise all translations are mine.

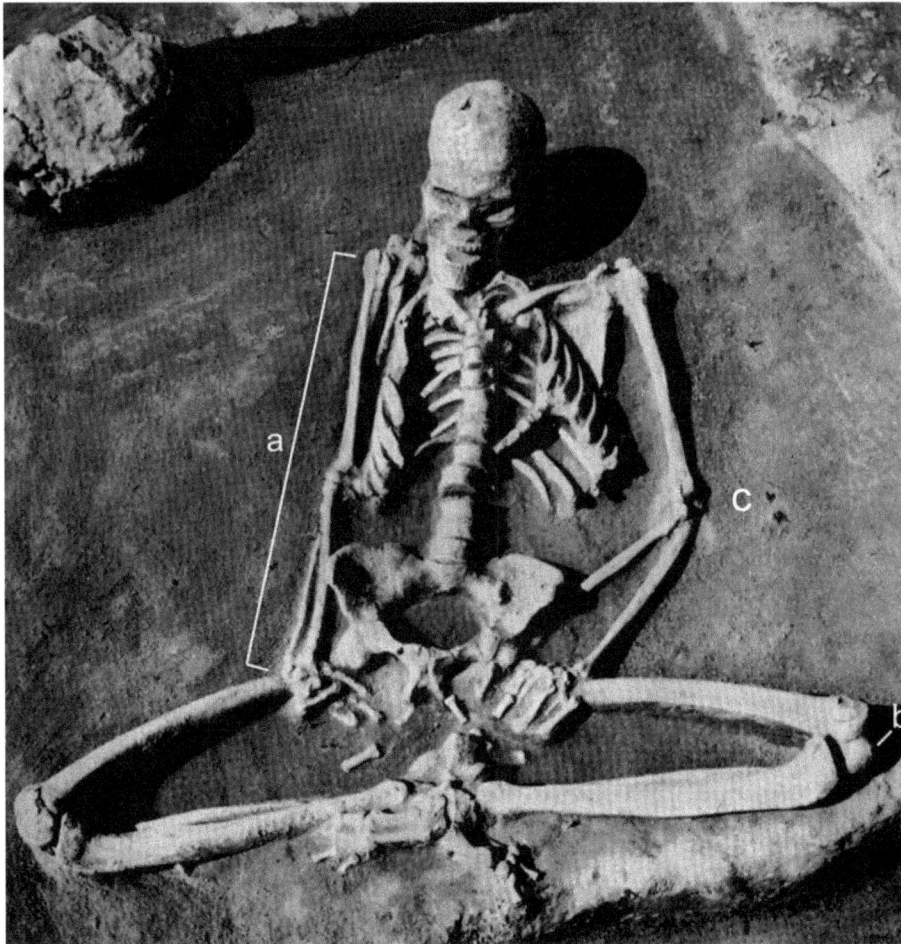

Figure 5. Photo of Lepenski Vir 69 burial (reproduced
with the permission of the Institute of Archaeology)

The burial is at the same level as the Proto-Lepenski Vir houses in the far downstream corner of the site. Lepenski Vir 69 is dated to the Lepenski Vir I phase by Srejović, while Radovanović (1996:177) places it into Proto-Lepenski Vir or early (phase 1) of Lepenski Vir I. There are no associated grave goods. This burial is an early example of the intramural disposal of the body with substantial burial construction marking a move from secondary to primary burials within the site. Therefore, it is likely that the individual held an important place within the community.

To summarize, the burial Lepenski Vir 69 is an early intramural primary burial of a mature adult male with evidence of multiple healed blunt force trauma on the frontal bone. The body was placed on a flat ground surface with a stone construction cover. The position and the orientation, evocative of the house-floor outline, signal this individual as an important member of the society.

Vlasac 69 (Figures 6,7,8; Table 3)

Description of the injury: Vlasac 69 exhibits one unhealed depressed fracture on the frontal bone (Figure 6). On the left half of the frontal bone, near *bregma,* the surface of the skull is depressed inwards. The dimensions of the depressed area are 15 mm x 9 mm, and thin fissures are seen in the region of the lower margins of the injury. The internal

surface of the cranial vault in the affected area is missing due to postmortem damage. (Roksandic *et al.* submitted). We cannot ascertain this injury as the cause of death, since there is no evidence that it did not occur immediately after death. The position of the fracture is otherwise concordant with interpersonal violence. Other pathology observed on this skeleton includes eburnation of the proximal humerus.

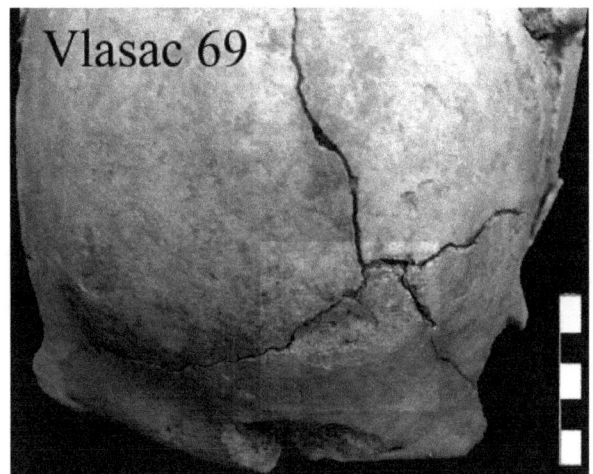

Figure 6. Vlasac 69. Evidence of perimortem blunt force
trauma on the frontal bone

60

Table 3. The individuals in association with the burial Vlasac 69.

Site	Grave no	Period	MNI	#	sex	age
Vlasac	69	M/N	3	1	m?	MA
Vlasac	69a	M/N	3	2	m	FA
Vlasac	69(1)+69a(1)	M/N	3	3	f?	A

Period: M=Mesolithic, M/N=Mesolithic in contact with Neolithic, N=Neolithic. MNI in the burial = minimal number of individuals for the burial from which the skeleton is issued, #of the individual = sequential number assigned to the individual within the burial, sex: m or f = male or female assigned based on pelvic remains, m?/f? male or female assigned based on postcranial robusticity; age: YA=young adult, FA=fully adult, MA=mature adult, SA=senile adult.

Figure 7. Vlasac 69/69a burial.
Photo courtesy of the Institute of Archaeology in Belgrade.

Skeletal data from the burial context: According to Srejović and Letica (1978: 72, Fig. 119, TXLVII), the burial Vlasac 69/69a consists of two crania with long bones piled up on top of them. The third individual was separated from the collected bones during the 1998 analysis on the basis of different size and robusticity. In terms of biological information, it was possible to discern only demographic data and a possible pathology of the left humeral head of Vlasac 69.

Burial interpretation: The published field drawings (Srejović and Letica, 1978: 72, Fig. 119) and photo documentation (Figures 7 and 8) do not provide many details on the position and arrangement of the bones, which are deposited on the substrate of small rocks, on a restricted quasi-square surface 0.42 m × 0.34 m. The postcranial elements, fragments of femoral and humeral shafts, a proximal femur, distal humerus, and a tibial shaft (visible in Figure 7) were piled on top of the crania and mandibles presented in Figure 8. Among the postcranial elements, long bones predominate, while very few fragments of ribs, pelves and vertebrae are also present. Some of the long bones show possible signs of weathering.[6] All of the above indicates a secondary burial of at least three adult individuals, two males and one female.

In summary, an adult male individual Vlasac 69, with a perimortem depressed fracture on the left frontal bone was deposited with at least two other adults (one male and one female) in a secondary burial of very small dimensions.

_____

[6] Caution should be applied until detailed study of taphonomy is finished, since some of the weathering could have happened during the excavations.

Figure 8. Vlasac 69/69a after the removal of long bones. The two skulls are visible in superior view.

Lepenski Vir 20. (Figures 8 a, 8b, 9 and 10)

Description of the injury: Lepenksi Vir 20 shows a different type of a healed blunt impact that is much deeper and narrower. It appears to have been produced by an object with conical sharp ending. A marked depression of the frontal squama is seen in the area of the right frontal protuberance. The fracture is pyramidal in shape with smooth walls and rounded margins. The dimensions of the lesion are 22 mm x 24 mm (Roksandic *et al.* submitted).

Skeletal data: Even though the drawing (Figure 10) shows nearly complete postcranial skeleton, only the skull was found during the 1998 analysis. Reconstructed, the skull is almost complete, with only fragments of the base missing. As in the case of the burial Lepenski Vir 69, it is likely that the postcranial bones were not collected during excavations (see above note 4). This is unfortunate since examination of the whole skeleton could give us a better understanding of the trauma itself.

Burial data: Individual 20 is a single burial in a circular stone construction assigned to either the Mesolithic/Neolithic Contact period (Lepenski Vir phase II) or the Early Neolithic (Lepenski Vir phase IIIa). Burial stone constructions are a common feature in the Mesolithic of the region, however, given that there is an observed strong continuity between Mesolithic and Neolithic burial practices in the region (Srejović 1969), we cannot exclude Neolithic provenience. The burial was in the western portion of the site between houses 39, 48 and 61 but not necessarily associated with them. According to the field documentation, the individual was positioned "on the left side of the body in a contracted position, legs flexed at 45° at different levels. Left arm, flexed at the elbow, was at the level of pelvis while the right was underneath the right femur." (Antunović, 1987: 37, my translation). As already noted, at the time of skeletal analysis in 1998, only the skull was available. The photo of the burial

clearly shows the circular stone construction. Unfortunately, it is impossible to ascertain the position of the individual as, except for the mandible and the proximal radius, no other bones are visible on the photo which was probably taken once the skeleton was partly removed.

Based on the drawing (Figure 10), the burial is a primary burial of a single individual in left lateral decubitus with the right leg contracted towards the rib cage and the left leg flexed. There is an indication of the 'effect of the wall' in the position of the right side of the thorax, and possible constriction at the level of the shoulder girdle. Both indicate architectural elements supporting the body during decomposition. The position of the deceased was not uncommon in the Early Neolithic of the Iron Gates Gorge including Lepenski Vir phase IIIa (Antunović, 1990), however this is not sufficient indicator of the individual's affiliation.

The conical object that produced the injury could have been any sufficiently hard stone, wood or antler tool with conical working surface. According to Antonović (personal communication 30/03/03), it could have been similar to the stone tool reproduced here in Figure 11. The tool was found in 1970, "near house 13" in the central portion of the site, dated to the early phase of Lepenski Vir I by Radovanović (1996a: 101). Unfortunately, the association of the object with the house is not clear, as there are no further provenience data. The tool, made of polished limestone, was substantially damaged by burning. It is the only such object found either at Lepenski Vir, or at any of the sites in the Iron Gates Gorge. The 'working end' of the tool was carefully faceted and polished. The actual tip is slightly broken, chipped by an impact with a hard object. While we cannot assume that the object that caused the injury would be found at the site, polished stone objects are associated with the appearance of the Neolithic in the region and could have belonged to either the Mesolithic/Neolithic Contact period or the Neolithic of the site.

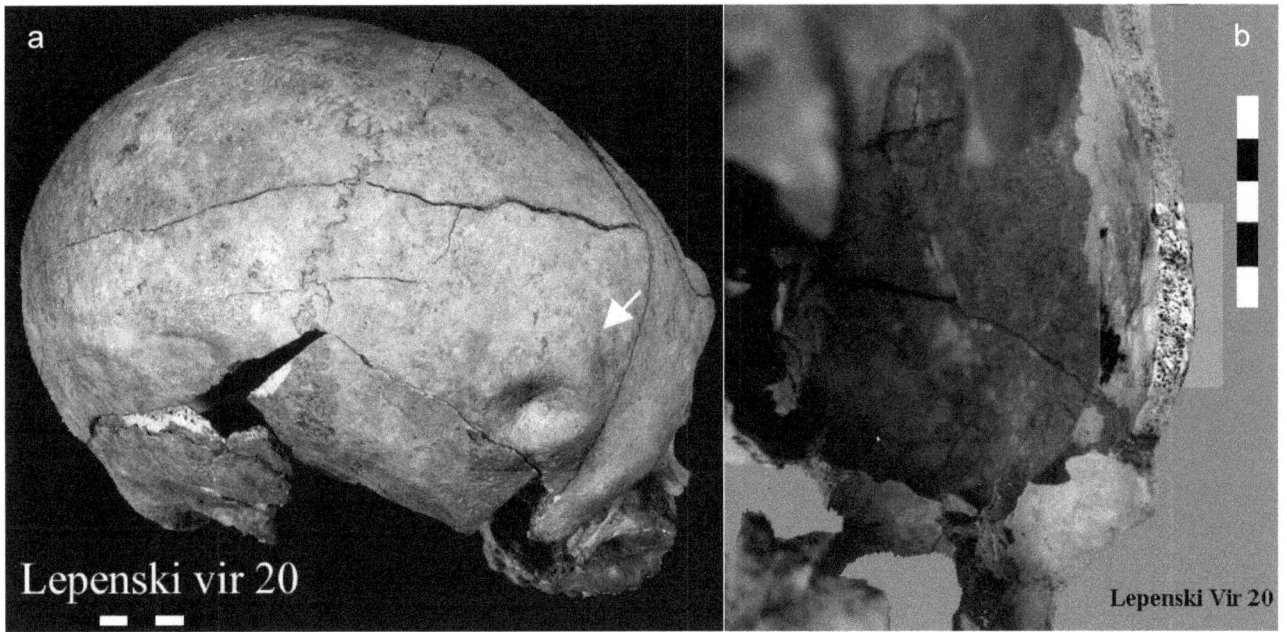

Figure 9 Lepenski vir 20. a) Arrow points to the depressed frontal impact caused with a conical object. b) the inner table of the frontal bone shows some relief as impact was strong enough to damage the inner table.

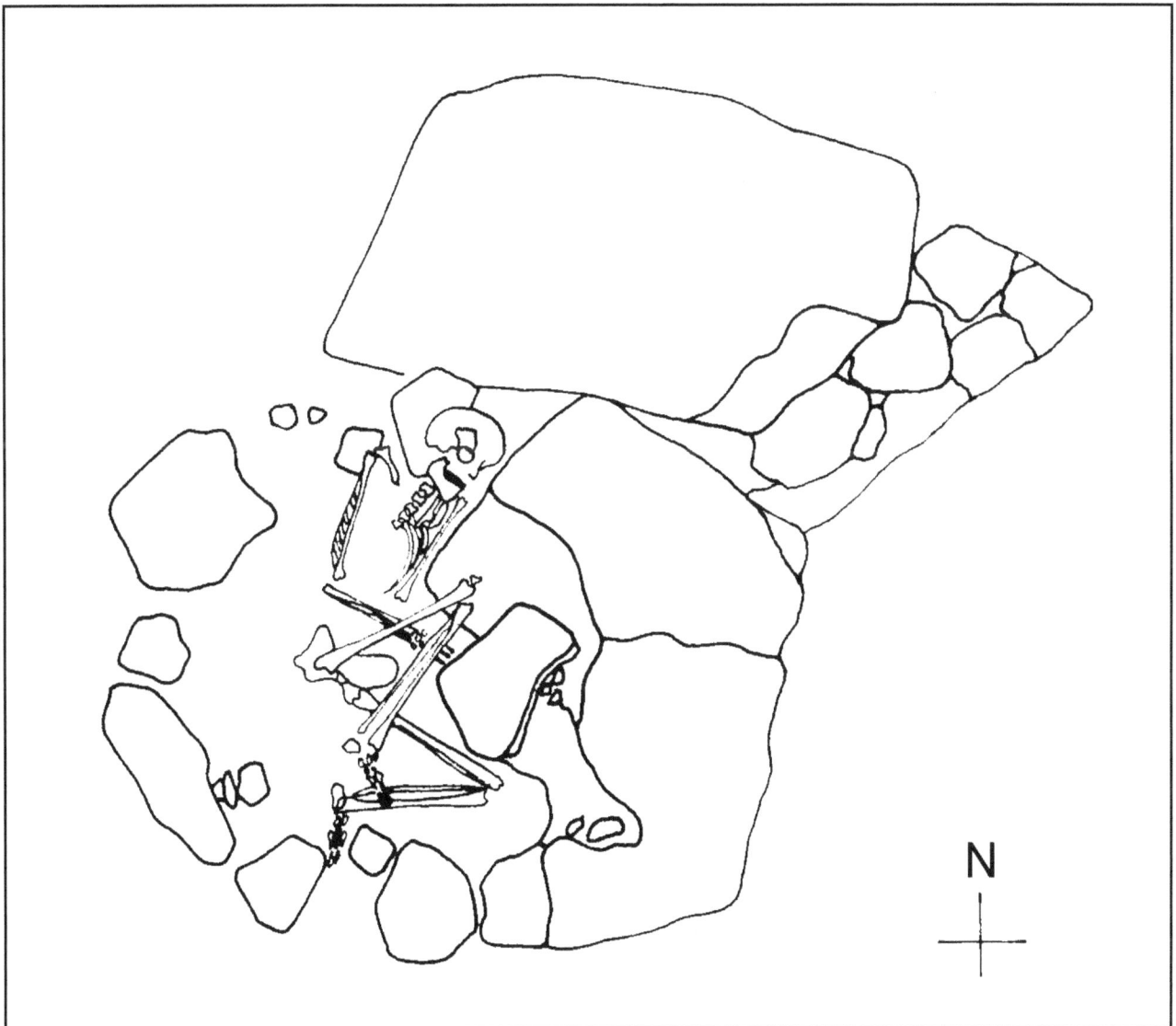

Figure 10. Field drawing of the burial 20 from Lepenski Vir.
Courtesy of the Archaeological Institute in Belgrade.

Figure 11. Possible object that caused the blunt force trauma. While we cannot ascertain this to be the object with which the injury was made, it is possible that an object of this type was used in conflict. Courtesy of D. Antonovic, Archaeological Institute of Belgrade.

To summarize, the mature adult male individual Lepenski Vir 20, displaying deep blunt force injury on his frontal bone, was found in a single primary burial of either Mesolithic/ Neolithic or Early Neolithic period. The blunt object that could have produced the lesion was most probably similar to a limestone object found in the central sector of the site.

5. POSTCRANIAL INJURIES

Only two individuals have postcranial injuries, which might be associated with violence.

Vlasac 51 a: (Figures 12 and 13; table 4)

Description of the injury: The lower third of the right ulnar shaft displays an un-united transverse fracture. Two fractured surfaces are remodeled into a pseudoarticulation, induced by lack of immobilization during the callus formation. The compact bone lining the involved ends shows areas of pitting and an irregular surface. There are no pathological changes on the right radius (Roksandic *et al.* submitted). No further pathologies are associated with this skeleton. This type of fracture suggests a direct trauma. It could have resulted from a blunt object breaking the bone in a defense movement of the arm raised to protect the head. According to Smith (1996: 84), in cases where the potentially corroborative craniofacial injury data are lacking, a violent aetiology for mid-shaft fractures becomes less likely. She lists a number of possible causes for this type of forearm fracture: accident, stress or fatigue, predisposition through an underlying pathological condition, or interpersonal violence. Unfortunately, only a mandible, left maxilla and a left zygomatic bone represent the face of the individual 51a; thus it is hard to ascertain whether or not there were any craniofacial injuries. Since we cannot exclude a violent aetiology, violence has to be considered as a possible explanation for the observed trauma.

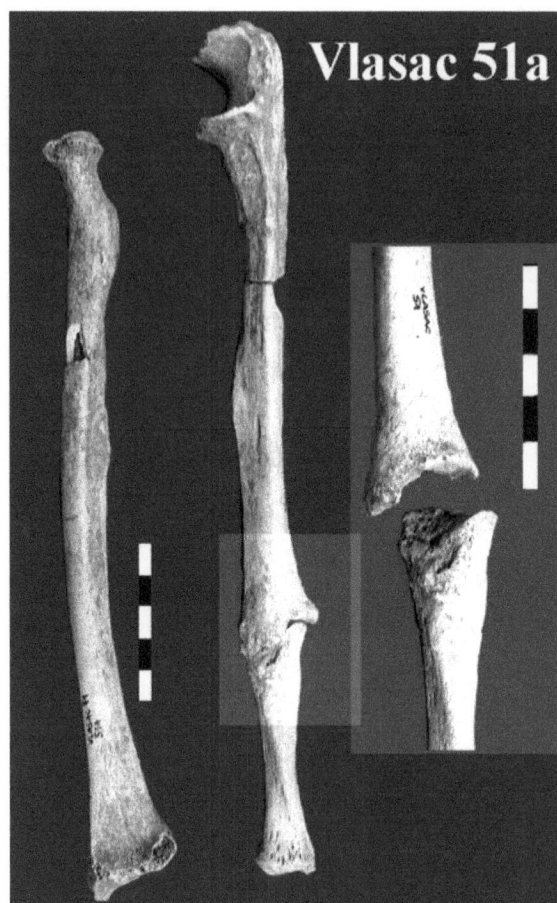

Figure 12. Vlasac 51a: radius and ulna, pseudoarticulation of the right ulna highlighted and in detail

Skeletal data from the burial context: The burials marked as 51, 51a and 51b and 52 represent a group of nine individuals buried on a flat surface. A field drawing published by Radovanović (1996:192, Fig. 4.9) shows another associated skeleton (52a) that was not found during the 1998 analysis. Of the six adults the more or less complete individuals 51a and 52 are both females. Another partially preserved adult, pieced together from fragments in 51, 51a and 51b, was also determined as a female based on the morphology of the preserved coxal bone. According to Zoffmann, (1983), the missing individual 52a was also an adult female.[7] Sex could not be determined for the cremated adult (51,a,b/2) and two fragmentary individuals associated with the burial 52 (52/1 and 52/3). On the basis of doubling of the arm and foot elements of a pre-pubertal child, another individual (52/2) was separated and determined as a young child or a pre-pubertal child (more likely the latter on the basis of the talus size).

Burial interpretation: All of the individuals were buried on a flat surface with no evidence of a burial pit. They were subsequently partially disturbed by hearths 19 and 19a (Srejovic and Letica, 1978: 56, Fig. 67, T. XII, XIII). Data on position are available for four of them: 51, 51a, 51b, and 52. According to the published photos (Srejović and Letica,

---

[7]   It could not be taken into account here since no bones associated with this number were found. The additional female could (at least theoretically) belong to this skeleton.

Table 4. Demographics of the individuals in burial association with the individual 51a at Vlasac.

site	burial no	MNI	#	sex	age	Age	Notes
Vlasac	51	5	1	NA	ppc	7-11	
Vlasac	51a	5	2	f	FA		
Vlasac	51b	5	3	NA	ppc	6-10	
Vlasac	51+51a+51b(1)	5	4	f	MA/SA		
Vlasac	51+51a+51b(2)	5	5	n	A		Cremated
Vlasac	52	4	1	f	YA		
Vlasac	52(1)	4	2	n	FA		
Vlasac	52(2)	4	3	NA	yc,ppc	2-12	
Vlasac	52(3)	4	4	n	A		
Vlasac	64a	3	2	NA	ppc	8-12	
Vlasac	64b	3	3	NA	ppc	8-12	
Vlasac	64 or 64(1)	3	1	NA	ppc/pc	9-13	

Period: M=Mesolithic, M/N=Mesolithic in contact with Neolithic, N=Neolithic. MNI in the burial = minimal number of individuals for the burial from which the skeleton is issued, #of the individual = sequential number assigned to the individual within the burial, sex: m or f = male or female assigned based on pelvic remains, m?/f? male or female assigned based on postcranial robusticity; age: yc=young child, ppc=pre-pubertal child, pc=pubertal child, YA=young adult, FA=fully adult, MA=mature adult, SA=senile adult.

1978: T. XII, XIII,) individuals 51a and 52 were buried in the extended dorsal decubitus with inverse orientation, the feet of individual 51a positioned at the head of individual 52. Complete splaying of the rib cage, pelvis and feet of individual 51a and the rib cage of individual 52 indicate some architectural element delineating an open space in which decomposition took place (Roksandic, 2002). Given the position of the relatively complete burials 51a and 52, and the fact that the fracture was visible and in a perfect alignment position even on the photo of the grave (see Figure 13 highlighted square), no externally induced post-

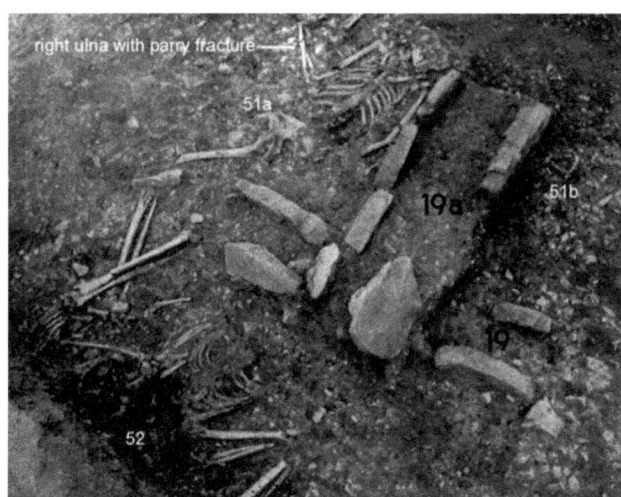

Figure 13. Vlasac 51 and 52 burial group with hearths 19 and 19a discussed in the text.

depositional movement can be envisaged for either of the skeletons. This could indicate their synchronicity, but this argument could not be pushed further given the lack of fine-grained information on internal spatial arrangement of the bones.

Two of the associated pre-pubertal children (nos. 51, 51b) are represented by a number of bones in anatomical connection: arm bones of individual 51b and vertebra and legs of individual 51. Field drawings further confirm that they were primary burials on the bare soil; however, they are not observed on the photo, except possibly for the mandible of 51b. Over these burials, the hearths 19 and 19a were built. Hearth 19a completely covers individual 51b, except for the mandible mentioned earlier. The building of hearth 19 seems to have disturbed the burials and removed some of the bones from the context, since no bones are indicated on the drawing in the area underneath the hearth. However, hearth 19a was oriented perpendicularly to the previous one, and covered the bones of the individual 51b, which, while looking 'disturbed' were not missing from the context.

Radovanović (1996a) further associates the burial group 64a, 64b and 64 with this group and with house 2. This group (64a, etc) consists of 3 pre-pubertal children. They postdate the earlier hearth and the described burial group (51-52) and could be associated with the later hearth (i.e. 19a).

In conclusion, a number of individuals (Vlasac 51, 51a, 51b, 52, 52, 64, 64a and 64b) were primary burials on a flat surface with some architectural cover allowing for the decomposition of the body in an open space. They were in a probable association with hearths 19 and 19a that were built once the decomposition of the bodies was complete. The group consists of six pre-pubertal children, three adult females of different ages, and three more adults of undetermined sex of which one was represented by several cremated bones. The fully adult female 51a with the parry fracture is the only individual showing any traces of trauma in the group.

Vlasac 4a sharp impact: projectile point in the ilium (Figures 14, 15, 16; Table 5)

Description of the injury: There is only one case of a sharp force trauma in the whole series. Careful examination and reconstruction of pelvic bones of the individual Vlasac 4a from bone fragments, revealed an ilium with an embedded bone projectile in the *iliac fossa* at the level of gluteal surface (Figure 12). The bone projectile has penetrated the *gluteus medius*, and both the external and internal laminae of the ilium. Subsequently, the tip of the bone projectile was broken off, and the rest of the projectile was broken at the point of penetration. The embedded portion of the projectile is 12 mm long, 4mm in diameter at the point of penetration and 3 mm at the point of exit. It is impossible to ascertain whether the breakage of both the tip and the lower portion of the projectile happened during the impact or post mortem (Figure 13). No microtraumatism that could indicate a failed attempt to remove the projectile from the bone *in vivo*, could be observed, which makes the postmortem scenario for the projectile breakage more likely. There is no clear macroscopic evidence of bone remodelling around the wound, although there is some inconclusive indication of remodelling on the external table around the entrance point of the projectile[8], further obscured by the accumulation of fine sediment in the area.

The projectile point penetrated the individual from the posterolateral side. It might have been shot at a high velocity (as an arrow or a dart) given that it managed to penetrate both *gluteus medius* (one of the bigger and stronger muscles) and the ilium. Experimental work by Lowrey suggests that bone projectiles of both the spindle and the triangular types had better penetrating value than either stone or iron points, and required less pull. However, most of the embedded projectiles in Mesolithic Europe represent different types of lithic tools: 12 out of 18 recorded by Vencl (1995: 220-222). When new data from Schela Cladovei (Boroneant et al., 1999) and Vlasac 4a are included, the same proportion is retained (14 out of 21 burials have lithic projectiles). Bone projectiles are found to be more strongly represented in projectile assemblages of the Northwest Coast hunter-gatherers, where intertribal warfare was evidenced archaeologically and ethnohistorically (Lowrey, 1999). No comparison is available for the bone *vs.* lithic projectiles for the Iron Gates Mesolithic, although Radovanović (1996a: 259-261) gives information on the number of bone projectiles of different types in the assemblage. The most common ones, pointed at one end and obliquely cut at the other (type a), and pointed with oval

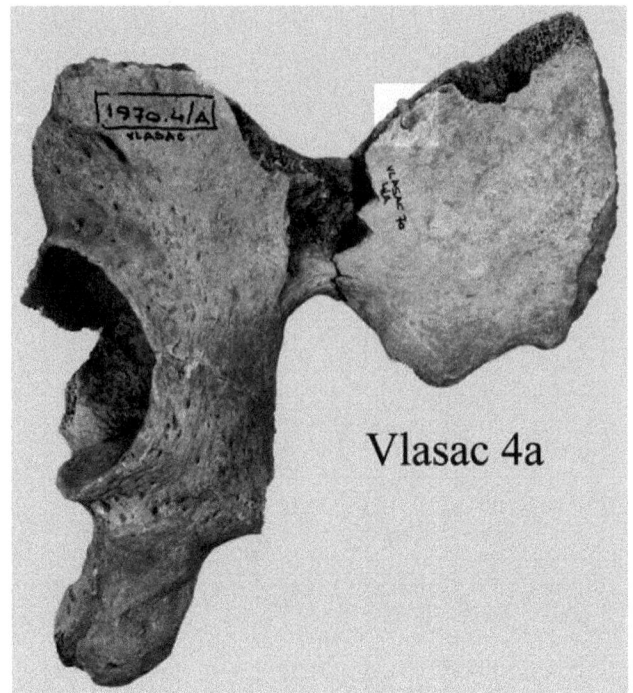

Figure 14. Reconstructed coxal bone of the individual 4a with projectile point in the ilium.

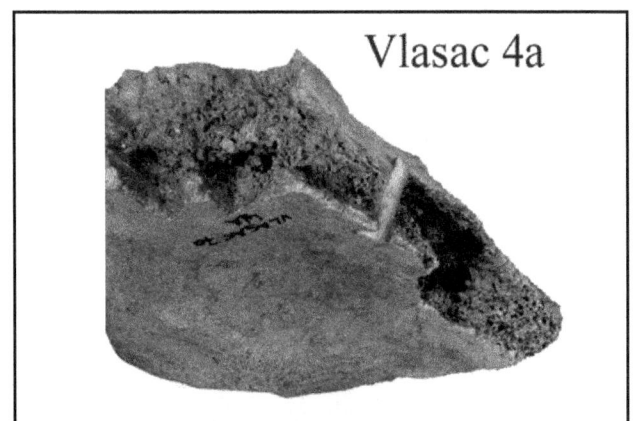

Figure 15. Detail of a broken fragment of the ilium showing the position of the bone projectile still firmly embedded in the bone, penetrating both external and internal tables, with broken tips.

section (type b), are represented at all of the sites in the Iron Gates Gorges except for Veterani Terace and Ostrovul Banului. They are most numerous in Vlasac II and III (Radovanović 1996a: 260-261). However, the presence of bone projectiles does not indicate warfare in itself, since they could be – and were – used for hunting (Choyke and Bartosiewicz, this volume).

Lack of explicit bone remodelling around the impact area with the projectile point indicates that this individual did not survive the incident for more than two weeks (Aufderheide and Rodriguez-Martin, 1998: 23). Blood loss would be an unlikely cause of death given the placement of the wound. An attempt to remove the projectile could have resulted in the micro-traumatism around the point of penetration, but of this there is no evidence. If this injury was indeed the cause

---

[8]   Fine sediment accumulated at this area obscures the possible remodeling. It couldn't be removed without causing damage to9 the bone.

Table 5. Demographics of the individuals in burial association with the individual 4a at Vlasac.

site	burial no		MNI	#	sex	age	notes
Vlasac	4a	M	3	1	m	pc/YA	skull/pcs
Vlasac	4b	M	3	2	m?	FA/MA	pcs
Vlasac	4b(1)	M	3	3	NA	n	left femur
Vlasac	9	M	2	1	f	MA	skull/pcs
Vlasac	9(1)	M	2	2	NA	sc	left neural arch of thv

Period: M=Mesolithic, MNI= minimal number of individuals in the burial, #of the individual = sequential number assigned to the individual within the burial, sex: m/f = male /female assigned based on pelvic remains, m? = male based on postcranial robusticity; NA= subadult sexing not attempted, age: n = newborn, sc=small child, pc=puberal child, YA=young adult, FA=fully adult, MA=mature adult, SA=senile adult.

of death, which is impossible to ascertain since a number of other possible injuries that did not leave any trace on the skeleton could have co-occurred, two scenarios could be proposed: 1) the projectile tip was poisoned – a relatively common practice for hunting larger prey or 2) the penetration of the point caused damage to the internal abdomen lining. Following the same line of reasoning, several possible explanations can be offered: 1) hunting accident, 2) homicide, 3) execution, or 4) warfare. Given the position of the impact – lateral and posterior in the lower part of the body – execution would be the least likely scenario. Hunting accident, homicide, or warfare were equally likely as they could all result from an ambush. While hunting accidents were probably not very common, they cannot be excluded on the bases of available evidence. Warfare, on the other hand, cannot be deduced from a single case, and will be discussed in comparison with data from Schela Cladovei below.

Skeletal data from the burial context: Burials 4 and 9 belong to the same grave structure made of rocks (Figure 14 based on Srejović and Letica 1978: Table XLII). A MNI of five individuals was found within the burial construction. Two previously unnoticed immature individuals: one newborn and a small child represented by very fragmentary remains were recorded in 1998.

Individual 4a: Based on the morphology of the pelvis, the greater sciatic notch and the general robusticity of the postcranial skeleton, the individual was male. The iliac crest is still not fused, indicating an older sub-adult or a young adult, since the fusion commences at around 17 years of age (Scheuer and Black, 2000: 372). Teeth eruption corresponds with postcranial data: 38 and 48 (Fédération Dentaire Internationale, 1971)[9] are erupted while 18 and 25 still remain in the alveolar sockets, indicating an age of 18 ± 3 years (Ubelaker and Buikstra, 1994). The individual 4b was fully adult (based on the presence of line of the epiphyseal union

on the available cross-section of the proximal humerus) or a mature adult (indicated by lipping on proximal ulna and foot bones). It was a remarkably robust individual – a good indicator of male sex in this series. Together with these two individuals (4a and 4b), a proximal fragment of left femur of a newborn was found: individual 4a(1). The bone is not complete, but compared to the rest of the neonatal skeletons (with complete femora, maxilae and mandibulae) it seems to be in the peri-natal stage. This determination should be taken with extreme caution, however, as size variation among the newborn can be substantial (Scheuer and Black, 2000: 393-395).

For skeleton number 9, Nemeskeri and Szathmary (1978d:9) note that the pubic angle has female values. No pubic bones were found during our examination of the material in 1998, most probably due to inadequate storage. On the other hand, the greater sciatic notch was present on both sides. Although the notches are of ambiguous morphology, a relatively rare case in the Iron Gates series, deep *prearicular sulci* on both sides confirm this individual as female. When all age markers (excessive tooth wear, available femoral head cross-section, morphology of the auricular surface, degenerative joint disease on the cervical and lumbar vertebrae, no senile pitting) were taken into account, the individual was determined as mature adult. Within the burial, among the bones of this adult woman, one fragmented neural arch of a thoracic vertebra of a young child (2-6 years) was found and designated as 9(1).

Burial interpretation: The group grave 4a-4b-9 was assigned to the Vlasac I chronological phase by Radovanović (1996a: 355). The two graves are found in a circular stone enclosure in a natural hollow divided by stone slabs (Figure 16). For grave 4a-4b, Srejović and Letica (1978: 67-68) give following description: "Inhumation in quadrant 1/6 on the relative depth of 1.88m (absolute depth 63.83m). The skeleton was deposited into a natural depression in the ground approximately 0.40m deep. A large inclined stone slab protected the cranium. The sides of the depression were outlined by stones (one large stone of an irregular shape, three stone slabs and a large stone slab perpendicular to and above the adjacent grave no. 9). The skull lay with the face towards the ground. Mandible and maxilla were dislocated.

---

[9] Dental recording system used by Fédération Dentaire Internationale is a two digit system, where the first digit indicates quadrant and dentition (1-4 adult; 5-8 deciduous) and the second digit indicates the tooth. Because of rapid entry into computer database and avoidance of special characters, this system is ideal for recording large anthropological collections. Hillson S (1996) Dental Anthropology. Cambridge: Cambridge University Press.

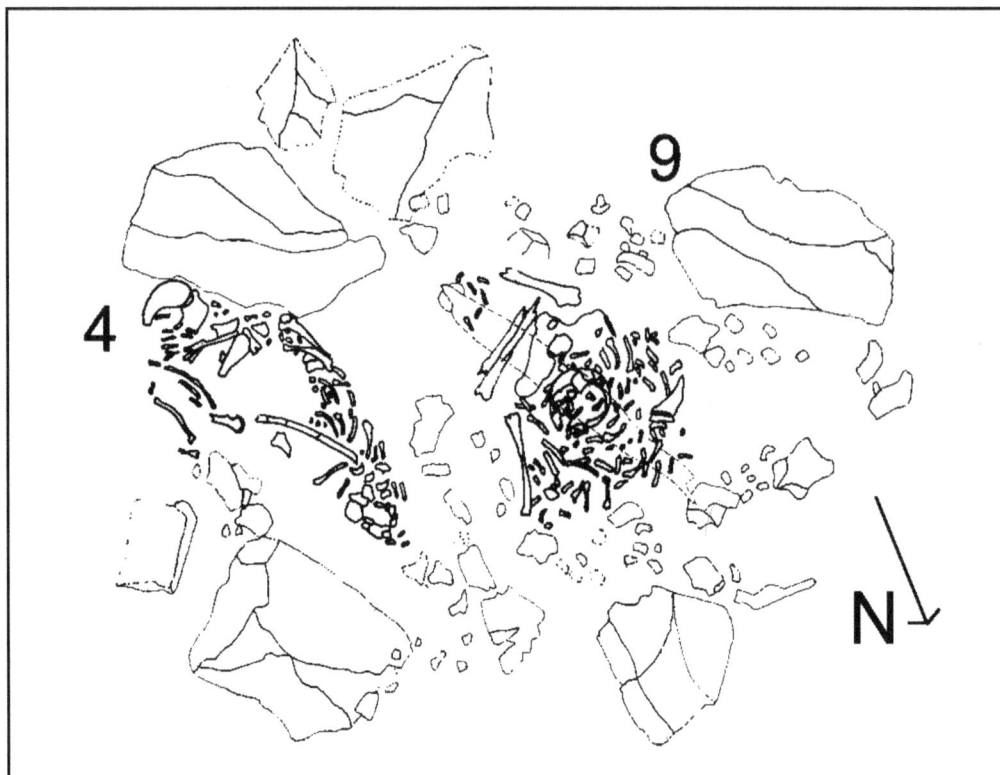

Figure 16. Field drawing of Vlasac 4 and 9 in a circular stone concentration.
Courtesy of the Archaeological Institute in Belgrade.

The left hand was positioned behind the back of the skull, while the right one was dislocated. The vertebral column and the ribs were arched. The impression was that the deceased was positioned on the right side of the body. The position of the legs is not clear. One of the legs was probably flexed at the knee. Grave goods: near the legs, fragments of bone awl [...] Some fragmented long bones of a male individual, designated as skeleton 4b were found in the same depression with skeleton 4a."

Although relatively detailed, this description is not easy to understand and the position of skeleton 4a seems to be more complex than reported. The available photo (figure 17) does not show the skull described by Srejović and Letica, but only the posterior aspect of the upper body with substantial disturbance of the rib cage, and the lateral portion of the lumbar vertebrae. The individual looks as if the upper body was deposited face-down, with torsion at the lumbar level. The legs could have been flexed underneath and to the left of the body axis, but there is a number of non-identified long bones that do not easily conform to this explanation. Unfortunately we have only one photo of this grave on which the details are not easy to distinguish, and successive layers of excavations of the body that could provide exact relationship between anatomical elements were not recorded photographically. The unknown position of the skeleton 4b further complicates the picture. Some of the long bones of this individual are visible underneath the removed skull and the upper body of individual 4a, while, in addition, a right anterior portion of the rib cage (very similar to the actual seated burials at the site), intermixed with some metatarsals can be discerned in the same area.

The fact that a number of carpals, metacarpals, tarsals and metatarsals were present in burials 4a and 4b, points to a likely primary burial of both individuals. Based on age and robusticity it was possible to further distinguish between the mixed bones of these two individuals. Some fragments of the skull were present that could not be assigned to the skeleton 4a and were accordingly attributed to the burial 4b. Among the bones recorded as 4b by excavators, there was a

Figure 17. Photo of the burial Vlasac 4a 4b.
Courtesy of the Archaeological Institute in Belgrade.

left branch of a hyoid bone. This bone is regarded as a strong indicator of primary burial, however, since the skull of 4a overlaid the bones of the 4b, it is also possible that it belongs to the skeleton 4a. Nevertheless, both skeletons are likely primary burials, with skeleton 4b buried first in the sequence, with skull removed and postcranial skeleton disturbed by the burial of the individual 4a.

The following description is given for burial Vlasac 9: "Skeletal inhumation, in quadrant a/6, relative depth 1.81m, (absolute depth 63.89m). The skeleton is deposited in a shallow natural depression with circular stone construction made of larger blocks of stone. The deceased was buried in a flexed position, the body, or rather the vertebral column with legs, overlying the head. The pelvis lay on the skull, retaining the proper anatomical position in respect to the head of the left femur. Right femur, fragmented and with dislocated head, lay next to the right coxal bone. The bones of the left foot were underneath the left humerus. The bones of the distal part of the right leg were fragmented and foot bones were underneath the base and the back of the skull. The left humerus was found in anatomical position in respect to the scapula, while the right one was overturned. A bone projectile was found among the bones of the left foot." (Srejović and Letica 1978:69, my translation).

The description of burial Vlasac 9, even more complicated than burials 4 and 4a, is difficult to understand and the available photo (Figure 18) shows little detail. Several

Figure 18. Photo of the burial Vlasac 9.
Courtesy of the Archaeological Institute in Belgrade.

preserved anatomical connections, left coxal bone with left femur, left humerus, radius and ulna (discernible in the photo), and left humerus with scapula, otherwise an unstable articulation (Duday, 1985), would indicate decomposition within the burial site, while their mutual relationship as well as the positioning of the skull underneath the pelvis could not be explained by any natural taphonomic process resulting from a primary interment. The removal of the skull and its rearrangement underneath the rest of the body must have been effected early in the decomposition sequence and could indicate dismemberment. While systematic assessment of the taphonomic changes has not been completed, no traces of dismemberment were found on the preserved bones during the 1998 analysis.

Here we propose one of the possible scenarios for the burial events in chronological order: Burials 4b and 9 could have been independent burial episodes of a mature female (9), and an adult male (4b) into the same grave construction, either simultaneously or diachronously. Burial 4a is best explained as a subsequent re-opening of the construction, retrieval of the skull of the adult male 4b (for possible reburial at another spot) and the burial of a young adolescent male 4a, with the positioning of a stone slab on top of the adjacent grave 9. The fragment of the vertebra of the young child 9(1) was most likely a secondary burial simultaneous with the interment of the adult female 9. Accordingly, it can be proposed that the secondary burial of the fragment of femur of a newborn 4a(1) was simultaneous with the burial 4a or 4b. The meaning of secondary burials of small fragments of human skeletons within primary burials remains open, as no systematic examination of these remains has been done so far. Their great number sugests that disturbance of previous burials is not necessarily the only, or the most plausible explanatory mechanism for this phenomenon.

Both burials contained bone implements as "grave goods:" a fragmented bone awl in burial 4a and a bone projectile in burial 9. Bone awls of small dimensions could have been used as projectiles (Mihailović, 1996) and, based on the size of the 'awl' it could have been a fragment of the embedded projectile point in the individual 4a. The projectile point in Vlasac 9, reported as a "grave good," could have, accordingly, had a different association with the body. It was found within the bones of left foot, which were themselves underneath the left humerus, potentially close to thorax. While this evidence is not conclusive, it could indicate that both Vlasac 4a and 9 were victims of violence. Their burial in the same enclosure complicates the picture and opens up many more possible interpretations. While only individual 4a shows evidence of an incontestable projectile wound, individual 9 could also have been a victim of violent death. Interment face down for burial 4a and potential dismemberment and the unusual position of burial 9 corroborate further their special treatment. Were they unceremoniously discarded victims of violence? Placing of the skull underneath the long bones is further evidenced in Vlasac 69, another potential victim of violent death with a perimortem blunt force depressed fracture on the frontal bone. In the case of Vlasac 69, decomposition was well advanced before the arrangement of the bones took place, suggesting that no immediate

Table 6. All recorded incidences of skeletal trauma possibly caused by violence in the Iron Gates Gorge sample. burial no refers to the number assigned to the burial by excavators.

Site	burial no	period	MNI	#	sex	age	Trauma
Vlasac	82a	M	5	4	m	MA/SA	Frontal (R)
Lvir	69	M	1	1	m?	MA/SA	Frontal, repeated (R,L)
Vlasac	51a	M	5	2	f	FA	Ulna parry fracture (R)
Vlasac	4a	M	3	1	m	YA	Projectile point in the ilium (R)
Vlasac	69	M/N	3	1	m?	MA	Frontal, perimortem (L)
Lvir	20	M/N? N?	1	1	m?	MA	Frontal, deep (R)

Period: M=Mesolithic, M/N=Mesolithic in contact with Neolithic, N=Neolithic. MNI in the burial = minimal number of individuals for the burial from which the skeleton is issued, #of the individual = sequential number assigned to the individual within the burial, sex: m or f = male or female assigned based on pelvic remains, m?/f? male or female assigned based on postcranial robusticity; age: YA=young adult, FA=fully adult, MA=mature adult, SA=senile adult.

connection between death by violence and the particular burial pattern could be established.

Discussion of the evidence of violent trauma on the right bank of the Danube

A total of six skeletons on the right bank in the Iron Gates Gorge exhibit traces of *probable* violent trauma (table 6). While violence as aetiology is the most likely explanation in the case of the five men, it is more doubtful in the case of ulna parry fracture recorded in the female individual Vlasac 51a. The latter is concordant with both accident and violence.

Two injuries could have been lethal: the projectile point in the ilium of the young male Vlasac 4a, and a perimortem cranial trauma of the Vlasac 69. The perimortem cranial fracture of Lepenski Vir 69 is more ambiguous and is more likely a postmortem trauma. In addition, individual Vlasac 9 could have died from a bone projectile found within the burial, but the evidence is circumstantial.

All of the cranial depressed fractures are on the frontal bone, which is consistent with the 'face to face' fighting. Side evidence is less convincing: two of the healed impacts are on the right side of the skull (Lepenski Vir 20, Vlasac 82) while the unhealed trauma of Vlasac 69 is on the left. Lepenski Vir 69 has two healed injuries, one on each side of the frontal bone.

Associated burial data

The Iron Gates Mesolithic group shows impressive variability in burial ritual (noted already by Srejović, 1972) in all periods under consideration. This observation is valid for all of the sites on the right bank, including the Early Neolithic sites of Ajmana and Velesnica. This makes it hard to separate the individuals with special status solely on the bases of burial ritual. The placement of certain individuals/skeletal elements in the houses, association with hearths in all of the sites, spatial

association with sculptures at Lepenski Vir, as well as the inclusion of 'extra individuals' or small fragments of bone into primary burials, provide a strong indication of the importance of ancestral ritual. It is probable that both complete and fragmentary skeletons represent family and lineage ancestors, i.e. individuals who occupy or claim certain of the Lepenski Vir houses as 'lineage essence' that establishes the corporate aspect of the dead person (Bloch, 1988).

Among the burials presented here only Lepenski Vir 69 and possibly Lepenski Vir 20 are single burials. Given that no postcranial elements were collected in the case of Lepenski Vir 20, and only the two femora in the case of Lepenski Vir 69, we cannot exclude the possibility that burials contained additional, uncollected/unrecognised individuals. Lepenski Vir 20 is the only *potentially* Early Neolithic burial with evidence of violent trauma. Neolithic burials from the region represent a continuation of the Mesolithic tradition of the Iron Gates Gorge. Both single and group burials are known from Lepenski Vir Neolithic and Velesnica, while diachronous group burials are found in Ajmana and Velesnica (Antunović, 1990). Even if the Lepenski Vir 20 individual is a single burial, given the paucity of data, no special status could be envisaged on this basis alone.

The situation is different for the Lepenski Vir 69. While we are definitely impeded by quasi-complete lack of postcranial skeleton, the drawing and the photo are detailed and clear enough to leave little doubt that it is indeed a primary single burial with no additional skeletal elements. This individual is signalled out by Srejović (1969) as representing an early (or even the first) occurrence of intra-mural primary burial at Lepenski Vir. According to him, all of the previous burials are partial secondary burials of already exposed bodies. However, this claim will remain unconfirmed until checked against the taphonomic information on weathering. In addition, the position of this individual is evocative and proportional to the trapezoid outline of the house-bases that are to predominate the subsequent periods at Lepenski Vir (Srejović and Babović 1983: 45, Fig. 18). Superimposed, a typical house with a hearth, sculpture and crucial constructive elements corresponds well to the outline of the body. This observation further links the house, the hearth, the sculpture and burial, providing us with a connection between the dead (the ancestor) and the house of the living, between the spiritual (the sculpture) and the mundane (the hearth). It is reasonable to suggest that the individual was an important member of his group. The question remains, can we link his ability and his special status to the evidence of healed depressed fractures on his forehead? Before attempting to answer this question, we need to look into burials of other individuals that were subject to violence.

All other cases of violent trauma come from group burials: Vlasac 82, Vlasac 51a, Vlasac 4a (with the associated potential victim of violence Vlasac 9) and Vlasac 69 each are represented by a number of individuals in a closed burial context. Their diverse demographics, and a whole array of burial rituals – primary, secondary, a combination of the two, and inclusion of extra individuals – as well as their strictly delimited burial space, indicate family or lineage tombs. This is further corroborated in Vlasac 82 by the presence of 'accetabular mark' on all three observable ilia – an otherwise rare discrete trait in this population.[10] The young man (Vlasac 4a) who most probably died a violent death, shot by a projectile point, is buried in a stone enclosure with another adult male, an adult female (another possible victim of violence) and the remains of a small child and a new-born baby. There is no indication that any of the individuals with evidence of violent trauma enjoyed a special status, suggesting that the status of Lepenski Vir 69 was most probably associated with some other accomplishments.

While the sample in the Gorges is very small and, given all the cautionary notes at the beginning of the article, can not be assumed to be representative, it is noteworthy that most of the violent interactions happened during pre-contact or Mesolithic times. There is little doubt that these skeletons are properly assigned to the period, even in this complex archaeological record. Two of the individuals (Vlasac 51a and Lepenski Vir 69) are characterized by an 'early diet' (Bonsall et al., 1997: 64-65, Tables 3 and 4) indicative of the pre-contact Mesolithic in the region (Radovanović, 2000). In addition, Vlasac 51a was dated by C14 to 7949-7585 BC calibrated. Only two of the burials with evidence of violence belong to the period when the contact with farming communities becomes established.

It can therefore be concluded that the evidence for violent interactions on a larger scale, which could indicate feuding/ warfare in the region, is minimal in both the pre-contact and contact times inside the Gorges on the right bank of the Danube.

Outside the Gorges, evidence from Schela Cladovei

In comparison with the area inside the Gorges, downstream from the Ključ region, on the left bank in the fertile flood-

plane, the site of Schela Cladovei shows a very different picture both in terms of prevalence of violent trauma – especially the number of projectile points embedded in the bone – and in terms of burial ritual. At Schela Cladovei zone III – excavated during the joint Romanian/British excavations in the early 90s – two skulls (female 42 and male 48) show evidence of blunt force trauma. Two individuals, one male (46) and one female (49) had parry fractures, while embedded bone projectiles were found in the male individuals 48 and 50, and a flint projectile in individual 47 for which the sex was not reported. (Boroneant et al., 1999: 389). In terms of dietary information, they all form a tight cluster, interpreted by Bonsall et al., (1997) as predominantly aquatic or by Radovanović (2000) as an 'early diet type,' indicating Mesolithic pre-contact times. However, C14 dates are more ambiguous as they fall between 7307-7545 BC calibrated, concordant both with pre-contact Mesolithic or the very beggining of possible contact with Neolithic. In addition, a skeleton of an adult male (3) with two projectile points: one in a rib cage and one in a femur, and another male (3a) with a bone projectile in the temporal bone – for which we do not have any precise dates or dietary information – were unearthed in previous excavations in the late 60s. They are considered to be the final Epi-paleolithic by Nicolaescu-Plopsor and Boroneant (1976). McSweeney and colleagues (2000) report a total of five individuals (four males and one female) with possibly fatal projectile wounds, 14 individuals with evidence of trauma of which five are blunt force trauma to the skull and several cases of lower arms fractures for the total of 57 individuals from both excavation campaigns.

A closer look at the burial pattern in the area III of the site, for which we have well published information, reveals a group burial with eight well articulated primary disposals, some with heads removed, several articulated but partial skeletons, and a number of isolated bones. MIN was calculated to be 25 individuals, most of them adults of both sexes (Boroneant et al., 1999). Similarly to the other Mesolithic sites in the region, there is a clear association of these burials with the "hearth" structure. All of the articulated skeletons were buried lying on their backs, along the same axis; two of them were in an inverse orientation to the others. Similar uniformity in position and orientation is found only in the central burial area of Hajdučka Vodenica, dated to the Contact period, but without any evidence of violent death.

Such striking differences in the prevalence of violent trauma – 7/25 in Area III of Schela Cladovei, (19/57 for the whole site) as opposed to 6/263 on all six sites on the right bank of the Danube in the Gorges – indicates a very different pattern of behaviour associated with violence. Given the geographic position of the sites on the right bank, they could have been harder to access and therefore less exposed to violent attacks by other groups. However, the sites of Velesnica and Ajmana are also situated on the flood plane beyond the Gorges and show no evidence of violence. Alternatively, death by violence could have resulted from different behaviours, or could have been treated differently by local groups.

On the basis of evidence presented above, the violent interactions on sites on the right bank of the Danube in the

---

[10] While raw data on discrete traits can not be taken at face value, such a situation is quite indicative.

Gorges could be explained as a series of unrelated and diachronous episodes. These incidents could have as easily happened within the community as with members of other groups. The evidence for violent interactions at Schela Cladovei, on the other hand is restricted in time and the burial ritual is rather uniform. It could represent either a single episode of group violence, or a series of related events. Either way, it is reasonable to suggest that the whole group was involved.

CONCLUSION

Violent interactions in Iron Gates Gorge during Mesolithic, and Mesolithic/Neolithic Contact period are confirmed by a restricted number of skeletal elements with traumatic injuries for which violence is a likely aetiology. There is an important difference in the pattern of violence between the right bank of the Danube in the Gorges area from that in the flood-plain downstream from the Gorges. When viewed separately, the Gorges area shows sporadic violence without any special status associated with individuals who engaged in violent interactions. The only likely 'special status' individual with violent trauma is Lepenski Vir 69. However, it cannot be confirmed that the status of this individual was specifically due to his involvement in violent interactions. All other individuals exhibit substantial variability in terms of burial ritual, which is a predominant pattern in the Iron Gates Gorge Mesolithic and Early Neolithic. While no trend towards increase or decrease of violence can be discerned given the restricted numbers of individuals with trauma, it is certain that violence on the right bank is not associated with the contact with farmers.

Schela Cladovei data offer a different picture, since we have a combination tight clustering of individuals that were subject to violence, Mesolithic type diet, and C14 dates that are borderline between precontact and contac period. Even if we accept that the dates indicate that the contact with Early Neolithic cultures further south in the Balkans was possible, it was most probably on the small scale evidenced by trade that brings the obsidian and the Pre-Balkan plateau flint to the area. Large displacement of farming communities that would shrink the territory of Mesolithic peoples is unlikely at this very early stage. The *causa belli* that was most often evoked: decrease in territory under pressure from Neolithic communities in the region, increase in population and other stresses associated with contact with farmers, can therefore be excluded as explanatory mechanisms for these violent interactions in the Gorges, but can not be excluded for this site.

While, based on the presented evidence, warfare cannot be excluded; it remains unlikely on the right bank of the Iron Gates Gorge. If there indeed was organized violence and warfare, as suggested by the Schela Cladovei data, it is localized and temporarily restricted (note the tight clustering of C 14 dates) and we cannot talk about endemic warfare. Furthermore, a closer look into the burial pattern at Schela Cladovei has to be taken in order to understand the high prevalence of violent interactions at the site. Warfare caused

by advancing Neolithic farmers can be excluded on the basis of the evidence presented here since most of the violent interactions happened during pre-contact or very early contact times.

Acknowledgements

The observations on the violent trauma were made during my research stay in Belgrade in 1998 funded by Wenner-Gren Small Research Grant no. Gr. 6250. I am indebted to Dr. Djurić and J. Kelečević for their help in identification and interpretation of violent trauma, Dr. Mikić for useful comments and the Faculty of Philosophy for the logistic support. I am also grateful to the researchers at the Institute of Archaeology in Belgrade for their help in providing necessary field documentation and especially to Mary Jackes, László Bartosiewicz and Malcolm Lillie for their valuable comments and criticisms on the first, barely legible draft.

Author

Mirjana Roksandic, Ph.D.
Department of Anthropology and Religion
University of Toronto at Mississauga,
3359 Mississauga Road North,
Mississauga, Ontario, Canada l5l 1C6
mroksand@utm.utoronto.ca

Bibliography

ANTUNOVIĆ M (1987) Grobovi i antropološki ostaci u starijem i srednjem neolitu Centralnog Balkana. Honours, University of Belgrade, Belgrade.

ANTUNOVIĆ M (1990) Anthropological and Archaeological Survey Concerning Mortuary Practices in the central Area of Balkan Peninsula During Early and Middle Neolithic. In M Otte (ed.): Rubane et Cardial. E.R.A.U.L. 39. Liège, pp. 39-50.

AUFDERHEIDE AC, and RODRIGUEZ-MARTIN C (1998) The Cambridge Encyclopedia of Human Paleopathology. Cambridge: Cambridge University Press.

BERRYMAN H, HAUN, S. (1996) Applying Forensic Technique to Interpret Cranial Fracture Patterns in an Archaeological Specimen. International Journal of Osteoarchaeology 6:2-9.

BLOCH M (1988) Introduction: Death and the Concept of a Person. In J Lindstörm (ed.): On the Meaning of Death. Upsala: Almquist & Wiksell International, pp. 11-30.

BOCQUET-APPEL J-P, and MASSET C (1982) Farewell to paleodemography. Journal of Human Evolution 11:321-333.

BONSALL C, LENNON R, MCSWEENEY K, STEWART C, HARKNESS D, BORONENAT V, BARTOSIEWICZ L, PAYTON R, AND CHAPMAN J (1997) Mesolithic and Early Neolithic in the Iron Gates: a Palaeodietary Perspective. Journal of European Archaeology 5:50-92.

BORONEANT V (1973) Recherches archéologiques sur la culture Schela Cladovei de la zone des 'Portes de Fer'. Dacia, N.S. CVII:5-39.

BORONEANT V, BONSALL C, MCSWEENEY K, PAYTON R, and MACKLIN M (1999) A Mesolithic burial area at Schela Cladovei, Romania. In A Thévien (ed.): L'Europe des Derniers

Chasseurs: Épipaléolithique et Mésolithique. (Actes du 5e colloque international UISPP, commission XII, Grenoble, 18-23 septembre 1995). Paris: Éditions du Comité des Travaux Historiques et Scientifiques, pp. 385-390.

BORONEANT VC, BONSALL K, MCSWEENEY R, and PAYTON MM (1995) A Mesolithic Burial Area at Schela Cladovei, Romania. Epipaleolithique et mesolithique en Europe, Paleoenvironement, peuplement et systemes culturels, 5eme Congres International U.I.S.P.P., Commision mesolithique.

BOTELLA M, ALEMÁN I, and JIMÉNEZ S (2000) Les huesos humanos, manipulación y alteraciones. Barcelona: Ediciones Bellaterra.

BUIKSTRA J, and UBELAKER D (1994) Standards for Data Collection from Human Skeletal Remains. Fayetteville: Arkansas Archaeological Survey.

CHOYKE AM, and BARTOSIEWICZ L (in press) Osseous Projectile Points From the Swiss Neolithic: Taphonomy, Typology and Function. In M Roksandic (ed.): Evidence and Meaning of Violent Interactions in Mesolithic Europe.: B.A.R.

CZARNETZKI A, KAUFMANN B, SCHOCH M, and XIROTIRIS N (1985) Definition der anatomichen Varianten, Unterlagen zur Diskussion. Basel.

De PAUW LG (1998) Battle cries and lullabies : women in war from prehistory to the present. Norman: University of Oklahoma Press.

DENNELL RW (1985) The Hunter-Gatherer/Agricultural Frontier in Prehistoric Temperate Europe. In SM Perlman (ed.): The Archaeology of Frontiers and Boundaries. Orlando, Fl.: Academic Press Inc., pp. 113-139.

DUDAY H (1978) Archaeologie funeraire et anthroplogie. Cahiers d'Anthropologie *1:*55-101.

DUDAY H (1985) Nouvelles observations sur la décomposition des corps dans un espace libre. Méthode d'étude des sépultures, pp. 6-13.

DUDAY H (1987) Contribution des observations osteologiques a la chronologie interne des sepultures collectives. In C Masset (ed.): Anthropologie Physique et Archaeologie. Paris: C.N.R.S., pp. 51-61.

EMBER M, and EMBER CR (1997) Violence in the Ethnographic Record: Results of Cross-Cultural Research on War and Agression. In DW Frayer (ed.): Troubled Times: Violence and Warfare in the Past. Amsterdam: Gordon and Breach Publishers, pp. 1-20.

Fédération Dentaire Internationale (1971) Two-digit System of Designating Teeth. International Dental Journal *21:*104-106.

FRAYER D (1997) Ofnet: Evidence for a Mesolithic Massacre. In DW Frayer (ed.): Troubled Times: Violence and Warfare in the Past. Amsterdam: Gordon and Breach Publishers, pp. 181-216.

GALLOWAY A (1999) Fracture Patterns and Skeletal Morphology: Introduction and the Skull. In A Galloway (ed.): Broken Bones: Antrhopological Analyses of Blunt Force Trauma. Springfield: Charles C. Thomas, pp. 63-80.

HILLSON S (1996) Dental Anthropology. Cambridge: Cambridge University Press.

JOVANOVIĆ B (1972) The Autochthonous and the Migrational Components of the Early Neolithic in the Iron Gates. Balcanica *III:*49-58.

JOVANOVIĆ B (1974) Praistorija Gornjeg Djerdapa. STARINAR N.S. *XXII:*1-22.

JOVANOVIĆ B (1984a) Hajducka vodenica, praistorijska nekropola. STARINAR N.S. *XXXIII-XXXIV:*305-313.

JOVANOVIĆ B (1984b) Padina, naselje mezolita i starijeg neolita. STARINAR N.S. *XXXIII-XXXIV:*159-167.

JOVANOVIĆ B (1984c) Stubica, naselje starijeg neolita. STARINAR N.S. *XXXIII-XXXIV:*177-178.

JOVANOVIĆ B (1987) Die Architektur und Keramik der Siedlung Padina B am Eisener Tor, Jugoslawien. Germania *65:*1-16.

JUDD M (2002) Ancient Injury Recidivism: an Example from the Kerma Period of Ancient Nubia. International Journal of Osteoarchaeology *12:*89-106.

KEELEY LH (1997) Frontier Warfare in the Early Neolithic. In DW Frayer (ed.): Troubled Times: Violence and Warfare in the Past. Amsterdam: Gordon and Breach Publishers, pp. 303-320.

KELLY RC (2000) Warless Societies and the Origin of War. Ann Arbor: The University fo Michigan Press.

LOVE B, and MÜLLER H-G (2002) A solution to the problem of obtaining a mortality schedule for paleodemographic data. In JW Vaupel (ed.): Paleodemography : age distributions from skeletal samples. Cambridge, New York, Cambridge University Press, pp. 181.

LOWREY NS (1999) An Ethnoarchaeological Inquiry into the Functional Relationship Between Projectile Point and Armor Technologies of the Northwest Coast. North American Archaeologist *20:*47-73.

MANN R, and MURPHY SP (1990) Regional Atlas of Bone Disease. Springfield, Il., C.C. Thomas.

MCSWEENEY K, BORONEANT V, and BONSALL C (2000) Warfare in the Iron Gates Stone Age: The evidence from Schela Cladovei. The Iron Gates in Prehistory, pp. 21.

MERBS CF (1989) Trauma. In KA Kennedy (ed.): Reconstruction of Life from the Skeleton. New York: Alan R. Liss, pp. 161-189.

MIHAILOVIĆ B (1996) Orudja od kosti, roga i zuba u procesu neolitizacije Centralnog Balkana. B. A. Honors, University of Belgrade, Faculty of Philosophy, Belgrade.

NEMESKERI J (1978) Demographic Structure of the Vlasac Epipaleolithic Population. In D. Srejović and Z Letica (ed.): Vlasac. Mezolitsko naselje u Djerdapu. Beograd: SANU, pp. 97-134.

NEMESKERI J, and LENGYEL I (1978a) Laboratory Examination on the Vlasac Bone Finds. In D. Srejović and Z Letica (ed.): Vlasac. Mezolitsko naselje u Djerdapu. Beograd: SANU, pp. 261-284.

NEMESKERI J, and LENGYEL I (1978b) The Results of Paleopathological Examinations. In D. Srejović and Z Letica (ed.): Vlasac. Mezolitsko naselje u Djerdapu. Beograd: SANU, pp. 231-260.

NEMESKERI J, and SZATHMARY L (1978a) Analysis of the Variation of Quantitative Traits. In D. Srejović and Z Letica (ed.): Vlasac. Mezolitsko naselje u Djerdapu. Beograd: SANU, pp. 157-176.

NEMESKERI J, and SZATHMARY L (1978b) Anthroposcopic and Epigenetic Variation. In D. Srejović and Z Letica (ed.): Vlasac. Mezolitsko naselje u Djerdapu. Beograd: SANU, pp. 135-156.

NEMESKERI J, and SZATHMARY L (1978c) Individual Data on the Vlasac Anthropological Series. In D. Srejović and Z Letica (ed.): Vlasac. Mezolitsko naselje u Djerdapu. Beograd: SANU, pp. 285-426.

NEMESKERI J, and SZATHMARY L (1978d) Sex and Sexualisation. In D. Srejović and Z Letica (ed.): Vlasac. Mezolitsko naselje u Djerdapu. Beograd: SANU, pp. 77-96.

NEMESKERI J, and SZATHMARY L (1978e) Taxonomical Structure of the Vlasac Mesolithic Population. In D. Srejović and Z Letica (ed.): Vlasac. Mezolitsko naselje u Djerdapu. Beograd: SANU, pp. 177-229.

NICOLAESCU-PLOPSOR D, and BORONEANT V (1976) Deux cas de mort violente dans l'Epipaleolithique final de Schela Cladovei. Annuaire Roumain de l'Anthropologie *13:*13-54.

PHENICE TW (1969) A newly developed visual method of sexing the *Os pubis.* American Journal of Physical Anthropology *30:*297-302.

RADOSAVLJEVIĆ-KRUNIĆ S (1986) Resultats de l'étude anthroplogique des squélettes provenant du site Ajmana. Djerdapske sveske - Cahièrs des Portes de Fer *III:*51-58.

RADOVANOVIĆ I (1996a) The Iron Gates Mesolithic. Ann Arbor: University of Michigen Press.

RADOVANOVIĆ I (1996b) Mesolithic/Neolithic Contacts: a Case of the Iron Gates Region. Poročilo o raziskovanju paleolitika, neolitika in eneolitika v Sloveniji *XXIII:*39-48.

RADOVANOVIĆ I (2000) Houses and Burials at Lepenski Vir. European Journal of Archaeology *3:*330-350.

ROKSANDIC M (1999) Transition from Mesolithic to Neolithic in the Iron Gates Gorge: Physical Anthropology Perspective. Ph.D., Simon Fraser University, Burnaby.

ROKSANDIC M (2000a) Between Foragers and Farmers in the Iron Gates Gorge: Physical anthropology Perspective. Documetna Prehistorica *XXVII:*1-100.

ROKSANDIC M (2000b) Velesnica Osteological Report. The Iron Gates in Prehistory.

ROKSANDIC M (2002) Position of Skeletal Remains as a Key to Understanding Mortuary Behavior. In MH Sorg (ed.): Advances in Forensic Taphonomy. Boca Raton: CRC Press, pp. 99-117.

ROKSANDIC, M., M. DJURIC, Z. RAKOCEVIC, J. KELECEVIC, AND K. SEGUIN. submitted. Interpersonal Violence at Lepenski Vir Mesolithic / Neolithic Complex of the Iron Gates Gorge.

SAUNDERS SR (1978) The Development and Distribution of Discontinuous Morphological Variation of the Human Infracranial Skeleton. Ottawa: National Museums of Canada.

SCHEUER L, and BLACK S (2000) Developmental Juvenile Osteology. London: Academic Press.

SIMONS A (1999) War: Back to the Future. Annual Review of Anthropology *28:*73-108.

SJØVOLD T (1984) A report on the Heritability of Some Cranial Measurements and Non-Metric Traits. In WW Howells (ed.): Multivariate Statistical Methods in Physical Anthropology. Dorchester: D.Reidel Publishing Company, pp. 223-246.

SKINNER M, and LAZENBY R (1983) Found! Human Remains. Burnaby, B.C.: Archaeology Press, S.F.U.

SREJOVIĆ D (1966) Lepenski Vir, Boljetin - neolitsko naselje. Arheološki Pregled *8:*94-96.

SREJOVIĆ D (1968) Lepenski vir (Boljetin) - predneolitska i neolitska naselja. Arheološki Pregled *10:*85-87.

SREJOVIĆ D (1969) Lepenski vir. Nova praistorijska kultura u Podunavlju. Beograd: SKZ.

SREJOVIĆ D (1971) Predneolitske i neolitske kulture u Djerdapu. Materijali VIII kongresa arheologa Jugoslavije *VI:*21-.

SREJOVIĆ D (1972) Europe's First Monumnetal Sculpture: New Discoveries at Lepenski Vir. Aylesbury: Themes and Hudson.

SREJOVIĆ D, and BABOVIĆ L (1983) Umetnost Lepenskog Vira. Beograd.

SREJOVIĆ D, and LETICA Z, eds. (1978) Vlasac. Mezolitsko naselje u Djerdapu. Beograd: SANU, Odeljenje istorijskih nauka.

STALIO B (1986) Le site prehistorique Ajmana a Mala Vrbica. Djerdapske sveske - Cahiers des Portes de Fer *III:*27-35.

THORPE N (2000) Origins of War. Mesolithic Conflict in Europe. British Archaeology:9-12.

UBELAKER DH (2002) Approaches to the Study of Commingling in Human Skeletal Biology. In MH Sorg (ed.): Advances in Forensic Taphonomy: Method, Theory and Archaeological Perspectives. Boca Ratton, Fl: CRC Press, pp. 332-351.

UBELAKER DH, and BUIKSTRA JE, eds. (1994) Standards for data collection from human skeletal remains : proceedings of a seminar at the Field Museum of Natural History, organized by Jonathan Haas. Fayetteville, Ark.: Arkansas Archeological Survey.

VASIĆ R (1986) Compte-rendu des fouilles du site préhistorique à Velesnica 1981-1982. Djerdapske Sveske, Cahièrs des Portes de Fer *III:*271-285.

VENCL S (1995) Interprétation des blesseures Causes par les armes au Mésolithique. L'Anthropologie *95:*219-228.

VENCL S (1999) Stone Age Warfare. In A. Harding (ed.): Ancient Warfare, Archaological Perspectives. Phoenix Mill: Sutton Publishing Ltd., pp. 57-73.

WALKER PL (1989) Cranial Injuries as evidence of violence in prehistoric Southern-California. American Journal of Physical Anthropology *80:*313-323.

WALKER PL (2001) A Bioarcheological Perspective on the History of Violence. Annual Review of Anthropology *30:*573-596.

Workshop of European Anthropologists (1980) Recommendations for Age and Sex Diagnosis of Skeletons. Journal of Human Evolution *9:*517-549.

ŽIVANOVIĆ S (1975a) Mesolitic Population in Djerdap Region. BALCANICA *VI:*1-9.

ŽIVANOVIĆ S (1975b) A note on the Anthropological Characteristics of the Padina Population. Z. Morph. Anthrop. *66:*161-175.

ŽIVANOVIĆ S (1975c) Prvo saopštenje o rezultatima antropološkog proučavanja skeletnih ostataka sa Padine u Djerdapu. Starinar N.S. *IIIV-XXV:*139-153.

ŽIVANOVIĆ S (1976a) Cromagnon in the Iron Gate Gorge of the Danube. Nature *260:*518.

ŽIVANOVIĆ S (1976b) The Masticatory Apparatus of the Mesolitic Padina Population. Glasnik Antropološkog društva Jugoslavije *3:*79-96.

ŽIVANOVIĆ S (1976c) Ostaci ljudskih skeleta iz praistorijskog nalazišta na Hajdučkoj vodenici. STARINAR, N.S. *XXVI:*124-129.

ŽIVANOVIĆ S (1979a) Apsolutna starost skeletnih ostataka kromanjonaca sa Padine u Djerdapu. 26-30.

ŽIVANOVIĆ S (1979b) Further Evidence on Cromagnon in the Iron Gate Gorge of the Danube. Current Anthropology *20:*805.

ŽIVANOVIĆ S (1986) Restes des ossements humains à Velesnica. Djerdapske Sveske, Cahiers des Portes de Fer *III:*286-288.

ŽIVANOVIĆ S (1988) The Temporal Region and the Supramastoid Ridge in Mesolitic Skulls from Padina in the Iron Gate Gorge of Danube. Human Evolution *3:*329-334.

ZOFFMANN Z (1983) Prehistoric Skeletal Remains from Lepenski Vir (Iron Gates, Yugoslavia). Homo *34:*129-148.

OSSEOUS PROJECTILE POINTS FROM THE SWISS NEOLITHIC: TAPHONOMY, TYPOLOGY AND FUNCTION

Alice M. CHOYKE and Laszlo BARTOSIEWICZ

Abstract: Except in situations where a bone projectile point is found embedded in a human body, osseous projectile points tend to be unreliable artifacts for quantifying their relative importance as weapons in conflicts. Owing to their relatively softer raw materials, however, bone and antler points are less frequently found in direct contact or actually penetrating the victims' bone compared to lithic projectiles. This study of the typical and easily recognized projectile points from St. Blaise on the shore of Lake Neuchâtel (Western Switzerland) shows that even if these points originated from hunting weapons, most of them were perfectly suited to killing humans as well. These projectiles come from a finely excavated, water-sieved site. The role of taphonomic loss related to the way these projectiles were used is reviewed. In addition, the divergent mechanical properties of bone and antler projectile points, especially as this relates to their penetrating properties, is discussed. A certain group of points from St Blasie and elsewhere in the late Neolithic of Switzerland is characterized by a tight uniform iconic style and dimensions. This may very well reflect strong identity with an important grouping within society as opposed to fulfilling the role of social markers between groups. Thus, although the use of these points for hunting in these Neolithic societies is clear, their occasional use on humans and the degree of human conflict in this period must remain ambiguous.

Keywords: Late Neolithic Switzerland, antler and bone projectile points, penetration efficiency, taphonomy, social identity, ad hoc production

INTRODUCTION

Most remains of projectile points actually found embedded in the victims' bone tend to be made of stone. Rare finds of bone points also occur, while antler artifacts found stuck in bone tend to be least common. As for the use of such projectile points in warfare, incapacitating the enemy efficiently is a priority that explains the apparent preference for harder materials such as stone or bone. This hypothesis inspired the functional study of a major assemblage of bone and antler projectile points, as well as a number of other bone artifacts possibly used as projectiles, from the late Neolithic lacustrine settlement of St. Blaise, Bains des Dames located on the northwestern shore of Lake Neuchâtel (Western Switzerland; Horgen to Auvernier cultures; Figure 1).

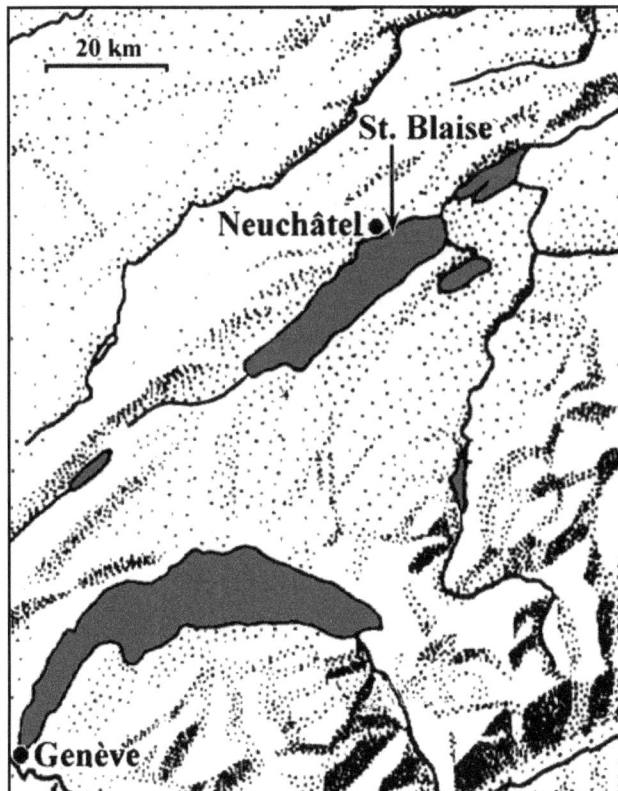

Figure 1. The location of St. Blaise–Bains des Dames along the shore of Lake Neuchâtel, Switzerland

WEAPONS OF WAR OR HUNTING GEAR?

Given the small number of bone points found embedded in either animal or human skeletal remains, and the fact that the anthropological and zoological finds are seldom discussed synthetically, typological distinctions between hunters' and warriors' projectile points have remained unreliable at most sites. Inferences, thus, must remain fundamentally indirect in nature. On the other hand, while one may speculate about whether cognitive aspects of killing humans and/or medium size game with arrows differed, the technical similarities involved are obvious.

Due to the virtual absence of human remains from the St. Blaise settlement, the primary interpretation of the projectile points under discussion here would be as parts of hunting gear, probably being used on humans only opportunistically. This coincides with the high proportion of wild animal bones in the refuse bone sample from this settlement (Figure 2). However, even if certain types of weaponry were not used in hunting, virtually all weapons made for the hunt could be turned on humans (Shepherd 1999: 223, Fig. 2) in both individual conflict and organized warfare. According to Chapman (1999: 109), the same technical qualities in [stone] arrowheads apply to warfare as to hunting. For purely technical purposes, therefore, he suggested that the 25 m

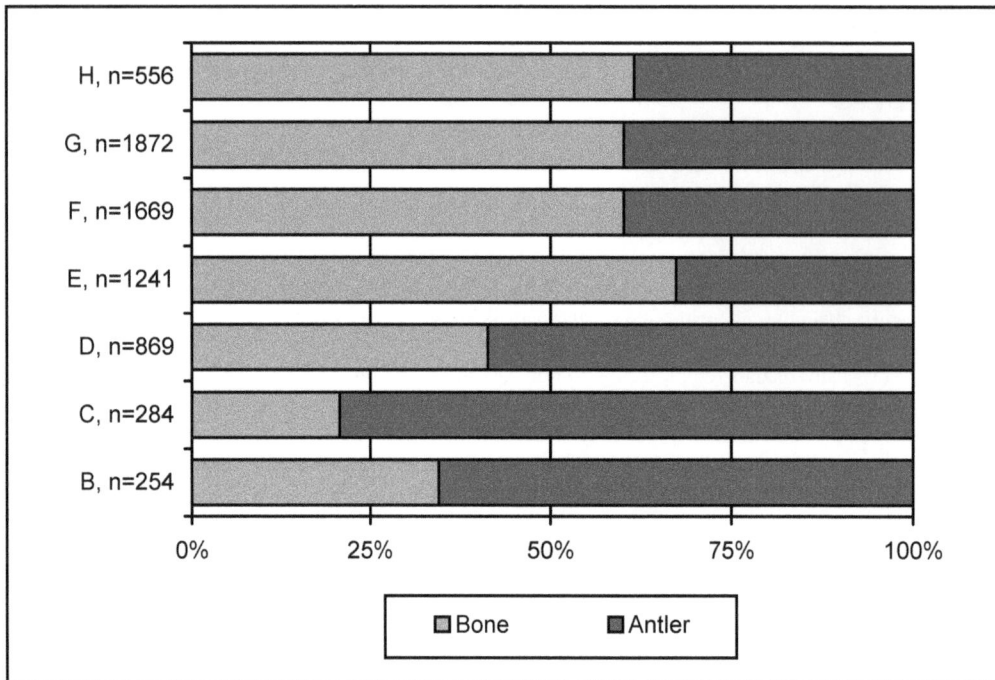

Figure 2. Diachronic increase in the proportion of bone tools

optimum hunter-prey distance established by Fischer (1985) be taken as the average for a comparable human conflict.

The two osseous raw materials under discussion here have different properties when used in hunting and warfare as was suggested by Pape (1982, 135) in his study of the more elaborate projectile points of the Late Neolithic and Bronze Age. Bone points are more destructive, while the more resilient, elastic antler (Currey 1970; MacGregor and Currey 1983; MacGregor 1985,26-28) tends to last longer. The large assemblage of worked bone and antler recovered at St. Blaise offered a unique opportunity for the appraisal of differences between bone and antler carved into projectile points.

ASSEMBLAGE COMPOSITION

The unusually rich assemblage of bone and antler artifacts from St. Blaise was collected using water sieving (mesh size= 5 mm). A total of almost 7000 artifacts, made from both materials were recovered and identified by the authors. This study concentrates on bone arrowheads (Type 3/2), two potentially relevant types of double bone points (Types 2/1, and 2/2) and antler arrowheads (Type P5d) as defined in Jörg Schibler's 1980 typology (to be discussed below).

Chronologically the site was sub-divided into sedimentological blocks B to H. The cultures present at this site included Horgen (Block B), Lüscherz (Blocks [C], D) and Auvernier (Blocks E to H). Block X contained mixed material near the top of the stratigraphic sequence. The Horgen Period occupation, dating to 3160–3100 BC, represents a small part of the original village and is located mostly in the northwestern corner of the excavated area. Layer C, contained sporadic artifacts from both the Horgen and

subsequent Lüscherz stylistic groups. Lüscherz deposits at this site represent a time span between approximately 2700 and 2670 BC. Due to overlapping effects of sedimentation and erosion, Horgen and Lüscherz elements could not always be separated. Thus, the exact length of the Lüscherz occupation is difficult to determine.

The dominant stylistic group is the Auvernier culture which lasted from approximately 2550 to about 2510 BC at this settlement. This archaeological culture marks the very end of the Late Neolithic in Western Switzerland. Apparently, the excavation area exactly covered that part of the settlement abutting the water front. The unexcavated portion of the Late Neolithic settlement continued inland towards the lakeside hills beneath the railway line. The diachronic distribution of bone and antler implements by sedimentological blocks is shown in Table 1.

The percentual composition of this material shows a diachronic increase in the proportion of bone tools at the expense of worked antler (Figure 2). The number of worked pieces of bone is less than 50% in provenances associated with the Horgen and Lüscherz Periods. The Auvernier Period (as well as the probably related top layer, Block X), on the other hand, is characterized by a slight dominance of bone tools.

Using the wild/domestic dichotomy, the faunal lists of these periods (Barbara Stopp, personal communication) show a clear increase in the relative frequency of wild animal bones at the St. Blaise settlement. A consistent decline in the contribution of domestic animal bones from almost 75% (Horgen Period) to only slightly more than 50% (Auvernier H Block; Figure 5) incorporates a range below which hunting might be considered substantial within the subsistence economy (Matolcsi 1982: 77). Earlier shifts in the

Table 1. The numbers of worked bone, antler and point types discussed in this study

All worked	B	C	D	E	F	G	H	X	Total
Bone	88	59	360	835	1003	1125	342	31	3843
Antler	166	225	509	406	666	747	214	56	2989
Total	254	284	869	1241	1669	1872	556	87	6832
Point type									
Bone 3/2	9	5				1		2	17
Bone 2/1	3	2	5	5	12	23			50
Bone 2/2	1	1	5	6	9	10	1		33
Antler P5d	18	8	1	2				2	31
Points total	31	16	11	13	21	34	1	4	131

proportions between domestic to wild animal remains at many Swiss lake dwellings does not mean an absolute decline in animal keeping: it should rather be attributed to the intensification of hunting (Hüster-Plogmann and Schibler 1997).

In this sense, it is interesting that the number of bone/antler tool types clearly related to hunting activities or their degree of elaboration decreases in later periods at this site. There is also little perceivable change in variability or style in comparison with other sites of the same archaeological cultures (Horgen, Lüscherz, Auvenier; Ramseyer 1985, Winiger 1992: Abb.1-3, Fig.10-11; Wolf 1993: Tables 98/3, 122/3; Schibler 1987: Tables 21/10, 21-23). This is in contrast, for example, with the Mesolithic situation in the Upper Volga region, where the major emphasis on hunting seems to have produced a great variety of beautifully made, elegant projectile points (Zhilin 1998, 173). Such stylistic variability may be related to function as well as to the fundamental importance of hunting in the Mesolithic. Thus, hunting societies might well decide to use projectile points to mark ethnic boundaries. Sackett (1990, 33) describes this as the 'isochrestic' model in which a social group chooses a particular way of making or forming an object out of the many possibilities available. The cluster of choices which produce a tool style are unique to individual social groups. These choices lie as much in the schedule of manufacturing as in the formal characteristics of, in this case, projectile points.

The uniformity of the Swiss arrowheads, thus, suggests that they may have been associated with a well-defined group of hunters/warriors within the settlement. On the other hand, neither hunting nor warfare seems to have been important enough during these periods for the tools associated with these activities to be used to express differences between groups across Switzerland. Stylistic differentiation in points again appears at the very end of the Neolithic (although not at the site under discussion here) and during the Bronze Age in many places in Europe when elaborated bone points (from the late Neolithic to the middle Bronze age) appear as copies of bronze types (Pape 1982: 145).

This trend toward reduction in the typological variability of projectile points at St. Blaise is of particular interest, since it coincides with the intensification of red deer (*Cervus elaphus* L. 1758) hunting, suggesting that antler manufacturers in the earlier periods relied to a greater extent on the carving of shed antler.

Similarly strange is the fact that the percentual contribution of projectile points also decreases diachronically at St. Blaise. Relatively speaking, most such artifacts came to light from the earliest, Horgen Period provenances (Figure 3), when animal keeping seems to have been better established. It remains even more of a mystery whether they were intended for killing humans or animals?

TAPHONOMY AND THE DEGREE OF EXPLOITATION

Understanding the function and socio-cultural meaning of projectile points would be hopeless without a brief critical survey of our source material. Our perception and interpretation of these artifacts may be distorted by at least three factors.

Loss related to artifact function

As is shown by the aforementioned trend at St. Blaise, owing to the basic function of projectile points, their representation in site materials is rather unreliable. At least, these less elaborated projectile points, displaying few signs of curation, seem to have been of the 'disposable' kind. The finely worked, labor intensive projectile points discussed by Zhilin (1998: 163) show definite signs of having been repeatedly repaired. The St. Blaise projectiles typically belong to the category of portable artifact that is most commonly used and lost/discarded off site, often in the bodies of injured animals or humans who either escape or finally die in a completely different place.

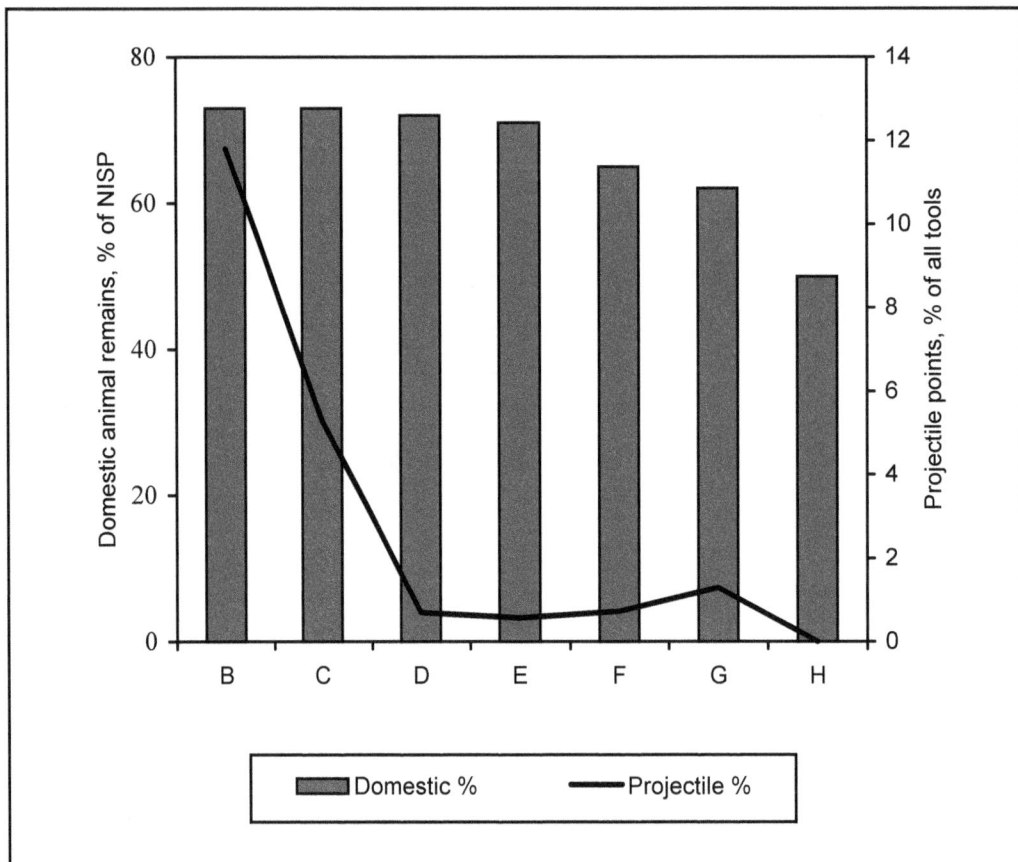

Figure 3. Diachronic decline in the exploitation of domesticates and in the presence of projectile points

Antipina (2001, 122; in press) has mentioned the possibility that elaborated projectile points from the Late Bronze Age, East European Steppe copper mining site of Gorny in the southern Urals were largely missing from the settlement material because they were exported as precious trade items.

The selectivity of evidence is also present in the discovery of specimens embedded in the victim's bone. As mentioned in our introduction, bone and antler projectile points are less commonly encountered in such contexts than are stone arrow heads, simply because they would penetrate bones only softer than themselves. In fact, to our knowledge, antler points have not yet been found in such unambiguous contact with either animal or human skeletons. The few embedded bone points penetrated skeletal parts softer than the bone points themselves. In addition to lighter and weaker human bones (at a definite taphonomic "advantage" from this purely mechanical point of view), flat bones of relatively small and usually young animals are most frequently damaged by points, typically made from splinters of the compact cortical bone of large ruminants.

Recovery bias

Fortunately, the points under discussion here are uniformly longer than 20 mm, the critical size threshold below which bone splinters are missed with great probability when finds are collected only by hand (Bartosiewicz 1988). The number of projectile points, however, still seems relatively low in the St. Blaise assemblage, in spite of 100% water-sieving.

A somewhat arbitrary parallel was used to help elucidating this potential taphonomic bias. Worked bone assemblages from Meso- and Neolithic sites in the Iron Gates Gorge of the Danube between Romania and Yugoslavia have recently been tabulated by Radovanovic (1996: 253-261). Sites in the Iron Gates region seem to contain a greater number of projectile points per worked bone unit than the Swiss collection under discussion here (Figure 4). The relationship between the number of worked bones (x) and projectile points (y) at St. Blaise and in the Iron Gates may be described by the regression equations in Table 2.

Superficially, the fact that almost ten times more projectile points per worked bone unit were identified in the Iron Gates (0.188/0.020; i. e. almost every fifth specimen, as opposed to every fiftieth at St. Blaise) may be interpreted either as a sign of the indubitably greater importance of hunting during the Mesolithic or, perhaps, a more violent way of life than at the lakeshore settlement of St. Blaise.

It must be emphasized, however, that the water-sieved collection from St. Blaise obviously contained many more small types of other bone artifacts than hand-collected assemblages in the Iron Gates region.[*] In light of this difference, the presence or absence of bone projectile points in and of itself should be considered a poor indicator of either the importance of hunting or even warfare.

---

[*] Of the Iron Gates sites, systematic water-sieving has been carried out during recent excavations at Schela Cladovei, not included in these calculations.

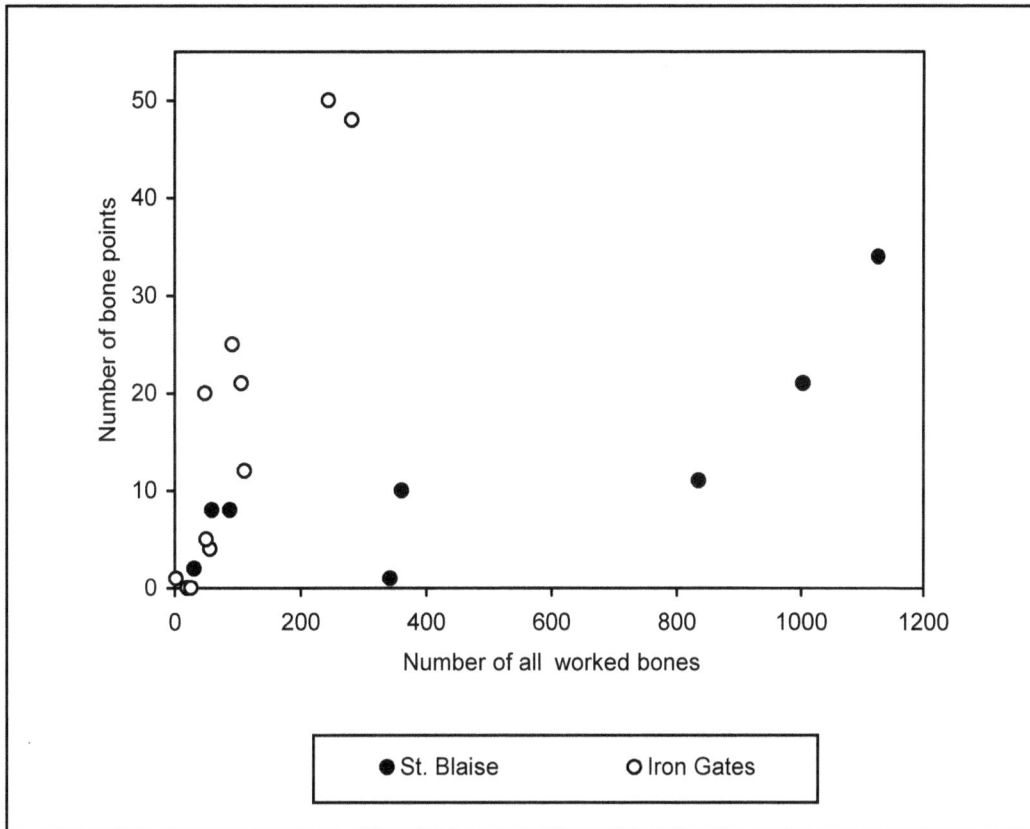

Figure 4. The relationship between bone tool assemblage size and the number of bone projectile points

Table 2. Contributions of projectile points to the worked bone assemblage in two regions

Site/Region	No. of assemblages	Regression equation	Correlation
St. Blaise	8	y = 0.020x + 2.124	r = 0.832***
Iron Gates	10	y = 0.188x - 0.832	r = 0.938***

Fragmentation and attrition

At St. Blaise, Type 3/2 bone points are characterized by tip polish and only moderate use wear relative to the degree of manufacture their production takes. As mentioned previously, more used and damaged pieces may have been lost or discarded off site. Wear traces evidenced on stone arrowheads from the Danish Mesolithic studied by Fischer (1985) suggested that most of them had not yet been used. The lack of reworking on bone projectile points from the site under discussion here seems to indicate that these planned artifacts were relatively unused or too small for any secondary use once they had became blunt or broken. This, once again, suggests that they were used in a context away from the settlement.

Type 2/1 double points were defined on the basis of purely morphological characteristics but almost certainly were used in a greater variety of ways. These may also have differed in terms of their hafting modes which could not be directly reconstructed in any of the cases under discussion here.

Type 2/2 double rib points were made from the compact outer surfaces of ribs. Smaller size, less intensive manufacturing and

overall handling polish on two of the Type 2/2 rib double points is indicative of a more limited use than was the case with long bone double points. At the same time, the greater homogeneity of this type suggests that it might have provided substitutes for smaller, less carefully crafted long bone double points which may or may not have served as casual projectile points.

Even the heterogeneous types of long bone and rib double points (Types 2/1 and 2/2) are characterized by a low intensity of use relative to the degree of labor investment required by their manufacturing.

TYPE DESCRIPTIONS

Bone arrow heads (Type 3/2)

The broadly defined Type 3/2 ("*Pfeilspitzen varia*") from Schibler's typology (1980: 47) represented by a rather uniform pointed and elongated form with smoothed edges, the only kind recognized at St. Blaise settlement. Tar remains occurring regularly on the basis and stem of these objects (12 of 17 specimens) as well as fortunate finds of shafted

Table 3. The distribution of raw materials within Type 3/2

	Cattle	Red deer	Large ungulate	Small ungulate
Rib			1	
Radius	1			
Metapodium		2	10	
long bone				1

projectile points confirm their morphological analogy to modern-day arrow heads.

With one exception, they were produced using long bone diaphysis splinters of large Ruminants (both cattle and red deer could be identified in one case each). As far as skeletal parts are concerned, straight metapodium fragments were clearly preferred, although usually no distinctions between metacarpus and metatarsus are possible. In the St. Blaise assemblage, a few other long bones and a rib point were found as well (Table 3).

Metapodium projectile points were produced using the "groove and split" technique. Plain carving with flint and grinding on abrasive materials such as sandstone were typical ways of finishing these artifacts, resulting in a high level of modification. Both tip and basis were carefully executed in most cases. The base was usually also sharpened, and even has a small crest left on it. The mode of shafting makes the pointed or crested basis of such arrow heads *de facto* "barbed": once inserted, the point can only be torn out of the wound causing further pain and damage.

Projectile points recovered from this site have almost uniformly symmetric long shouldered tips (Form 3 in Schibler 1981: 16, Abb. 3) although other broad symmetric forms (Forms 2, 5) are represented as well.

With the exception of two rectangular (Form 4) and a trapezoid (Form 8) cross-section (all stemming from the natural shape of bone splinters), tips were ground into a round cross-section. The only trapezoid tip was formed on a small Ruminant bone, which would have been probably too thin to produce a perfectly round cross-section.

This artifact type was recovered most commonly (with only two exceptional Lüscherz and one Auvernier specimens)

from the Horgen and mixed Block C layers of St. Blaise. Its exclusive contribution to that chronological subsample at this site makes it suitable for typo-chronological distinctions. Projectile points of this type, together with their antler counterparts discussed below, may be considered common in the Horgen culture.

Long bone double point (Type 2/1)

According to Schibler's typology (1981: 42) this group includes exclusively long bone points. It is important to note, however, that lower pig incisor double points, potentially grouped with this type (Schibler 1980: 34), do not occur in the St. Blaise material. In fact, long bone double points, so characteristic of the Cortaillod material from Twann (Schibler 1981), seem to have lost most of their importance at this late Neolithic site in comparison with other small point types.

This type is made of long bone diaphysis splinters of Artiodactyl bones. Small and large ungulates seem to have contributed almost equal numbers to the assemblage under discussion here, although a more precise identification of these heavily modified splinters is usually hopeless. Of the better recognizable specimens, remains of red deer, roe deer and Caprines (all metapodia) and one cattle radius were recognized.

As for skeletal parts, metapodium splinters again dominate. One third of the material, however, could only be described by the generic term "long bone diaphysis fragment". In this latter broad category, however, highly modified flat bone and especially rib splinters may have been included as well, although there is no way to ascertain this theoretical possibility (Table 4).

These points were produced by intensive carving with flint tools such as burins and scrapers and grinding with abrasive

Table 4. The distribution of raw materials within Type 2/1

	Cattle	Caprine	Red deer	Roe deer	Large ungulate	Small ungulate
radius	1					
metacarpus				1		
metatarsus			1			
stylopodium					4	1
metapodium		2	2	2	4	10
long bone					14	12

materials affecting most of the tools' surface. In spite of the high contribution of metapodia to the pool of raw materials for double points, marks of the groove and split technique could be recognized only in two (!) cases, probably because subsequent manufacturing obliterated the marks of primary flint scraping.

The refined typology developed by Schibler for these artifacts on the basis of their mid cross-sections (Schibler 1981: 42) to a great extent may be linked with the choice of raw materials as well as the intensity of manufacturing. While no long bones were turned into "tubular" double points (sub-type "f" by Schibler), lenticular and bean-shaped mid cross-sections (sub-types "b" and "e") were observed on less modified small Ruminant bone points, while rectangular mid cross-sections (sub-type "a") were more characteristic of large Ruminant metapodium double points.

Round mid cross-section (sub-type "c") was typical of heavily worked specimens in both size categories. It was characteristic of almost two thirds of metapodium (58.2 %) and one third of non-metapodium (32.4 %) double points. This round shape was achieved with more work on metapodium than on other, non-metapodium fragments.

Although both ends of these artifacts were sharpened into tips, only one of these served as an actual working end. In other cases, the presence of a "pointed base" may be recognized in the form of more cutmarks than manufacturing polish related to sharpening, and higher use wear on the working tip. One of the Horgen points even has tar remains around the base, which is, in most cases, regarded as evidence of hafting, as illustrated by Winiger (1992).

Among the working tips symmetric broad (Form 2) and sharp (Form 1) shapes were most common. Some shouldered (Form 3) and dull (Form 5) specimens occurred as well. The contribution of these latter two, however, is less than 15 %.

Cross-sections of the working tip are most typically round (Form 1) or lenticular (Form 2), although in this case a greater variability may be observed. The presence of rectangular (Form 4) and triangular (Form 10) tip cross-sections is particularly remarkable on points characterized by a relatively low intensity of manufacture.

In relative terms, this artifact type was recovered most commonly from the Horgen and C layers of the St. Blaise site. At the same time, its percentual contribution increases more-or-less consistently from the Lüscherz Period onwards.

Rib double point (Type 2/2)

This artifact type is defined using an morphological feature in addition to its raw material. A somewhat greater proportion were made on rib splinters of large Ruminants. In one case, a Horgen Period red deer rib double point could be identified. Since, however, all these points were made from the *substantia compacta* fragments of ribs, they are sometimes even difficult to assign to animal size categories.

Table 5. The distribution of raw materials within Type 2/2

	Red deer	Large ungulate	Small ungulate
Rib	1	17	15

With one exception, when grooving and splitting could be detected, all these points were produced by carving with flint tools and subsequent grinding on sandstone or other abrasive materials. The intensity of surface modification, however, falls well below that found on long bone double points. This is indirectly shown by the fact that many such points could be identified on the basis of spongiosa remains on the tools' mid-shaft.

Symmetric, sharp (Form 1) and broad (Form 2) tip shapes are equally common in this type. The only exception is a small Ruminant rib double point with a sabre-shaped (12) working tip: due to the small bone used as raw material, the tool retained some of the bone's original form. Cross-sections of the working tip are more variable with frequent occurrences of all flattish shapes (Forms 2, 5, 12, 13). Six round (Form 1) and four triangular (Form 10) tips were recorded as well.

This artifact type was recovered in comparable proportions from all major layers of the St. Blaise site. Its small numbers and homogeneous contribution to chronological subsamples make them unsuitable for defining developmental trends in themselves.

Antler projectile point (P5d)

Such slender projectile points (made either of bone or antler) are without question a tool type of the Horgen culture. They are usually about 60 mm long. One end has a round symmetrically pointed tip, while the other is trimmed into a thinned tang, ending in a raised barb to enhance attachment to the shaft. A great deal of care and energy was invested into manufacturing such projectile points. Many of the specimens have traces of tar and twine on their surfaces from the attachment to the arrow shaft.

Only about 10 mm of the tip is always left free (Plate I, middle). At St. Blaise, one of these antler points (Inv. No. 793) was found still attached to its hazelwood (*Corylus avelana* L. 1758) shaft.

Antler projectile points were evidently extracted from the thicker *substantia compacta* in the lower beam of the red deer antler rack. While antler seems to have been the preferred raw material for this tool type, numerous bone specimens (discussed previously under Type 3/2) were found.

First, a long slim strip of soaked antler was procured by grooving two parallel lines 60-70 mm long into the softened compact external layer of the beam. The strip was forced out and the rough shape was carved using a flint tool such as a burin. However, characteristically for all the more heavily worked, refined antler and bone objects at St. Blaise, the

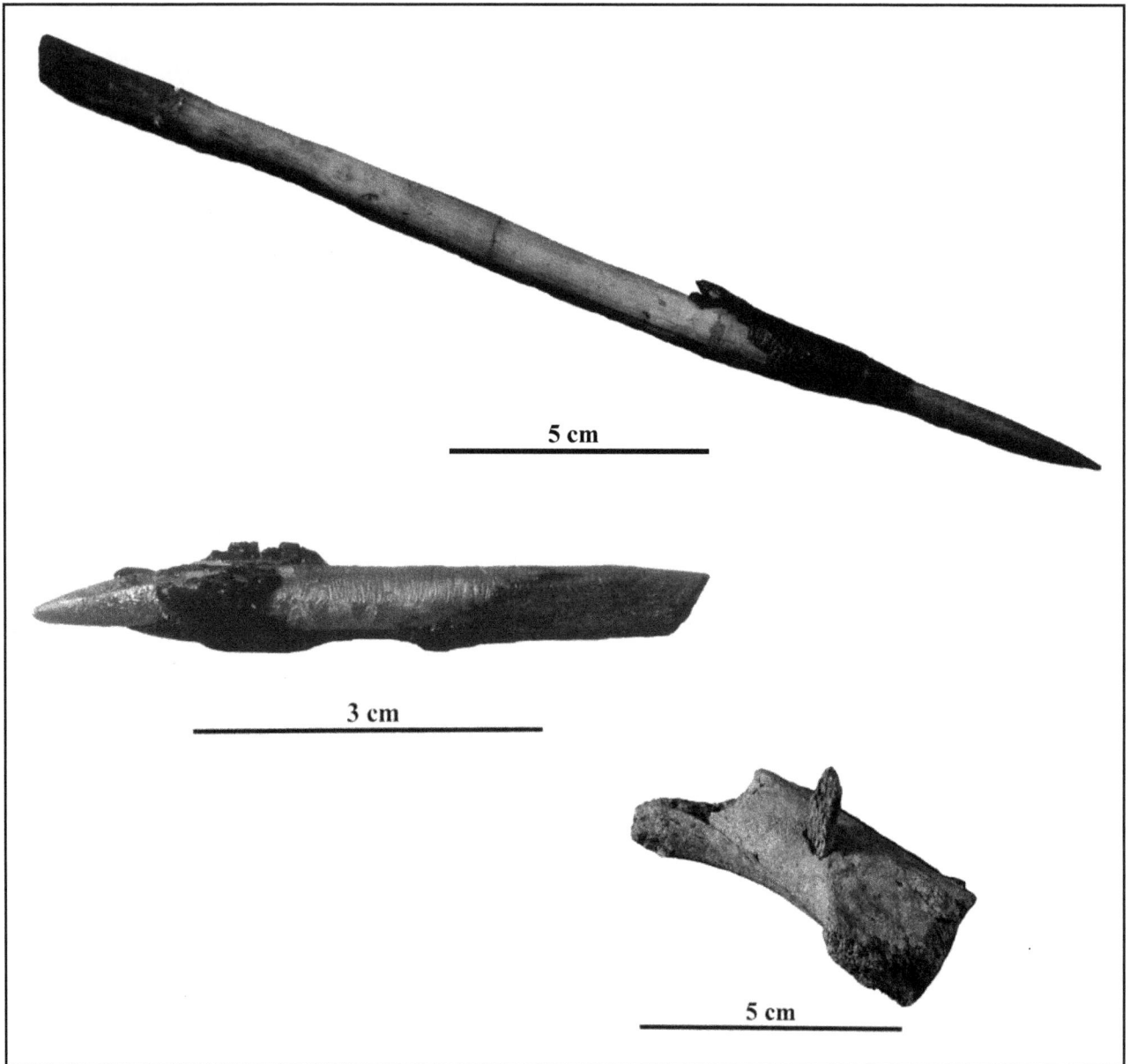

Plate I. Top: Type 3/2 bone projectile point with foreshaft (?) from the Horgen Period of St. Blaise
Middle: Type P5d projectile point with tar remains from the Horgen Period of St. Blaise
Bottom: Rib projectile point embedded in the pelvis of young pig from 15th century Vác, Hungary

final shaping was done by grinding on an abrasive surface, probably once the antler had begun to harden as it dried out. The thin tang of the projectile point was then laid against the wooden shaft or an extra piece at the end of the shaft. Cord made from sinew or bast was wrapped around it and the whole thing firmly fixed by a birch tar coating. The tips of these points are elongated and remarkably round in cross-section (Form 1) showing how easily this raw material can be worked in a softened state.

The P5 or P5d projectile points occur almost exclusively in the B (Horgen) and C (mixed Horgen and Lüscherz) sedimentological Blocks. There is one specimen from a pure Lüscherz deposit at St. Blaise, two from an uncertain context and two from the Auvernier sedimentological Block E. It is even possible that artifacts from the underlying strata, disturbed by a particularly deeply driven pile, were brought up into the Auvernier level.

THE RECONSTRUCTION OF FUNCTION

In addition to formal analogies of tool typomorphology, composite finds as well as ethnographic parallels must be briefly reviewed.

Bone point 3/2 and antler point P5d

Thanks to the good preservation of organic materials in the water-logged layers of St. Blaise, wooden shafts recovered with arrowheads make the identification of 3/2 bone and P5d antler points as such implements unambiguous. One open question, relevant to the actual use of such projectile points, is the possible use of foreshafts.

Ethnographic examples suggest that during use, less of an attempt may have been made to recover the points themselves than the shaft. High quality raw materials for bows (yew wood; *Taxus baccata* L. 1758) and arrow shafts (e. g. hazelwood or wayfaring tree: *Viburnum lantana* L. 1758) identified at other Swiss Neolithic sites (Gross et al. 1990: 90) also support this hypothesis.

When discussing a 230 mm long guelder rose (*Viburnum opulus* L. 1758) Neolithic arrow fragment found at Blackhillock Bog (Aberdeenshire, Scotland), Mercer (1999: 147, Fig. 2) referred to composite arrow shafts. These are made of a foreshaft that remained in the victim, while the back-shaft broke away, making its recovery easier. Foreshafts made from less special wood such as pine (*Pinus* sp.: Bokelmann 1999: 78; Guthrie 1983: 289) would also be indicative of the difference between the values of arrow shafts and projectile points.

A Yanomami bone double point studied by the authors was mounted on such a 228 mm long foreshaft. The butt end of a bone-tipped arrow fragment of similar length (c. a. 20 cm) from St. Blaise shows dark discoloration, a possible indication of attachment as a foreshaft (Plate I, top).

Even in the absence of wooden components, most projectile points brought to light at St. Blaise seem to have been directly attached to obliquely sharpened pieces of wood recovered from the waterlogged sediment. The 9-11 mm diameters of the prehistoric wooden shafts recovered, more-or-less, correspond to the 10-12 mm diameter of the main arrow shafts that belong to the aforementioned Amazonian point and foreshaft.

Foreshafts may have been especially advantageous in hunting when it was sufficient for arrows to cause pain, bleeding and subsequent exhaustion, thus, preparing large game to be killed by other means (Møhl 1978: 21). A "shoot to kill" policy, however, may have been preferred in warfare as part of self-defense, in the face of equal adversaries.

In the absence of wooden components, tar remains may also offer evidence of shafting that, together with characteristic size and shape, is of help in identifying projectile points. Chemical analyses showed that the tar used on the stone arrow heads in the *Iceman*'s quiver was produced by carbonizing either the wood or bark of birch (*Betula* sp.) in a reducing atmosphere. The asphalt-like tar thus obtained hardens as it cools (Spindler 1993:162). Birch tar, produced experimentally, was successfully used in shafting arrows (Neubauer-Saurer 1997: 43).

Bone points 2/1 and 2/2

Some of the Type 2/1 artifacts brought to light at St. Blaise may also have served as projectile points. Two Horgen Period and an Auvernier Block G double point from this settlement offer some indirect evidence of this. They have an overall shape very similar to that of P5d type antler projectile points, more-or-less exclusive to the Horgen layers. Another double point is covered with tar remains on the bone's original outer surface, while the inner side corresponding to the *cavum*

medullare remained clean as a possible attachment surface for an arrow shaft.

Such forms appeared in the Horgen layers of the Twann settlement as well (Furger 1981: 60). Most importantly, a Neolithic specimen found near the Lake of Biel was embedded in the ventral surface of the sacral bone from a red deer (Jörg Schibler, personal communication).

A remarkably different, alternative use for double points, fishing (Schlenker 1994: 45), deserves particular attention. At least two symmetric Auvernier Period (Blocks F and G) double points had equal size tips and showed minor transversal indentations in the middle which may be indicative of their use as fish gorges. It is also remarkable that a stratum within the Auvernier layer with two fish hooks contained three long bone double points and four rib double points without signs of hafting. The symmetric specimen with attachment marks in the middle was found in the proximity of this deposit as well. Many double bone points from the Paleolithic to the recent past have been used as fish gorges (Riek 1959; Vilsteren 1987: 31). Some were used in catching both fish and waterfowl in the area of Lake Konstanz (von Tröltsch 1902).

The great size variability in fish gorges is clearly illustrated by typologically identical, 100-130 mm long Medieval wooden cod gorges (Szabó et al. 1985; Heinrich 1986: 52), as well as expedient modern "gorges" for small fish made from matchsticks in southwestern France (Cleyet-Merle 1990: 85). Bone double points from St. Blaise represent the lower range of this broad size interval. The mean length of 77 double points (Types 2/1 and 2/2 combined) was only 54.2 mm. Several Auvernier specimens (Blocks F and G) were as long as 60-80 mm, while the largest double point recovered from Block G measured 106.9 mm.

An unique early Mesolithic find assemblage from Federsee – Forschner (Torke 1993: Abb. 5) contained a 67 mm long pointed bone object in association with a score of pike bones (*Esox lucius* L. 1758) and remains of a large tench (*Tinca tinca* L. 1758). This latter, with the gorge hidden inside, may have been the bait used in catching the 4-5 kg pike. The indentation in the middle of that artifact even displayed polish wear left by the fishing line.

METRIC PROPERTIES AND EFFICIENCY

Neolithic archery developed into a highly sophisticated technique that permitted kills to be made from a distance from 5 to 50 m (Stodiek and Paulsen 1996: 15), thereby reducing the imminent risk involved in warfare and hunting dangerous game. The characteristics of the ideal flint projectile listed by Fischer (1985: 37) are valid for its bone and antler counterparts.

These qualities are reviewed in light of a metric analysis and experimental results published in the literature.

Longitudinal symmetry, directional stability

From this point of view, long and slender bone/antler points are unquestionably superior to most lithic projectiles. Given the great deal of uniformity in this respect, rather than overall shape, sizes of the four types under discussion here may be of interest.

In order to appraise homogeneity within the set of artifacts tentatively identified as projectile points in this study, Student's t-tests were carried out to identify statistically significant differences between types. The measurements compared included the three greatest dimensions of each point (length, breadth and depth) and two tip measurements: length (SPI) and diameter measured at a distance of 5 mm from the tip (GSB).

Bone double points show the greatest degree of heterogeneity. They even differ significantly by their raw material: rib double points (Type 2/2) are on average half the weight, significantly thinner and their tips are also shorter. Of these, the more numerous group, long bone double points (Type 2/1), was compared to that of Type 3/2 arrowheads. In this case, double points were significantly thinner with shorter tips. Most importantly, no significant metric differences could be established between the morphologically similar Type 3/2 bone and P5d antler projectile points.

Of the values listed in this table, the mean weights of 0.8-2.4 are of special interest. What is significant is the concept of a relatively light, pointed armature (<10 g and in practice usually <2g; Fischer 1985). A heavier tip would have unbalanced the arrow. Owing to the smaller specific weights of bone and antler (1.5 to 1.8; Fábián 1973) than stone, they could be used in making longer arrowheads with better directional stability. The most "professional" points could thus, on average, weigh slightly over 2 g. The lengths of individual points in the four types are plotted against their respective weights in Figure 5. According to this graph, Type 3/2 and P5d points tend to be stouter than double points above the 2 g weight limit.

During experiments with stone projectile points (Rozoy 1985: 18), ca. 90 cm arrows (shaft diameter 1 cm) were fitted with 0.5-2 g points to produce a total weight of ca. 20-30 g. Such arrows can be best used in shooting medium to large sized game (comparable to a human being in terms of physical makeup), which it would pass through completely. Such weapons could be generally used over distances of 20 to 50 m, whose lower limit corresponds to Chapman's (1999: 109) aforementioned average range for prehistoric armed conflict.

Table 6. Pairwise metric differences between the four point types (measurements in mm)

Measurement, mm	n	Mean value	Standard Deviation	n	Mean value	Standard Deviation	t-value	df	p-value
Type		2/1			2/2				
W, g	51	1.6	1.2	28	0.8	0.6	3.209	77	0.002
Greatest length	48	55.6	18.3	29	51.9	18.4	0.846	75	0.400
Greatest breadth	56	6.4	2.0	32	5.8	2.3	1.243	86	0.217
Greatest depth	57	4.2	1.2	33	3.1	1.0	4.401	88	0.000
SPI	48	29.4	10.3	28	30.1	13.1	-0.265	74	0.792
GSB	50	3.2	1.1	30	2.4	0.5	3.618	78	0.001
Type		2/1			3/2				
W, g	51	1.6	1.2	9	2.4	1.4	-1.980	58	0.052
GL	48	55.6	18.3	9	55.0	14.6	0.090	55	0.929
GB	56	6.4	2.0	9	6.7	1.8	-0.441	63	0.661
GD	57	4.2	1.2	9	5.9	1.6	-3.821	64	0.000
SPI	48	29.4	10.3	9	38.5	17.3	-2.170	55	0.034
GSB	50	3.2	1.1	9	3.2	1.3	-0.091	57	0.928
Type		3/2			P5d				
W, g	9	2.4	1.4	22	2.6	1.2	-0.333	29	0.742
GL	9	55.0	14.6	27	63.2	14.7	-1.462	34	0.153
GB	9	6.7	1.8	28	6.8	1.0	-0.258	35	0.798
GD	9	5.9	1.6	27	6.4	2.0	-0.691	34	0.494
SPI	9	38.5	17.3	17	38.3	19.6	0.021	24	0.984
GSB	9	3.2	1.3	24	3.2	0.8	0.158	31	0.876

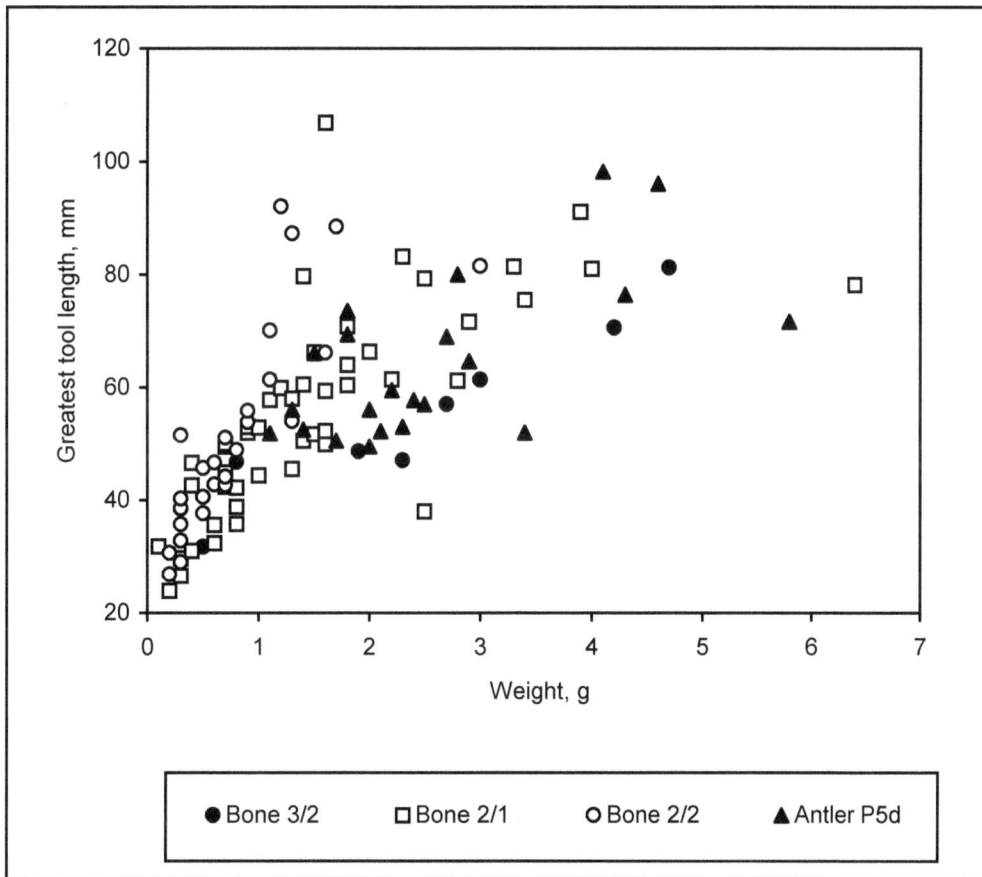

Figure 5. Weight/length relations in the four types of points in the assemblage from St. Blaise

Optimum penetrating qualities

Experimental work, testing the penetration parameters of projectile points has been limited to animal carcasses. Live prey would make the standardization of technical parameters difficult. From the large number of shootings at whole and still warm animals, it can be concluded that Stone Age [stone-tipped] arrows had extremely good qualities of penetration, often forcing their way through the ribs of a sheep and even of a full-grown boar (Fischer 1985: 36-37). While recently, human corpses were reputedly used in a blockbuster war movie to better imitate shot wounds, a similar practice would be ethically unacceptable in experimental archaeology.

The analogy of what are termed medium size mammals (preferably killed prior to target shooting) should indeed be perfectly sufficient for simulating the effects of projectile points, even in human conflict. An experiment in the Duisburg Zoo has shown that antler projectiles shot into a dead fallow deer (*Dama dama* L. 1758) penetrated, on average, 20 cm into the animal, while the mean penetration depth was 32 cm for stone arrow heads. Even antler points may have proven lethal in this case, although when hitting bone, they sometimes chipped (Stodiek and Paulsen 1996: 35, Abb. 34 and 35). In general, however, their life span surpassed those of more brittle stone projectile points used in the same experiment.

On the other hand, experimental work by Lowrey (1999) among native Americans of the Pacific Northwest Coast (see Roksandic this volume) showed that bone projectiles of both the spindle and the triangular types had better penetrating value than either stone or iron points, and required less pull. These seemingly contradictory results may be dependent on how the different experiments were conducted and what their aims were.

Evidently the ribs of the large game provide some protection against arrows, but hits inbetween or behind them offer a good chance of killing a red deer, an elk (=moose, *Alces alces* L. 1758) or even an aurochs (*Bos primigenius* Boj. 1827) with a single shot. Perforated and sometimes healed red deer scapulae also bear witness to the power of some of these shots (Noe-Nygaard 1974, 1975).

Experiments on elk carcasses carried out by Guthrie (1983: 284, Fig. 5) suggest that points with diameters of <10-11 mm all penetrated to 20 cm or beyond into the animal. Thicker points had a smaller mean penetration depth, below 20 cm. The shaggy hair and thick skin of a dead European bison (*Bison bonasus* L. 1758) used in another experiment in the Duisburg zoo prevented any projectile points from penetrating deeper than 120 mm. Antler points, potentially lethal when used on smaller creatures, proved remarkably ineffective in this experiment (Stodiek and Paulsen 1996: 34, Abb. 29). One must remember, however, that the same meager performance would have been more damaging to a smaller, thin-skinned human torso. Bundles of prehistoric clothing or even some sort of leather armor would have withstood the impact of the same projectile points a lot less efficiently than the bison's natural defenses.

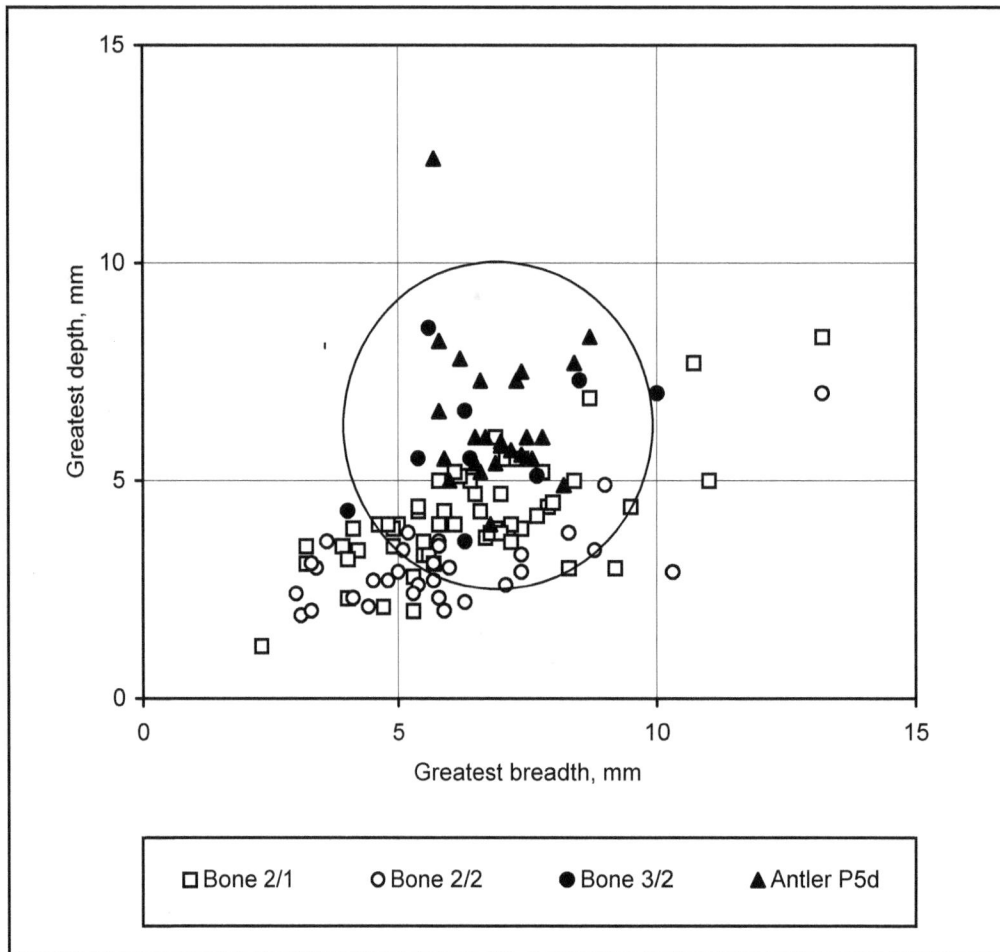

Figure 6. The greatest transversal dimensions of point types.
Groups within the circle are of optimal penetration capacity

As for the points recovered from St. Blaise, their greatest transversal diameters were plotted against each other in Figure 6, in order to appraise penetration capacity. Most Type 3/2 and P5d points falling below the 10 mm upper limit of 200 mm penetration into elk, therefore could have served as a most potent missile against humans [as well]. Some of the double points also fall within these limits, however, their small and variable thickness may have been a disadvantage, reducing the life span of such points when used as projectiles.

The capacity to produce the sharpest cut possible

This trait of the projectile points is related to heavy bleeding. The functionally decisive mean thickness (greatest breadth = 6.7 mm, greatest depth = 6.4 mm) of these bone points, however, is below the 7-8 mm range at which a sharp decline in durability was measured in archery experiments (Guthrie 1983: 285). Since, however, Guthrie used longer points on a robust game animal, fracturing was probably more of a problem than in the case of the smaller St. Blaise specimens, possibly used on smaller prey.

The small projectile points with a thinned, slightly hooked base represent a tool type which is emphatically characteristic of the Lüscherz and, even more, the Horgen settlement materials. Similarly to the projectile points from Yvonand (Voruz 1984), the Lüscherz specimens are more elongated compared to the short dense Horgen points. Comparable small points occur in the Horgen levels from the nearby Twann settlement but not in the Middle Neolithic Cortaillod levels either here or, for example, at the Cortaillod Period site of Burgäschisee-Süd (Bleuer 1988). These all may have been equally dangerous for small game or fellow human beings.

CONCLUSIONS

Osseous projectile points tend to be unreliable artifacts for quantifying their relative importance as weapons in conflicts. Owing to the fundamental taphonomic nature of projectile points, their relative frequency in settlement assemblages (uneven spatial distribution related to use, chancy recovery) is a poor, although piquant, indicator of prehistoric violence. Shafted specimens or those embedded in the victims' flesh or bones offer rare but convincing evidence of the mode of use. Owing to their relatively softer raw materials, however, bone and antler points are less frequently found in direct contact or actually penetrating the victims' bone than lithic projectiles.

Although the function of the most typical projectile points from St. Blaise may be relatively easily recognized, in the absence of external evidence, the prospective victims of these arrowheads could not be precisely identified. Metric analyses have shown, however, that even if these points originated from hunting weapons, most of them were perfectly suited to killing humans as well.

Some Type 3/2 bone points show such a striking similarity to P5d antler projectile points that distinguishing between the raw material of these two highly worked types was sometimes difficult. According to experimental evidence, however, more brittle bone points would have a 1/6 shorter mean life expectancy than their antler counterparts of the same size. At the same time, the mean penetration of corresponding antler points was only 80% of those of bone projectile points (Guthrie 1983: 288). Less lacerating/lethal [antler] arrowheads therefore may have been more suitable for hunting than combat. Efficiency, availability and labor investment (manufacturing and possible curation) together may have influenced the designed function of these projectile points.

The Type 3/2 and P5d projectile points, most characteristic of the late Neolithic Horgen settlement at this site, were probably used by men and boys, widely presumed to have been the warriors or hunters in this Late Neolithic society. But, does this explain why here they have such a tight uniform iconic style and dimensions? Stylistic similarity beyond functional necessity, is a mirror of social comparison. The choice of strong emulation may reflect strong identity with an important social grouping. Although this class of artifacts cannot be said to be decorative, the uniformity in style argues for a deliberate adherence to a very particular form and may be described as a kind of active communication about social identification.

Type 3/2 bone and P5d antler projectile points are carefully planned, finely worked and standardized in size. They represent the "high end" of the so-called manufacturing continuum (Choyke 1997). A notably greater variability of forms and raw materials is evident among the two types of double points under discussion here, many of which may still have been used as projectile points.

Rib double points (Type 2/2), which may also have been used as projectiles, represent the far less sophisticated "expedient" or Class II end of the manufacturing continuum. A curious example of a much later specimen may serve here as the juxtaposition against which the warrior/hunter image of better made arrowheads can be better appreciated. A small ungulate rib projectile point, distinctly expedient in nature, was found embedded in the ventral side of an ilium fragment from a young pig (Plate I, bottom) at a late medieval (13th-15th century) site in Vác, Hungary (Bartosiewicz 1995: 178, Plate 18). This specimen dates to a time by which prehistoric bone manufacturing was long forgotten in Hungary. A low status person, such as a poacher or a child, however, may have improvised this "primitive" weapon for killing the pig, whose wild or domestic status could not be established, owing to the animal's young age. Found outside this context, however,

the haphazardly carved rib splinter probably would not have been recognized as a projectile point. Bone projectile points, intended as a vital part of "serious" weaponry designed for warfare, must have been a lot more carefully planned and executed in prehistoric times.

Authors

Alice M. Choyke
Medieval Studies Department
Central European University
9 Nador St.
1051 Budapest
Hungary

Laszlo Bartosiewicz
Institute of Archaeological Sciences
Loránd Eötvös University
1088 Budapest, Muzeum krt. 4/B
Hungary

References

ANTIPINA Ye. 1999. Kostnye ostatki zhivotnykh s poseleniya Gorny (biologicheskiye i arkeologicheskiye aspekty issledovaniya). *Rossiiskaya Arkeologiya* 1, Moskva: 103-116.

BARTOSIEWICZ, L. 1988. Water-sieving experiment at Örménykút, Site 54. In Járó, M. and Költö, L. eds.: *Archaeometrical research in Hungary*. National Centre of Museums, Budapest: 267-274.

BARTOSIEWICZ, L. 1995. *Animals in the urban landscape in the wake of the Middle Ages*. BAR International Series 609, Oxford.

BLEUER, E. 1988. Die Knochen- und Geweihartefakte der Siedlung Seeberg, Burgöschisee-Süd. *Acta Bernensia II, Seeberg, Burgäschisee-Süd* Teil 7, Verlag Stämpfli & Cie AG, Bern.

BOKELMANN, K. 1999. Eine Stielspitze mit Schäftungspech der Ahrensburger Kultur aus Stellmoor. In E. Cziesla, Th. Kersting and St. Pratsch eds. *Den Bogen spannen... Teil 1. Festschrift für Bernhard Gramsch zum 65. Geburtstag*. Beier & Beran, Archäologische Fachliteratur, Weissbach: 77-81.

CHAPMAN, J. 1999. The origins of warfare in the prehistory of Central and Eastern Europe. In J. Carman and A. Harding eds.: *Ancient warfare. Archaeological perspectives*. Sutton Publishing, Stroud: 101-142.

CHOYKE, A. M. 1997. The bone manufacturing continuum. *Anthropozoologica* 25-26: 65-72.

CLEYET-MERLE, J.-J. 1990. *La prehistoire de la peche*. Collection des Hesperides. Editions Errance, Paris.

CURREY, J.D. 1970. *Animal Skeletons*. Studies in Biology 22, London.

FÁBIÁN, Gy. 1973. *Állattan* (Zoology). Mezõgazdasági Kiadó, Budapest.

FISCHER, A. 1985. Hunting with flint-tipped arrows: Results and experiences from practical experiments. In C. Bonsall ed.: *The Mesolithic in Europe*. Edinburgh, John Donalds Publishing Ltd. 29-39.

FURGER, A. R. 1981. *Die Kleinfunde aus den Horgener Schichten. Die neolitischen Ufersiedlungen von Twann*. Band 13. Staatlicher Lehrmittelverlag, Bern.

GROSS, E., JACOMET, S. and SCHIBLER, J. 1990. Stand und Ziele der Wirtschaftsarchäologischen Forschung an Neolithischen Ufer- und Inselsiedlungen im unteren Zürichseeraum (Kt. Zürich, Schweiz). In Jörg Schibler, J. Sedlmeier & H.-P. Spycher eds.: *Festschrift für Hans R. Stampfli. Beiträge zur Archäozoologie, Archäologie, Anthropologie, Geologie und Paläontologie.* Helbing & Lichtenhahn, Basel, 76-100.

GUTHRIE, R. D. 1983. Osseous projectile points: biological Considerations affecting raw material selection and design among Paleolithic and Paleoindian peoples. In C. Grigson and J. Clutton-Brock eds.: *Animals in archaeology: 1. Hunters and their Prey.* BAR International Series 163, 273-294.

HEINRICH, D. 1986. Fishing and consumption of cod (Gadus morhua Linnaeus, 1758) in the Middle Ages. In: Dick C. Brinkhuizen and Anneke T. Clason eds.: *Fish and archaeology.* BAR International Series 294: 42-52.

HÜSTER-PLOGMANN, H. and SCHIBLER, J. 1997. Archäozoologie. In J. Schibler et al. eds. *Ökonomie und Ökologie neolitischer und bronzezeitlicher Ufersiedlungen am Zürichsee. Band A: Text.* Monographien der Kantonsarchäologie Zürich 20. Zürich und Egg: 40-121.

LOWREY, N.S. 1999. An Ethnoarchaeological Inquiry into the Functional Relationship Between Projectile Point and Armor Technologies of the Northwest Coast. *North American Archaeologist,* 20(1): 47-73.

MACGREGOR, A. 1985. *Bone, Antler, Ivory and Horn: The Technology of Skeletal materials Since the Roman Period.* Croom Helm, London.

MACGREGOR, A. and CURREY, J.D. 1983. Mechanical Properties as conditioning factors in the bone and antler industriy of the 3rd to the 13th century AD, *Journal of Archaeological Science* 10: 71-77.

MATOLCSI, J. 1982. *Állattartás öseink korában* (Animal keeping in the time of our ancestors). Budapest: Gondolat Kiadó.

MERCER, R. J. 1999. The origins of warfare in the British Isles. In J. Carman and A. Harding eds.: *Ancient warfare. Archaeological perspectives.* Stroud Sutton Publishing: 101-142.

MØHL, U. 1978. Elsdyrskeletterne fra Skottemarke og Favrbo. Arbøger for Nordisk Oldkyndighed og Historie, 1978: 5-32.

NEUBAUER-SAURER, D. 1997. Birkenpechproduktion im Neolithikum (Ein mögliches Verfahren). In W. Brzeziczki and W. Piotrowski eds.: *Proceedings of the First International Symposium on Wood Tar and Pitch.* Biskupin, Poland 1993: 41-44.

NOE-NYGAARD, N. 1974. Mesolithic hunting in Denmark illustrated by bone injuries caused by human weapons. *Journal of Archaeological Science* 1: 217-248.

NOE-NYGAARD, N. 1975. Bone injuries caused by human weapons in Mesolithic Denmark. In A. T. Clason ed.: *Archaeozoological studies.* North Holland and American Elsevier, Amsterdam – New York.

PAPE, W. 1982. Au sujet de quelques pointes de flèches en os. In H. Camps-Fabre ed. *Industrie de l'Os Neolithique et de l'Age des Metaux 2,* C.N.R.S., 135-172.

RADOVANOVIC, I. 1996. *The Iron Gates Mesolithic.* International Monographs in Prehistory, Archaeological Series 11, Ann Arbor, Michigan.

RAMSEYER, D. 1985. Pieces emmanchee en os et en bois decervides. Decovertes Neolithiques Recentes du Canton de Fribourg, Suisse Occidentale. In H. Camps-Fabre ed.: *Industrie de l'Os Neolithique et de l'Age des Metaux 3,* C.N.R.S., 194-211.

RIEK, G. 1959. Das Federmesser führende Magdalénien der Burkhardtshöhle bei Westerheim im Kreis Münsingen (Schvöbische Alb). *Fundberichte aus Schwaben,* NF 15, 9-29.

ROZOY, J-G. The revolution of bowmen in Europe. In C. Bonsall ed.: *The Mesolithic in Europe.* Edinburgh, John Donalds Publishing Ltd. 13-28.

SACKETT, J. 1990. Style and ethnicity in archaeology: the case for isachrestism. In M. Conkey and C. Hastorf eds.: *The Uses of Style in Archaeology.* Cambridge University Press, Cambridge, 32-43.

SCHIBLER, J. 1980. *Osteologische Untersuchung der cortaillodzeitlichen Knochenartefakte. Die neolithischen Ufersiedlungen von Twann.* Band 8. Schriftenreihe der Erziehungsdirektion des Kantons Bern, herausgegeben vom Archäologischen Dienst des Kantons Bern, Staatlicher Lehrmittelverlag, Bern.

SCHIBLER, J. 1981. *Typologische Untersuchungen der cortaillodzeitlichen Knochenartefakte. Die neolithischen Ufersiedlungen von Twann.* Band 17. Schriftenreihe der Erziehungsdirektion des Kantons Bern, herausgegeben vom Archäologischen Dienst des Kantons Bern, Staatlicher Lehrmittelverlag, Bern.

SCHIBLER, J. 1987. Die Hirschgeweihartefakte und Die Knochenartefakte. In E. Gross et al. eds.: *Zürich "Mozartstrasse", Neolithische und bronezeitliche Ufersiedlungen.* Orell Füssli Verlag, Zürich: 156-176.

SCHLENKER, B. 1994. Knochen- und Geweihgerät in der Jungsteinzeit. In M. Kokabi, B. Schlenker and J. Wahl. eds. *Knochenarbeit.* Stuttgart: Landesdenkmalamt Baden-Württemberg: 41-56.

SHEPHERD, D. 1999. The elusive warrior maiden tradition: bearing weapons in Anglo-Saxon society. In J. Carman and A. Harding eds.: *Ancient warfare. Archaeological perspectives.* Stroud Sutton Publishing: 219-243.

SPINDLER, K. 1993. *Der Mann im Eis.* Wilhelm Goldmann Verlag, München.

SZABÓ, M., GRENADER-NYBERG, G. and MYRDAL, J. 1985: Die Holzfunde aus der frühgeschichlicher Wurt Elisenhof. Studien zur Küstenarchäologie Schleswig-Holsteins. Ser. A. Vol. 5. Frankfurt-Main – Bern – Las Vegas.

STODIEK, U. and PAULSEN, H. 1996. *Mit dem Pfeil, dem Bogen...* Isensee Verlag, Oldenburg.

TORKE, W. 1993. Die Fischerei am pröhistorischen Federsee. *Archäologisches Korrespondenzblatt* 23, 49-66.

von TRÖLTSCH, E. 1902. *Die Pfahlbauten des Bodenseegebietes.* Verlag Ferdinand Enke, Stuttgart.

Van VILSTEREN V. T. 1987. *Het benen tijdperk. Gebruiksvoorwerpen van been, gewei en ivoor 10.000 jaar geleden tot heden.* Drents Museum.

VORUZ, J.-L. 1984. Outillages osseux et dynamisme industriel dans le Néolithique jurassien. *Cahiers d'archéologie Romande* No. 29, Lausanne.

WINIGER, J. 1992. Beinerne Doppelspitzen aus dem Bielersee. *Jahrbuch der Schweizerischen Gesellschaft für Ur- und Frühgeschichte* 75: 65.

WOLF, C. 1993. *Die Seeufersiedlung Yverdon, Avenue des Sports (Kanton Waadt).* Cahiers d'archéologie romande 59, Lausanne.

ZHILIN, M. 1998. Technology of the manufacture of Mesolithic arrowheads on the Upper Volga. *European Journal of Archaeology* Vol.1/2: 149-176.

FIGHTING FOR YOUR LIFE?
VIOLENCE AT THE LATE-GLACIAL TO HOLOCENE TRANSITION IN UKRAINE

Malcolm C. LILLIE

Abstract: The restructuring of the fauna and flora in the steppe and forest-steppe zones of Europe at the transition to the Holocene period appears to have resulted in the potential for periodic resource stress among the indigenous hunter-gatherer populations. Existing published sources for the Dnieper Rapids region of Ukraine, in particular from three cemeteries dating to this transitional period, supports the notion that resources were being competed for to a degree that resulted in violent interaction. The skeletal evidence from these cemeteries suggests that the increased use of the bow and arrow in hunting was accompanied by its increased use in inter-group violence. The osteological and lithic analyses carried out by Russian researchers to date on these skeletal remains, highlight a prevalence of injury unattested in the later Mesolithic and Neolithic cemeteries from this area, as studied by the present author.

Keywords: Ukraine, Epipalaeolithic, fisher-hunter-gatherers, territoriality, cemetery, violent interactions

INTRODUCTION

This paper presents an overview of the published sources relating to three Epipalaeolithic cemeteries from the Dnieper Rapids region of Ukraine, and outlines the evidence for violence that has been recorded on the human skeletal remains from these cemeteries. Reference to the Epipalaeolithic cemetery of Vasilyevka III includes more recent studies by the present author, and all later (Mesolithic-Neolithic) cemeteries have also been investigated by the author (Lillie 1998a & b).

The Dnieper (Dniepr[1]) Rapids region of Ukraine has been a focus for the siting of a series of large cemetery complexes since the Epipalaeolithic and earliest Mesolithic periods (Figure 1). It is likely that three cemeteries from this area relate to these particular stages, which are characterised by an abrupt shift in the vegetation and fauna of Europe at the transition from the Late-glacial and into the Holocene period. Amongst the significant faunal changes in evidence bison (*Bison priscus*), a key 'mass drive hunting' animal was replaced by auroch (*Bos primigenius*), and the Pleistocene horse (*Equus latipes*) was replaced by the east European wild horse (*Equus gmelini*) (Nuzhinyi 1998: 102).

The cemeteries, which are located to the south of the town of Dniepropetrovsk on the Dnieper (Dolukhanov 1996), are unusual in that they are unaccompanied by any associated settlement evidence.Unfortunately, to date only one of these cemeteries, Vasilyevka III (Vassil'evka) has been the subject of radiocarbon dating by Jacobs (1993), to between 10,080 to 9980 BP. The three radiocarbon determinations obtained, 10,080±100 BP (OxA-3809), 10,060±105 (OxA-3807), and 9980±100 BP (OxA-3808), when calibrated to 2σ using the OxCal program, indicate an age range of 10,400-9200 cal BC. The other Late-glacial, or earlier Holocene cemeteries from this area, Voloshkoe (Voloshki) and Vasilyevka I (Vassil'evka I) remain undated in absolute terms.

According to Telegin (1982), Voloshkoe is viewed as the earliest of these cemeteries, with Vasilyevka III occupying the more recent chronological position. Danilenko (1955) assigned a Late Upper Palaeolithic age to part of the Voloshkoe cemetery on the basis of the stratigraphical position of the skeletons within the loess of the island upon which the cemetery was located. In addition, the character of the stone tool inventory was considered to comprise both Epipalaeolithic and Mesolithic elements. Nuzhinyi (1989, 1990 and *pers. comm.* 1993), while investigating the projectile damage on Upper Palaeolithic and Mesolithic microliths, concluded that the chronological affinities of a number of these objects was pre-Holocene in derivation (1990:117). The impact damage analyses carried out by Nuzhinyi (1989, 1990, 1993) provide a basis for the current discussion.

Alongside the evidence from Vasilyevka I (Stolyar 1959: 78-165) and Vasilyevka III (Telegin 1961: 3-19), Voloshkoe enables consideration of the elements of conflict, and their pathological expression. This evidence is occurring during a stage of major restructuring of the landscapes in the European mainland and more specifically in this context, the Dnieper region. Broadly, the available evidence relates to both this region, and also to the evidence for inter-group conflict within the wider European context (e.g. Price 1991: 223-4).

The changes in the flora and fauna of a region, due to climatic parameters such as the Late-glacial to Holocene transition, would have stimulated technological developments and a reorientation of hunting strategies. While this is a generally accepted supposition (e.g. Balakin and Nuzhinyi 1995), the idea that 'all evidence of intensive collection of fish and, especially, plant food resources, both by modern and prehistoric societies, is a clear-cut sign of a general crisis in

---

[1]   Many of the names relating to this region have been given alternative spellings by Russian/Ukrainian and Western European writers. This is due in part to the transfer of spelling from Cyrillic. As such, where alternatives exist these are presented in brackets in order to ensure comparability between sources.

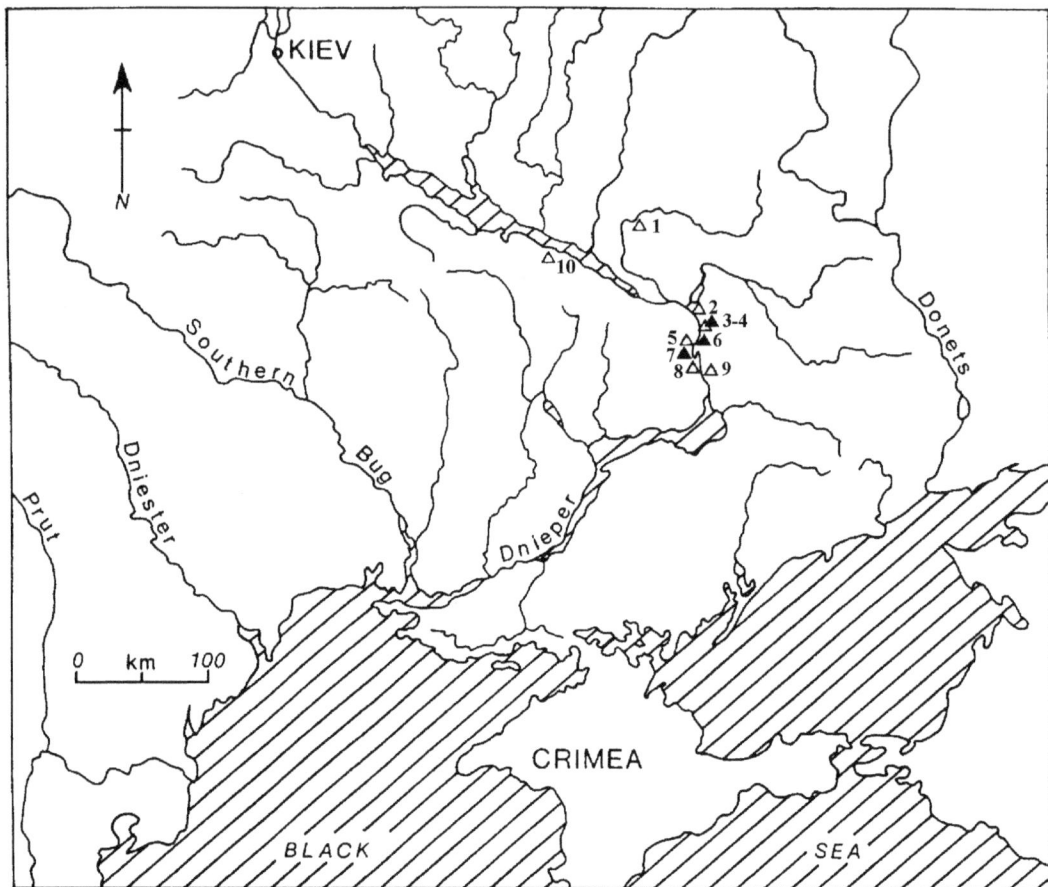

Figure 1: The Dnieper Rapids region, showing location of key cemeteries.
1. Osipovka, 2. Igren VIII, 3. Vasilyevka V, 4. Vasilyevka III, II, and I, 5. Nikolskoye, 6. Marievka,
7. Voloshkoe, 8. Vovnigi II, 9. Yasinovatka, 10. Derievka I. ▲ = Mesolithic, △ = Neolithic.

the hunter-gatherer economy' (*ibid.* 1995:192) appears somewhat counterintuitive. In the Dnieper region the evidence from stable isotope analysis of late Mesolithic (Marievka,) and Neolithic (Igren VIII, Osipovka, Vasilyevka V, Yasinovatka and Dereivka I) diets indicates that a broad range of resources were incorporated into what was in essence a fisher-hunter-gatherer resource procurement strategy (Lillie and Richards 2000). Unpublished data from the Vasilyevka II (Mesolithic) and Vovnigi II (Neolithic) cemeteries supports fish as a key dietary element during both periods. Palaeopathological analysis of these populations confirms the presence of very low levels of dietary stressors (Lillie 1996, 1998b), which would equate to the European Mesolithic and Neolithic levels as outlined by Meiklejohn and Zvelebil (1991).

While periodic food shortages would have occurred throughout the earlier Holocene, at least on a seasonal basis, it is apparent from the palaeopathological and isotopic studies carried out to date, that the resource spectrum in the Dnieper region was diverse enough to deflect any short-term impacts. The continued focus of large-scale cemeteries at the Rapids argues for a seasonal aggregation of population at this location in order to exploit a stable resource. However, it is apparent from the cemetery evidence presented below, that at the Late-glacial/early Holocene boundary, some conflict arose, possibly due to competition for the available resources at the Dnieper Rapids.

THE CEMETERIES OF THE DNIEPER RAPIDS

Voloshkoe

The cemetery of Voloshkoe (Figure 2) was published in the Russian language journal *Sovetskaya etnografiya* (Vol. 3, pp. 56-61) by V.N. Danilenko in 1955. Danilenko reports that the cemetery was located some 18 km to the south of Dnepropetrovsk, close to the village of Voloshkoe. The cemetery is located on the second loess terrace of the Dnieper, on the same level as the Palaeolithic sites of the Dnieper Rapids area. The burials were situated in a line running in a SE-NW direction for *ca.* 14m, being *ca.* 4 m in width. On excavation it appeared that the cemetery had been divided into two parts, a north-western part which contained Burials Nos. 1-12 (these occurred in short rows), and a south-eastern part which contained Burials Nos. 13-18 (these latter burials had no discernible order and differed in the burial ritual from those of Burials Nos. 1-12). Eighteen of the nineteen individuals buried were adults and one (Burial No. 18) was a child burial. Burial No. 8 was a paired grave. Two burials (Nos. 15 and 18) were in the extended position, a ritual previously ascribed a Neolithic periodisation by Telegin (1968). However, on the basis of the absolute dating of Vasilyevka III and II and Marievka (Jacobs 1993, Lillie 1998a) this burial rite has been shown

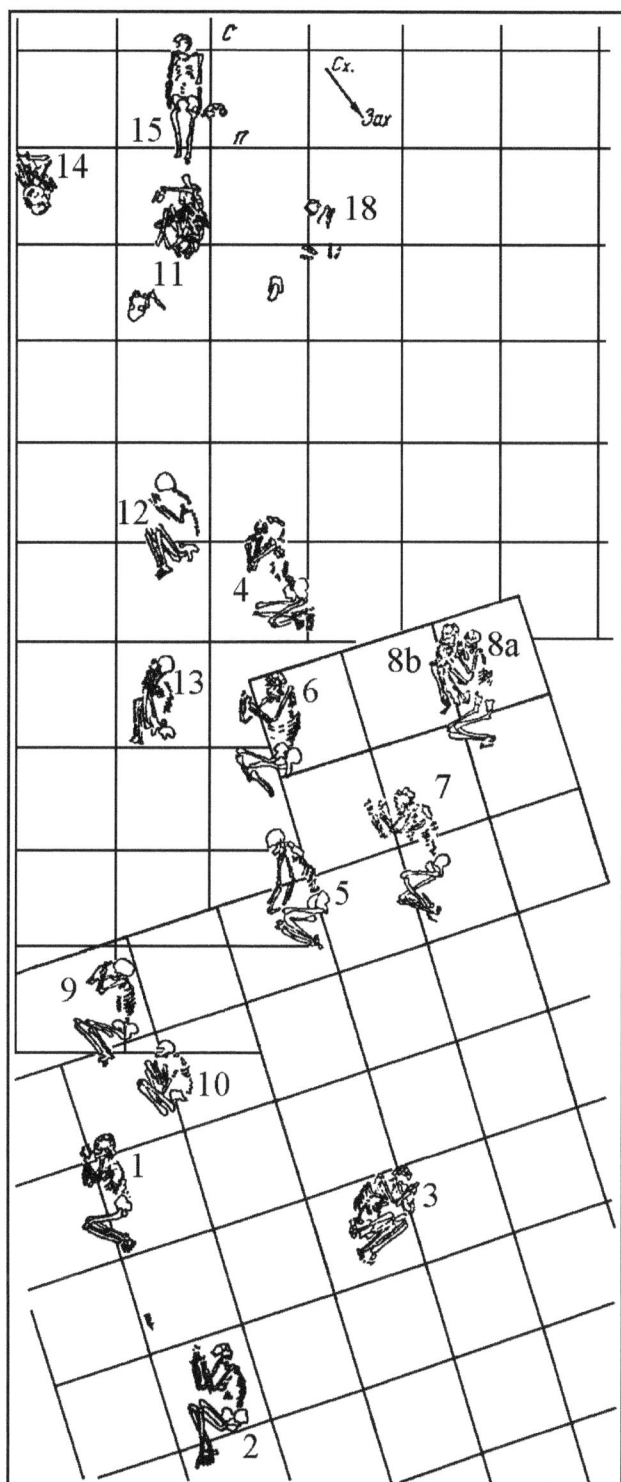

Figure 2: Voloshkoe Epipalaeolithic Cemetery
(Redrawn from Telegin 1982).

A small blade with backed retouch was found plunged into the atlas bone of the skeleton indicating that the individual in question was shot by someone using a bow and arrow. Danilenko (1955) concludes that on the basis of these observations bladelets with backed retouch are in fact arrowheads. Nuzhinyi (1989:90) reports that three arrowheads were associated with individual No.3, and considers this to be the earliest evidence for the use of the bow in the area covered by the modern boundaries of Ukraine (Figure 3).

Burial No. 5 (male) also exhibits signs of violence to the person in that, along with other examples, it appears that the hands were cut off prior to interment. In addition a small bladelet with a sharp end and backed retouch, i.e. an arrowhead, was found in the sternum. Burial No. 16 at Voloshkoe was found in a complicated ritual positioning comprising a considerable degree of disarticulation, with evidence to suggest that the right hand and adjoining long bones were cut off prior to burial. A piece of blade with backed retouch, and with bone mass adhering to its distal end (Nuzhinyi 1989: 90) was found in close proximity, and a second point was also in close proximity, although the mixing of elements from other individuals makes definite association difficult. Unfortunately no insight into why the evidence supports disarticulation is provided by Danilenko. However, a similar ritual removal of skeletal elements by cutting has been inferred for Burial No. 15, which has the hands and both legs below the knees missing. The combination of an absence of evidence for intrusion into the burials at this site, and the fact that three individuals were lacking specific body parts, led Danilenko to conclude that removal was deliberate and an integral element of the burial ritual associated with these individuals.

Analysis of the lithics associated with these interments (Nuzhinyi 1989, 1990) suggested that the fragments of microlithic points recovered from the human remains at this site, such as the fragment of point from the ribs of individual No. 10, displayed shattering associated with spin-off fractures at the point of impact (1990:117). A similar fracture pattern also occurred on the backed blade recovered from the cervical vertebra mentioned earlier. The vertebra exhibited the imprint from the shaft of the projectile weapon, which according to Nuzhinyi had 'clearly penetrated into the bone along with the microlith' (below Fig. 3: 4-5) (Nuzhinyi 1990:117). In the latter context the illustration (Fig. 3) clearly indicates a degree of fragmentation of the vertebra at the point of impact.

At Voloshkoe Burials 3 and 5 have direct evidence for impact damage on the bones, Burial 16 has both a point in close proximity to the skeleton and a backed blade with bone mass adhering to it, though its association is unclear, and burial 10 has a point which exhibits impact damage in association, but not in fact embedded in the bone. The precise nature of the associations remains uncertain in a number of instances as the excavation report does not provide sufficient resolution to enable an accurate determination of context. Obviously, this limitation is one that will be inherent in any literature review using a summary excavation report such as that of Danilenko (1955).

to have its origins in the Epipalaeolithic and subsequent Mesolithic periods.

According to Danilenko (1955), the stratification and flint industry associated with a number of the burials is indicative of a Final Palaeolithic age. While the significance of certain traits in the burial ritual is obvious, Danilenko (1955) concludes that societal influences may have been operating, especially in the case of the person in Burial No. 3, who was 'murdered'. This particular burial is located away from the others, and a number of artefacts were found in association.

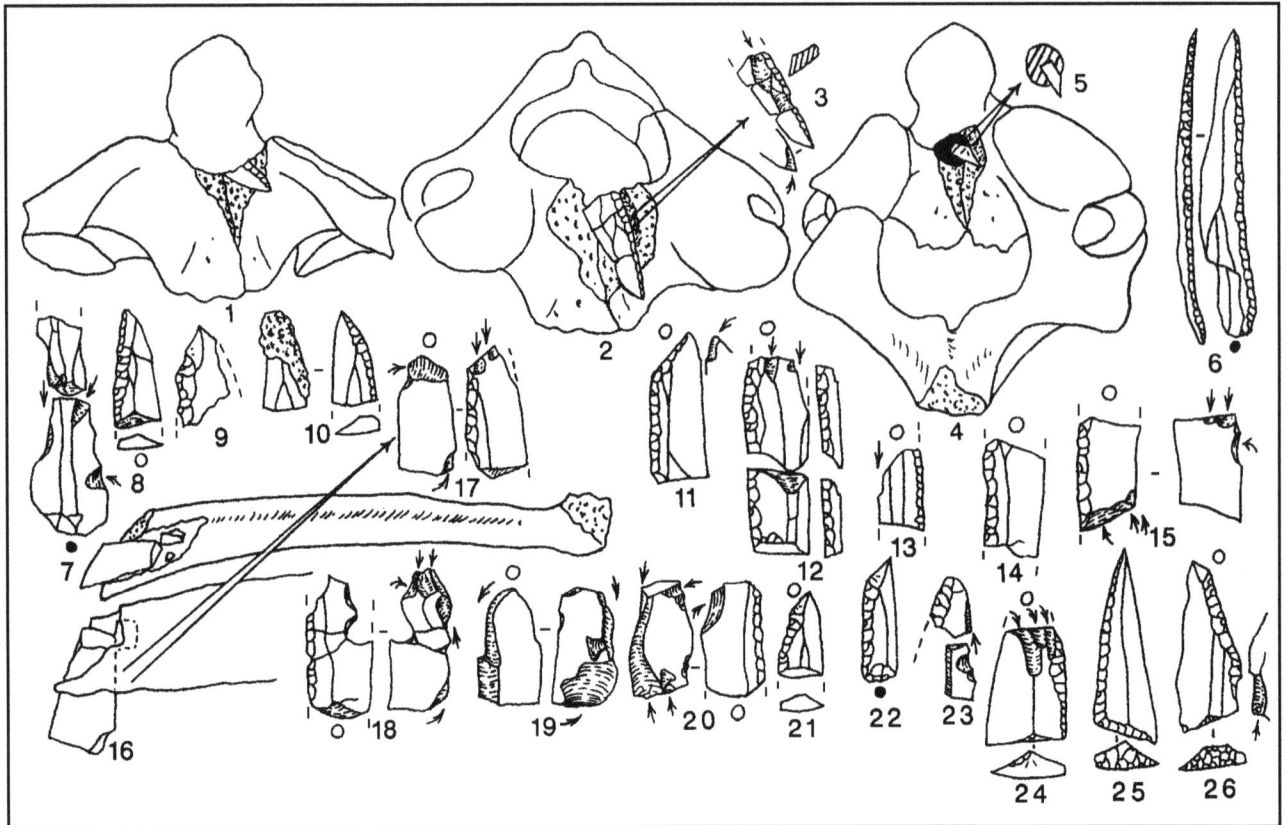

Figure 3: Microliths found among the human bones from the cemeteries of Voloshkoe (1-10), Vasilyevka I (11-15) and Vasilyevka III (16-26) (*after* Nuzhinyi 1990:118).

Vasilyevka I

The cemetery of Vasilyevka I (Figure 4) is situated on a steep slope on the present-day left bank of the Dnieper, apparently corresponding to the third terrace (Konduktorova (1974: 8-9). Twenty six burials were originally recovered (Stolyar 1959: 78-165), amongst which were three double interments, and an instance of the burial of only the lower half of an individual (which Stolyar interpreted as a discrete context due to a lack of any evidence for subsequent disturbances).

According to Nuzhinyi (1990:117), the lithics associated with the flexed skeletons from Vasilyevka I (Figure 3), which 'were located in the final Pleistocene loess-like clays, without humus in the burial pits, are 'geometrized' backed points (arrowheads). These particular artefacts are attributable to an Upper/Epi-Palaeolithic periodisation on the basis of counterparts in regional sites with post-Gravettian features. Two of the individuals interred in this cemetery had evidence for impact damage from microlithic projectile weapons.

Burial No. 17 (male) at Vasilyevka I had four weapon induced injuries in evidence, including a trapezoidal point, clearly shot into the body, fragments of two points with pronounced impact damage, and two pieces that could be reconstructed (Nuzhinyi 1989:91, 1995:196). The individual in Burial No.10 had a fragment of microlithic point with similar impact fracturing, which was located in the region of the ribs (*ibid.* 1989:91). The latter reference to Burial No. 10 is surprisingly

similar to that of Burial No. 10 at Voloshkoe (above), and as Nuzhinyi does not appear to reference this association in his 1990 paper, some caution must be adopted in this context, particularly as Danilenko (1955) makes an identical reference to Burial No. 10 at Voloshkoe.

Vasilyevka III

Vasilyevka III (Figure 5), was originally discovered by Danilenko in 1953 on the left bank of the Dnieper, on the slope of the third terrace. Excavations by Telegin in 1957 (1961: 3-19), and 1962, led to the discovery of forty-four graves. This is a figure that represents a minimum estimate of the number of interments due to the fact that the central area of the cemetery was destroyed by a ravine. It is anticipated that the original number of interments would have been in the region of sixty to seventy individuals (Konduktorova 1974: 9).

The majority of the burials at Vasilyevka III (thirty-seven), were in the crouched (flexed) position, whilst seven were in the extended position. The variation in burial ritual was interpreted by Telegin (1957) as reflecting differing chronological positions, with the crouched inhumations being considered Mesolithic and the extended inhumations supposedly reflecting late Mesolithic to Neolithic burials (Konduktorova 1974: 10). Both Stoylar (1955) and Gokhman (1966) disagreed with Telegin's viewpoint, asserting that both styles of burial were contemporaneous and wholly Mesolithic,

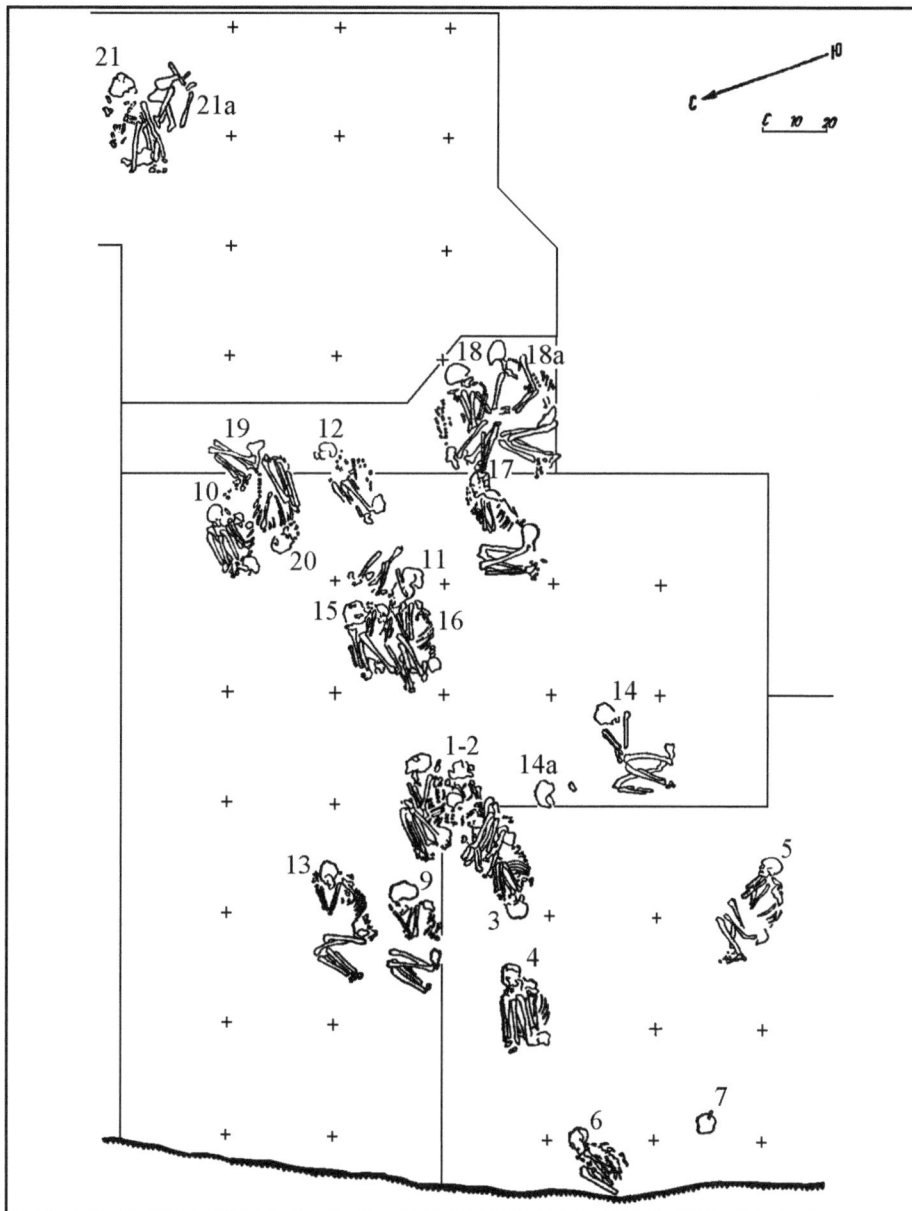

Figure 4: Vasilyevka I (Redrawn from Telegin 1982).

as opposed to Late Mesolithic/Neolithic (or more precisely Proto-Neolithic) in derivation.

As noted above, the work of Jacobs (1993) on the dating of the site of Vasilyevka III confirms Stolyar's and Gokhman's ideas concerning the contemporary nature of the interments. However, these dates indicate an age range of 10,400-9200 cal BC, which suggests an Epipalaeolithic as opposed to Mesolithic age for these burial traditions, a position previously suggested by Danilenko (1955).

According to Nuzhinyi (1990:117-8), the flexed skeletons from Vasilyevka III have similar chronological affinities to Vasilyevka I. However, it is the identification of microliths that had again functioned as pointed tips (arrowheads), but with a geometric shape (being that of an asymmetrical triangle) that suggested chronological variations between the modes of interment at the two cemeteries (Figure 3). One example of this later, 'Mesolithic', lithic type was found

among the ribs of an extended burial (No. 33) of a female aged 18-22, at Vasilyevka III, and Nuzhinyi (1989: 91) asserts that this object has typological similarities to examples from the Teviec burial ground. Burial No.36, possibly a female aged 20-25, had fragments of a similar point in association. In addition, macrowear evidence for bending and spin-off fractures occur on several microliths, while a lumbar vertebra of the individual in Burial No. 37, a male aged 25-35, had a microlith embedded in it (*ibid.* 1989: 91). This object had clearly been shot into the victim from behind, and shattered into numerous pieces on impact.

Another artefact that originally indicated a Mesolithic age for the extended burials at Vasilyevka III (Nuzhinyi 1990:118) is the fragment of a slotted bone point with two composite microblade edges, wedged in a lumbar vertebra of the individual in Burial No. 34, a female aged 18-22 (Nuzhinyi 1989: 91). The individual in Burial No. 5 (indeterminate age and sex) had both arrow and spear points, comprising a

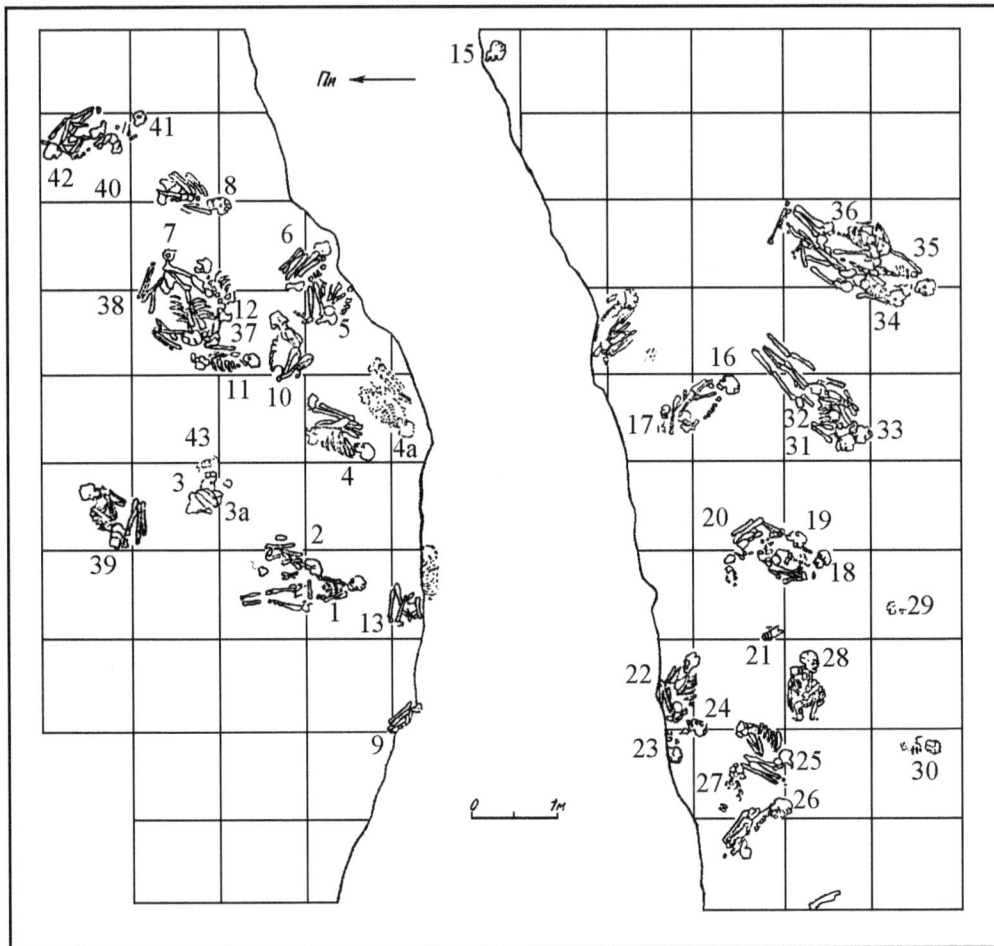

Figure 5: Vasilyevka III (Redrawn from Telegin 1982).

trapezoidal micro-burin, a fragment of a similar point, and a fragment of microlith with marked impact fracture pattern, embedded in the skeleton. These points are widely represented in Boreal age assemblages from the steppe zone (*ibid*. 1990:118). The new dating of the Vasilyevka III cemetery (Jacobs 1993) confirms Nuzhinyi's (1989) observations that many of the lithic points in evidence at the cemeteries of Voloshkoe, and Vasilyevka I and III have parallels at final Palaeolithic sites of Ukraine.

The evidence from Vasilyevka III suggests that we have one individual (Burial No. 5), with multiple points 'embedded' in the skeleton, Burial No. 37, an adult male aged 25-35 has a microlith embedded in the skeleton and Burial No. 34, a young female aged 18-22 has a slotted bone point in the region of the lumbar vertebrae. In addition Burials Nos. 33, a young female aged 18-22, and 36, a probable female burial aged 20-25 have arrowheads in association, possibly indicating flesh wounds that have not impacted on bone. The young age of those individuals identified is perhaps significant as the loss of women of child-bearing age and young adult males would conceivably be the most damaging to any Epipalaeolithic hunter-gatherer group. This evidence may suggest that if the evidence indeed reflects violence due to competition for resources, then a discrete portion of the group is being singled out in this activity. The evidence is clearly limited, but intriguing nonetheless.

DISCUSSION

In light of the above evidence, and the fact that the Dnieper Rapids have been shown to have remained pivotal in terms of fishing resources throughout the earlier Holocene, it is possible that the violence evidenced at Voloshkoe, and Vasilyevka I and III reflects competition for access to resources at the Late-glacial to Holocene transition. Balakin and Nuzhinyi (1995) note that many examples of cemetery sites are recorded at the rapids of the largest rivers of the world. Such sites include Jebel Sahaba (Sudan) where *ca.* 40% of the interred displayed evidence for a violent death, having been caused by microlithic projectile weapons, with at least three individuals (Nos. 20, 21, and 44) having the microliths still embedded in the bones (*ibid*. 1995:195-6).

Evidence for multiple impact damage as evidenced by flints and a single bone find embedded in a number of the victims, alongside the possible dismemberment of certain individuals at sites such as Voloshkoe in the Dnieper Rapids region, has parallels in recent ethnographic contexts (Balakin and Nuzhinyi 1995). Such 'ritual' dismemberment may be interpreted as an attempt to inhibit the passage of the deceased into the afterlife (*ibid* 1995).

The Dnieper Rapids cemeteries are an exceptional phenomenon, representing the collective burial grounds of the fisher-hunter-gatherer populations of the region from Epipalaeolithic through to Eneolithic/Copper Age contexts. Balakin and Nuzhinyi (1995:197) have suggested that there would have been periodic "economic stress" and a shift towards the exploitation of aquatic resources as a "typical" reaction to a crisis in the hunting economy (accompanying the shift from Glacial to Post-Glacial fauna's). However, to date, the skeletal evidence for dietary stressors at the Dnieper Rapids cemeteries does not lend support to this assertion (Lillie 1996, 1997, 1998a & b). There is no skeletal evidence for significant resource stress, nor for similar violent interactions at the end of the Mesolithic and into the Neolithic periods (Lillie 1998b), despite clear suggestions that a greater degree of population aggregation occurs at this transition. Indeed, it is at this time that the numerous large-scale cemeteries such as Dereivka I, Yasinovatka and Nikolskoye are becoming established along the Dnieper.

Furthermore, the evidence from stable isotopic studies on these populations (Lillie and Richards 2000), alongside the proliferation of cemetery sites into the Neolithic, suggests an increasing emphasis on the exploitation of the rich fish resources of the Dnieper into this period. The key point of note in this discussion is the fact that the bone (a single example from Vasilyevka III) and lithic points embedded in the interred humans at the Rapids are interpreted a representing the arrowheads from weapons used by a separate group, who were in competition with the Dnieper populations at the Late-Glacial to Holocene transition (Dvoryaninov 1978:11, Nuzhinyi 1998:113).

The violence in evidence on the skeletons of the Epipalaeolithic/earlier Mesolithic Dnieper cemeteries is clearly suggestive of conflict. Unfortunately, a number of limitations occur when using published sources, for instance, no indication of evidence for reactive bone has been forthcoming and certain associations of artefacts in relation to precise location on/in the skeleton is lacking. Similarly, the suggestion that dismemberment occurs is intriguing, but no indication of whether this was ante- or post-mortem in nature is forthcoming from the available evidence. Despite extensive studies of the available skeletal archive from the Dnieper Ragion by the present author, none of the osteological material reported as exhibiting evidence for trauma was available for study. All materials with such evidence appear to have been separated off from the stored collections and housed separately in museum collections for display purposes.

If we accept that violent interaction is indeed an element of the daily lives of the populations interred at Voloshkoe, Vasilyevka I and III, then the evidence from Vasilyevka III may be exceptionally significant in illuminating the nature of the violence that occurs. On the basis of the age and sex profile of those individuals with either direct, or indirect, indications of violence, it would appear that the younger age categories *ca.* 18-35, of both females and males were being targeted. As noted above, the loss of females of child-bearing age and young adult males could conceivably be seen by an aggressor as the most serious loss to any hunter-gatherer group.

Despite the above discussion, it is apparent that the continued exploitation of the Rapids alongside a perpetuation of inhumation in these cemeteries suggests that the Rapids represented a focal point of population, perhaps on a seasonal basis, that continues to be exploited by the Dnieper culture groups in spite of the conflict that may be reflected by the skeletal remains. The evidence for violence that characterises Epipalaeolithic and earlier Mesolithic cemeteries is accompanied by shifts in the nature of the toolkits that these populations used in their resource procurement strategies. Such changes reflect adaptability and re-orientation in response to changing climate and resource availability.

The rapids, pools and cascades on the Dnieper would clearly have been attractive locations for fishing, but the rapids also present a physical barrier to passage along the river, necessitating disembarking in order to negotiate them. In addition, the rapids occur at a point where the Dnieper crosses a swell in the crystalline basement, as occurs on the Volga at Kuibyshev, which results in a shift in stream flow (Figure 1) from a general southestern to a southwestern direction (Hoffman 1965:41). The combination of physical and resource factors occurring at the Dnepropetrovsk on the Dnieper creates a situation whereby the Rapids, by their very nature, predispose themselves towards becoming foci of activity.

As a consequence, the early absolute dates from Vasilyevka III, alongside the relative dates for Voloshkoe and Vasilyevka I, suggest that the inter-group violence in evidence potentially highlights the early stages of territoriality at a point where regional groups would have competed for a preferred location, primarily for the exploitation of freshwater resources. Once these territorial rights are established, it appears, on the current evidence, that the need for violent conflict in order to maintain them is unnecessary throughout the subsequent Mesolithic, Neolithic and Eneolithic/Copper Age periods in this region.

Acknowledgements

Colleagues in St.Petersburg and Kiev allowed me access to the Ukrainian skeletal series in 1992 and 1994. In Kiev Prof. Dmitri Telegin and Inna Potekhina not only looked after me but imparted much of their knowledge of the Ukrainian material culture and chronology. Their help proved fundamental to my understanding of this region, and these particular chronological periods. In St.Petersburg Prof. Gokhman and Alexander Kozintsev allowed me unimpeded access to the collections and Prof. Vladimir Timofeev, Lena and Ksenia cared for me and educated me in the ways of Russian culture. Similarily Inna and family in Kiev gave me their knowledge of Ukrainian traditions in a way that ensured that my research visits proved rewarding on numerous levels. The stable isotopes considered above were analysed and interpreted by Mike Richards while at ORAU, now at Bradford University. The author would particularly like to thank Vladimir Timofeev for his translation of Danilenko's 1955 text into English, and to acknowledge the observations of a reviewer who highlighted many of the inherent inconsistencies and limitations in the published sources used in this overview.

Author

Dr. Malcolm C. Lillie
Wetland Archaeology and Environments Research Centre
Department of Geography
University of Hull
Hull
HU6 7RX
M.C.Lillie@geo.hull.ac.uk
www.hull.ac.uk/wetlands

References

BALAKIN, S. and D. NUZHINYI. 1995. 'The Origins of Graveyards: The Influence of Landscape Elements on Social and Ideological Changes in Prehistoric Communities'. *Préhistoire Européenne* 7: 191-202.

DANILENKO, V.N. 1955. 'Voloshskiy Epipaleoliticheskiy Mogolnik'. (The Voloshkoye Epipalaeolithic Cemetery). *Sovetskaya etnografiya* 3: 56-61.

DOLUKHANOV, P.M. 1996. *The Early Slavs: Eastern Europe from the Initial Settlement to the Kievan Rus.* Essex: Longman Ltd.

DVORYANINOV, S.A. 1978. 'O Dneprovskih mogilnikah kamennogo veka'. In: *Arkheologicheskiye issledovaniya Severo-Zapadnogo Prichernomorya.* Kiev.

GOKHMAN, I.I. 1966. *Naselenie Ukrainy v Epokhu Mezolita I Neolita: antropogicheskiy ocherk.* Nauka: Moscow.

HOFFMAN, G.W. 1965. *A Geography of Europe: including Asiatic U.S.S.R.* London: Methuen & Co. Ltd.

JACOBS, K. 1993. 'Human Postcranial Variation in the Ukrainian Mesolithic-Neolithic'. *Current Anthropology* 34:417-30.

KONDUKTOROVA, T.S. 1974. 'The ancient populations of the Ukraine: from the Mesolithic age to the first centuries of our era'. *Anthropologie BRNO* XII (1&2): 5-149.

LILLIE, M.C. 1996. 'Mesolithic and Neolithic Populations of Ukraine: Indications of Diet from Dental Pathology'. *Current Anthropology* 37:135-42.

LILLIE. M.C., 1997. 'Women and Children in Prehistory: Resource Sharing and Social Stratification at the Mesolithic-Neolithic Transition in Ukraine'. In: J. Moore and E. Scott (eds.) *Invisible People and Processes: Writing Gender and Childhood into European Archaeology.* London: Leicester Univ. Press. pp.213-28.

LILLIE, M.C., 1998a. 'The Mesolithic-Neolithic transition in Ukraine: new radiocarbon determinations for the cemeteries of the Dnieper Rapids region' *Antiquity* 72:184-88.

LILLIE, M.C. 1998b. The Dnieper Rapids region of Ukraine: a consideration of chronology, dental pathology and diet at the Mesolithic-Neolithic transition. Sheffield University: Unpublished PhD thesis.

LILLIE, M.C. and M.P. RICHARDS. 2000. 'Stable Isotope Analysis and Dental Evidence of Diet at the Mesolithic-Neolithic Transition in Ukraine'. *Journal of Archaeological Science* 27:965-72.

MEIKLEJOHN, C., and ZVELEBIL, M. 1991. 'Health Status of European Populations at the Agricultural Transition and the Implications for the Adoption of Farming'. In Bush, H., and M. Zvelebil (eds.) *Health in Past Societies: Biocultural Interpretations of Human Skeletal Remains in Archaeological Contexts.* Oxford: B.A.R. (Int. Ser.) 567:129-44.

NUZHINYI, D. 1989. 'L'utilisation des microlithes géométrques comme armatures de projectiles'. *Bulletin de la Société Prehistorique Francaise* 86 (3):88-96.

NUZHINYI, D. 1990. 'Projectile Damage on Upper Palaeolithic Microliths and the Use of Bow and Arrow among Pleistocene Hunters in the Ukraine'. *Proceedings of the International Conference on Use-Wear Analaysis.* Sweden: Uppsala. pp. 113-24.

NUZHINYI, D. 1993. 'Projectile Weapons and Technical Progress in the Stone Age'. Traces et fonction: les gestes retrouvés Colloque international de Liège Éditions *ERAUL* 50: 41-53.

NUZHINYI, D. 1998. 'The Ukrainian Steppe as a Region of Intercultural Contacts Between Atlantic and Mediterranean Zones of European Mesolithic', In: Domañska, L. and K. Jacobs (Eds.) *Beyond Balkanization.* Poznań: Baltic-Pontic Studies 5. pp. 102-119.

PRICE, T.D. 1991. 'The Mesolithic of Northern Europe'. *Annual Review of Anthropology* 20: 211-33.

STOLYAR, A.D. 1959. 'Pervyi Vasilyevskii Mezolithicheskii Mogilnik'. (The Mesolithic cemetery of Vasilyevka I). *Arkheologicheskii Sbornik* 1: 78-158.

TELEGIN, D.YA. 1957. 'Tretiy Vasilyevskiy Mogilnik (The cemetery of Vasilyevka III). *Kratkiye Soobshcheniya Instituta Arkheologii Akademii Nauk: USSR Kiev* (Ukraine) 7: 9-12.

TELEGIN, D.YA. 1961. K voprosu o dnepro-donetskoy neoliticheskoy kulture'. (On the question of the Dnieper-Donets Neolithic culture). *Sovetskaya Arkheologiya* 9: 10-20.

TELEGIN, D.YA. 1968. *Dnipro-Donetska kultura.* (The Dnieper-Donets culture). Kiev: Naukova Dumka. pp.248-54.

TELEGIN, D.YA. 1982. *Mesolitichni pamyatki Ukraine (9-6 tisyacholitta do n.e.).* (Mesolithic Populations of Ukraine [9-6th Millennia]). Kiev: Naukova Dumka.

SOCIAL COMPLEXITY AND INTER-PERSONAL VIOLENCE IN HUNTER-GATHERER GROUPS OF THE ATLANTIC COAST OF URUGUAY

SEBASTIAN PINTOS BLANCO

Abstract: Mounds - many of them containing funerary remains - are one of the most conspicuous characteristics of the archaeological record of Eastern Uruguay. The groups occupying the coastal Atlantic border of Uruguay (Humedales) began to monumentalize the landscape and mark the death of certain members of the group from 5000 BP onward. The practice was continued until the arrival of European conquerors. In this paper, I focus on the evidence of interpersonal violence recovered from the burials of the easternmost Uruguayan Department of Rocha. Cut marks, secondary burials and burnt bones could be understood as expressions of inter- and intracommunity struggles. This evidence is interpreted within the context of such cultural features as space monumentalization, changes in diet, and variations in lithic and ceramic technology. The article proposes a positive correlation between the process of space hierarchization through monument construction (earthen mounds), and the monumentalization of death, the evidences of violent human interactions, and the production increase (processing cost, diet breath, domestication). Based on the presented evidence, I discuss the beginning of social complexity in the so-called "primitive" societies.

1. INTRODUCCIÓN

En este trabajo pretendo analizar la serie de evidencias provenientes del registro arqueológico de la cultura de los constructores de cerritos (mounds) de la Región Este de Uruguay, América del Sur (figura 1). Esta cultura de cazadores recolectores, presenta como uno de sus rasgos más destacados la de haber construido túmulos (cerritos). Muchos de estos monumentos realizados en tierra, frecuentemente contienen en su interior enterramientos humanos, los cuales, exhiben diferencias tanto en las modalidades de enterramiento como en los ajuares asociados.

Estos ambientes de humedales de las llanuras atlánticas de la región Este del Uruguay, comienzan a ser monumentalizados a partir del V mileño bp. (figura 2). Los grupos progresivamente irán connotando monumentalmente el paisaje, mediante el emplazamiento de cerritos en lugares "especiales". Los cerritos por lo general se ubican en puntos destacados topográficamente, visibles desde diferentes perspectivas y desde los cuales es posible el control visual de amplias superficies, siendo estas zonas de una alta concentración de recursos (López y Pintos 2000). El proceso de jerarquización espacial, tiene como rasgo particular el de ir asociado con la monumentalización de la muerte de ciertos individuos. En este texto, presentaré una serie de datos

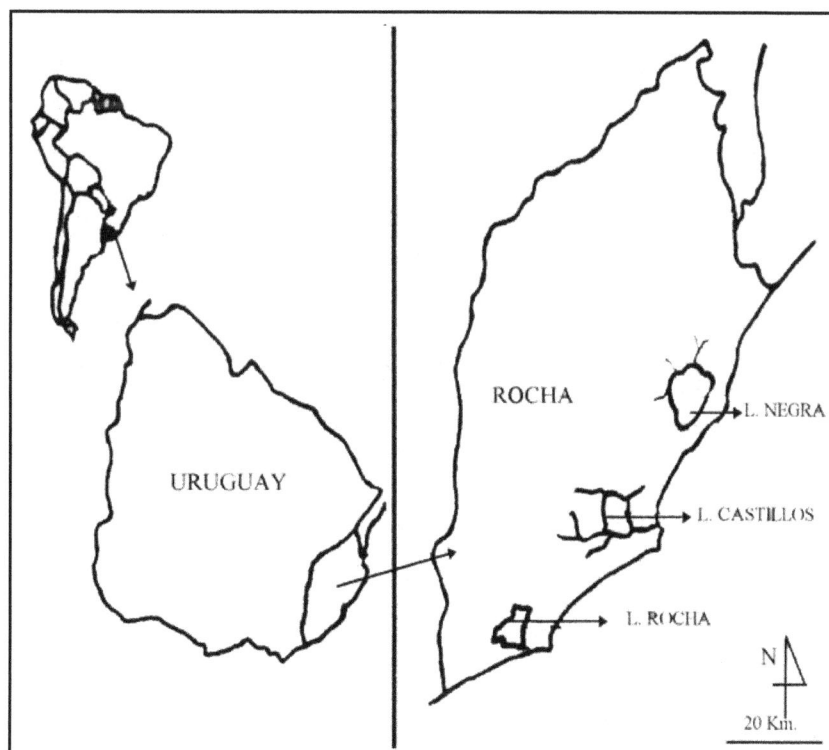

Figura 1. Mapa de ubicación general.

Figura 2. Distribución general de cerrtios para el Departamento de Rocha, Uruguay.
Cada punto indica su ubicación, tanto para túmulos aislados como para conjuntos.

generales sobre el registro material de esta cultura (Arcaica), haciendo especial hincapié en los enterramientos humanos de la región.

Intentaré poner de manifiesto la pertinencia de enfocar la investigación de este registro arqueológico, dentro de lineamientos teórico-metodológicos, que hacen al estudio de la emergencia de la complejidad social (Arnold 1992, 1996; Bender 1978, 1981; Binford 1980; Price y Brown 1985; Testart 1982a,b; Schnirelman 1992, 1994; Zvelebil 1986; entre otros). Los vestigios de estas sociedades cazadoras recolectoras no concuerdan con la tradicional caracterización de bandas simples (en el sentido de Lee y Devore 1968). Existen marcadas diferencias en relación con el manejo social

del medio, un manejo más intenso en cuanto a: producción de individuos, uso del espacio (monumentalización, sedentarismo y explotación de recursos), jerarquización y especialización social. La monumentalización del paisaje, la muerte monumentalizada y un muy particular manejo de especies (animales y vegetales), permiten sugerir para estos habitantes prehistóricos de Uruguay una percepción de la realidad más compleja en comparación con la caracterización tradicional de sociedades de caza y recolección.

Algunos de los enterramientos humanos, exhiben huellas asignables a violencia interpersonal o tratamiento traumático del individuo (Pintos y Bracco 1999). El incremento en el conflicto y la violencia interpersonal e intergrupal, han sido consideradas como variables que hacen al proceso de complejización social en sociedades cazadoras recolectoras. Se presenta la información referente a posibles situaciones de violencia/conflicto social y se discute la misma en un marco más amplio, estableciendo las posibles correlaciones con variables tales como: cambio ambiental, disponibilidad de recursos, transformaciones tecnológicas, entre otras.

2. EVOLUCIÓN AMBIENTAL Y OCUPACIÓN HUMANA

La región Este de Uruguay esta compuesta por extensas planicies costeras del litoral Atlántico. En estas zonas, distribuidos en buena parte del Dpto. de Rocha se localizan los cerritos (mounds), sobrepasando sus límites para adentrarse en territorio brasileño y departamentos limítrofes del propio Uruguay, en lo que ha dado en llamarse la "cultura de los constructores de cerrtios". El ambiente dominante en dichas planicies es el del humedal, sin desatender al pasado geológico remoto, los datos que se presentan están concentrados en el Holoceno y en especial en los últimos 7000 años, período clave en la conformación de estos humedales.

La región del Departamento de Rocha al igual que casi la totalidad del territorio uruguayo presenta un relieve suave, nada abrupto y sin elevaciones de importancia, existiendo una sucesión de lagunas costeras. La Laguna Merin es la de mayor importancia en la región, cercanas a ella se emplazan otra serie de lagunas litorales como ser : Laguna Negra, Laguna de Castillos y Laguna de Rocha . La Cuenca de la Laguna Merín se extiende entre los 31°30' y los 34° 30' de latitud Sur y los 52 ° y 55° de latitud Oeste. Lo deprimido de estas amplias planicies litorales, ha llevado a que la dinámica marina ejerciera gran influencia en la conformación y evolución de este paisaje. La alternancia de ingresiones y regresiones conjuntamente con periodos de mayor y menor pluviosidad, han sido variables de gran incidencia, tanto en la conformación/cambio de ambientes como en el poblamiento prehistórico de esta región en tiempos holocénicos. La dinámica marina ha generado un sistema de terrazas, vinculadas a las sucesivas ingresiones. Dichas terrazas evidencian variaciones locales asociadas a accidentes menores (paleolagunas, paleocauces, paleocrestas, entre otros), los cuales constituyen obstáculos topográficos ligeros, pero al ser esta una región extremadamente plana, los mismos influyen en gran forma sobre el régimen de drenaje, dando lugar a superficies saturadas de agua (bañados) (Bracco et. al. 2000), siendo zonas ecotónicas de muy alta concentración de recursos.

Para el lapso temporal de mayor interés desde una perspectiva arqueológica (Holoceno), existe una propuesta de dinámica paleogeográfica de gran utilidad (Ibidem.). Los investigadores toman como referencia general los modelos propuestos para la zona meridional Argentina (Irinondo y Garcia 1993) y la zona Sur del Brasil (Martin y Suguio 1989). La información para ambas regiones presenta importantes concordancias, las cuales han sido a su vez contrastadas con el registro del litoral uruguayo (Bossi et. al. 1995, Bracco

1993, Bracco et. al. 2000). Para el territorio uruguayo, en base a estos estudios, por el momento se pudo decir que el máximo de Wurm se situaría entorno al 18.000 bp. según análisis de polen y entre el 11000 y 13000 bp. si se atiende a isótopos de oxigeno en sedimentos oceánicos (Bossi et. al. 1995). El nivel del mar habría aumentado desde los -100/-140 m. en el 18000 bp., para situarse en 0 m. entorno al 7000 bp.. Alcanzado el 0 actual se registra una ingresión entorno al 6000 - 5000 bp. (Bracco et. al. 2000). Posteriormente tendrían lugar una serie de fluctuaciones que culminarían nuevamente en el nivel actual. En el siguiente cuadro se esquematiza esta dinámica de los niveles marinos:

Fecha (años bp.)	Dinámica costera atlántica.
Lapso 18.000-7.000	Paulatino ascenso de –100/-140 m. hasta alcanzar el 0 m.
Entorno al 5100	Máximo de cota + 5m.
Entorno al 4000	El mar se retira
Entre el 3500-3000	Ingresión a cota de entre + 2 y +3 m.
Entorno al 2600	La línea de costa se retira nuevamente
Entorno al 2100	Ingresión a cota + 2 m. y posterior descenso paulatino hasta el nivel actual.

Existe una clara vinculación entre la variación del nivel de base oceánico y la presencia de condiciones propicias para la consolidación de los diferentes humedales. Si bien esto es así, para el período que nos interesa, un nivel de mar alto solo aseguraría el funcionamiento de los humedales por debajo de la cota + 5 m. (Bracco et. al. 2000), alimentados por las mareas y los desbordes de las lagunas (L. Negra, L. Castillos etc.); los bañados ubicados en cotas más altas necesariamente debieron contar con un aporte pluvial similar al actual. Entre el 8500 bp. y el 5000 bp., la zona contó con un clima cálido y húmedo, lo cual, potencializado a su vez, con un nivel de base marino alto (desde el 7000 bp.), confluye en condiciones favorables para la presencia de bañados (humedales). Posteriormente entre el 5000 y el 2500-2000 bp. hay evidencias de un declive en las lluvias y una disminución de la temperatura, dinámica que queda resumida en el siguiente cuadro:

Período (años bp.)	Clima
? - 5000	Húmedo y cálido
5000/4000 - 2500/2000	Seco y frío
2500/2000 - 500	Húmedo y templado

A pesar de que el modelo no esté aún totalmente afinado para la región, se pueden extrapolar una serie de generalidades en cuanto a las condiciones ambientales que imperaron en el momento de la ocupación humana prehistórica de este territorio. La fecha más temprana para el poblamiento del Departamento de Rocha, se reconoce entorno al V mileño bp. (Pintos 1999). En este momento habría un nivel marino alto que potencializaría los humedales por debajo de la cota

+ 5m., dejando sujeto al régimen pluvial los bañados situados en cotas superiores. Entre el 4000 - 2000 bp. el descenso en las precipitaciones hace pensar en una reducción de las superficies del humedal en las cotas altas y una cierta permanencia de los bañados de tipo salino en cotas bajas a merced de las mareas y lagunas con conexión oceánica (por ejemplo: Laguna Merin, Laguna de Castillos y Laguna de Rocha). Estas condiciones de sequedad se interrumpen hacia el 2500-2000 bp., donde se daría un aumento de las superficies inundadas, situación que se agudizaría por encontrarse muchos de los drenajes obstruidos a causa de la sequía del período anterior, llegándose a una configuración de bañados y tierras emergidas no muy diferente de la que puede observarse en la actualidad. Existe una gran concordancia espacial entre los cerritos y los ambientes de humedal, todo indica que esta cultura de "los constructores de cerritos" aparece y permanece históricamente estrechamente vinculada a las grandes extensiones de ambientes ecotónicos (de alta productividad) del Departamento de Rocha (López y Bracco 1994) (figura 3 y 4).

Figura 3. Vista general de un cerrito, sitio Potrero Grande, Rocha - Uruguay.

Figura 4. Vista general de la excavación en el cerrtio A, sitio Guardia del Monte, Laguna de Castillos, Rocha - Uruguay. Se observa el dominio visual sobre amplias zonas de humedal.

3. EL MANEJO SOCIAL DEL MEDIO

En este texto sostengo que resulta más adecuado atender al concepto de manejo con la naturaleza, para una adecuada caracterización del grupo en estudio. El concepto de manejo social del medio, como aquí se lo quiere definir, atiende a tres cuestiones fundamentales:

I) la serie de actividades y técnicas, involucradas en obtener la energía y materiales necesarios para la subsistencia del grupo;

II) el orden de racionalidad presente en la serie de relaciones sociales que se establecen entre los individuos a la hora de la extracción (acceso), reparto y consumo de los recursos;

III) la actitud (ideacional/simbólica) del grupo para con el medio bajo la cual son realizadas estas actividades.

El estudio de la complejidad sociocultural, puede así , ser abordado atendiendo a cuestiones de manejo social de un determinado medio. Desde esta óptica, deberán ser tenidas en cuenta las correspondencias estructurales entre el sistema de relaciones ecológicas (tecnología), y los órdenes de racionalidad que den coherencia a la estructura, en sus relaciones tanto a nivel externo como interno. Entendiendo por externo la representación simbólica de la relación cultura/naturaleza, y por interno, a los factores ideológicos que legitiman las modalidades de acceso, reparto y consumo de los recursos que el grupo dispone (estructura de parentesco).

El concepto de manejo aquí redefinido, ha sido tomado de la ecología aplicada, la utilidad del mismo radica en que permite contemplar grados diferenciales de acción humana sobre el medio. Es decir, a partir de un mismo principio conceptual, es posible enfocar diferentes grados de complejidad social, sin que esto implique necesariamente la definición de tipos o divisiones culturales estrictas. Un análisis de grupos cazadores recolectores que parta del concepto de manejo social del medio, permite atender de forma correlacionada a cuestiones claves como: el uso del espacio, intensificación productiva, demografía, reciprocidad social, entre otros.

Como señalan Lee y DeVore (1968:11) : *"We make two assumptions about hunters and gatherers: 1) they live in small groups, and 2) they move around a lot. Mobility limits personal property to what can be carried, so society is generally egalitarian; group size is small, usually bellow 50; local groups do not own or identify particular resources; and food surpluses are rare"*. En mi opinión, mas allá de que esta caracterización sea correcta o no, lo interesante a destacar es que toda configuración sociocultural responderá a profundas opciones culturales o políticas tomadas por el propio grupo como estrategia vital. Es decir, estoy asumiendo así, que sea ya una dada demografía, un rango de movilidad, o bien cierto grado de intensificación productiva, estos descansan en definitiva en opciones o estrategias socialmente adoptadas. Con esto, no estoy negando las limitaciones materiales o constricciones sociales que puedan estar incidiendo en las opciones de un grupo dado, simplemente, se les da aquí un rol limitante, que no determinante. En este

sentido, parece más adecuado ver las diferentes estrategias de manejo social, como algo no absolutamente determinado por las condiciones objetivas del medio, sino que las mismas podrían estar respondiendo a complejas opciones y configuraciones ideológico/culturales del grupo en cuestión. Esto permite sostener que el destino o "futuro" de un grupo, sería el fruto o la síntesis de una serie de elecciones (políticas, morales, culturales, materiales, entre otras) aceptadas, o al menos respetadas, con mayor o menor agrado, por la mayoría de sus integrantes. Lo cual, refuerza la idea de un historia no determinada (en términos absolutos), sino que más bien limitada en sus posibles caminos. Limitada en el sentido de que muchas veces por coyunturas dadas, no son posibles ciertos caminos, pero, a su vez, una historia no determinada, ya que frente al espectro de opciones posibles (sedentarización, crecimiento demográfico, intensificación productiva, entre otras), toda sociedad tiene la capacidad histórica de negar o al menos obstaculizar posibles trayectorias.

Aumentar la producción de individuos, es algo que por decenas de milenios grupos humanos han evitado, en la misma dirección, no intensificar el uso del espacio (es decir, no monumentalizarlo, o incrementar su productividad), ha sido la conducta dominante hasta hace muy pocos miles de años, y en sí misma, la jerarquización y la desigualdad social, parecen ser perversiones sociales recientes en nuestra especie. Se plantea aquí, que no ha sido por incapacidad de "acción" que dichos fenómenos no acontecieran con anterioridad, por el contrario, fue por diversidad de opción que en la mayoría de los casos y por un lapso muy prolongado, las mismas no se adoptaron como estrategia de manejo social.

Teniendo como marco interpretativo general lo expuesto en los párrafos anteriores, pasaré ha exponer una serie de datos sobre el registro arqueológico de los constructores de cerritos de Uruguay, que a mi juicio, ilustran un proceso creciente de complejidad en el manejo social del medio. Se exponen datos acerca de la cultura material: tecnología lítica, cerámica y arqueofauna. Esta información, a su vez, se correlaciona con la procedente de los enterramientos humanos y la de los propios túmulos como construcciones que hacen a un paisaje monumental en estas sociedades cazadoras recolectoras.

4. CULTURA MATERIAL: POSIBLES INDICADORES DE COMPLEJIDAD

El registro arqueológico de estos cazadores recolectores del Arcaico Sudamericano (Uruguay), presenta una serie de particularidades que hacen que él mismo no concuerde con la arqueología tradicional de bandas de caza y recolección.

En lo referente al marco ambiental y a la oferta de recursos potenciales de estos humedales de la región este del Uruguay, resulta de sumo interés su configuración en numerosos "parches", esto supone que en extensiones de pocos kilómetros (no más de 10) uno pueda explotar diversas ofertas ambientales, complementarias temporalmente a lo largo del año. Por ejemplo, para el caso de la Laguna de Castillos, un grupo asentado en sus márgenes tiene acceso directo a los recursos de la propia laguna (peces, bivalbos, aves, etc.), de los bañados (nutrias, carpinchos, ciervo de los pantanos, etc.) de los campos (venado de campo, cocos de palmera butiá, madera, etc.), y a menos de una jornada de camino los recursos de las serranías (guazúbirá, frutos, lítico, madera dura, etc.) y de la costa atlántica (lobos marinos, peces, moluscos, crustáceos, etc.). De esta forma existe la posibilidad de una secuencia de explotación estacional-anual, que generaría una base continua y estable de energía, sustentada en un circuito de aprovisionamiento que no requeriría de grandes desplazamientos del grupo. Este particular marco ambiental, en su variedad y diversidad, redunda en una homogeneidad y estabilidad en cuanto a oferta de energía alimentaria se refiere. El estudio comparativo de las muestras procedentes de varios sitios de la región, permito establecer la riqueza en especies componentes de la dieta (amplitud de dieta) de estos cazadores recolectores (Pintos 1995, 1996, 2000, Pintos y Gianotti 1995). Se identificaron huesos pertenecientes al menos a 21 especies animales diferentes, con evidencias de procesamiento carnicero para su consumo. En este registro arqueofaunístico, resalta la presencia del perro (doméstico) única especie que no evidencia procesamiento carnicero y que frecuentemente se encuentra enterrada junto a los humanos (Pintos 2000). Los sucesivos análisis de muestras, permiten esbozar un modelo de cazadores recolectores con una dieta rica en especies, pero en la cual el aporte energético central vendría dado centralmente por los cérvidos (Venado de Campo y Ciervo de los Pantanos) seguidos por los carnívoros marinos (Lobo Marino) (Ibidem.). Esta importancia del lobo marino como presa, no solo ha quedado registrada en sitios costeros (Chagas 1995) sino que también en los de tierra adentro (Pintos 1996). A su vez, se plantea que el enriquecimiento de la dieta (aumento en el numero de especies cazadas) irá incrementándose con el tiempo. Desde una perspectiva diacrónica, el manejo de recursos faunísticos, se duplicaría en un lapso de 1500 años (2500 - 1000 bp.). En tiempos tempranos, la dieta estará muy centrada en la explotación de los cérvidos, para paulatinamente irse enriqueciendo con el uso de una variada gama de especies (de menor porte) , llegándose en tiempos tardíos a una fuerte representación de los roedores (nutria, ratón, apereá, peces) sin que esto implicara una disminución en los valores provenientes de los grandes mamíferos (cérvidos, lobo marino) (Pintos 2000). En cuanto a la flora para tiempos recientes (entorno al 1000 bp.) hay muestras en sedimento y adherencias en las cerámicas de especies domesticadas tales como: maíz, poroto, calabaza (Del Puerto y Campos 1998).

El proceso de intensificación en el manejo social del medio (mayor amplitud de dieta, domesticación), puede verse insinuado también en otras esferas de la cultura material como por ejemplo: tecnología cerámica e industria lítica. La presencia de material cerámico adquiere especial relevancia por el contexto cazador recolector en el que éste aparece, siendo así, el caso de la cultura de los constructores de cerritos es un ejemplo más de sociedades arcaicas cuya base tecnológica involucra el uso de la cerámica. Sin entrar en mayores detalles, se puede proponer la existencia recurrente para los sitios excavados de un nivel pre-cerámico. La presencia de cerámica (Tradición Vieira) se remonta al 2500 bp. (Schmitz 1967). Esta tradición, definida por colegas brasileños para el Sur de Brasil, se encuentra presente en sitios con cerritos de ambos países; con un origen fechado en el 2500 bp., y sucesivas fases hasta tiempos de contacto con elementos europeos (Naue 1968, 1971, Schmitz 1976). A partir de los estudios cerámicos disponibles la cerámica de estos constructores de cerritos, (asignable en líneas generales a la Tradición Vieira), es una cerámica de tecnología simple, con muy baja incidencia en la decoración, y con un predominio en el ámbito tecnológico de la cocción reductora y la manufactura por rodete (aunque existen casos de cocción oxidante y técnica de pastillaje). En relación con su funcionalidad, por las adherencias en cara interna así como externa, se la caracterizado como una cerámica de tipo utilitaria (Bracco et. al. 1993, Curbelo et. al. 1990, Pintos y Capdepont 2001). Nuevos trabajos en la zona Este de Uruguay comienzan a sugerir fechas entorno al 3000 bp. para los inicios de dicha tecnología (Capdepont 1997, Pintos y Capdepont 2001).

En cuanto al material lítico, como aspecto relevante de los conjuntos recuperados en las diferentes excavaciones, se señala el predominio en el uso de materias primas de origen local (radios de no mas de 20 Km.) (cuarzo y riolita) (Curbelo et. al. 1990, Curbelo y Martínez 1992, López 1994). Según estos autores, el cuarzo se presenta como la materia prima más abundante tanto a nivel geológico, como en los conjuntos arqueológicos. El mismo es de muy mala calidad para la talla, lo cual explicaría el control mediante el uso de talla bipolar, mientras que las materias primas de buena calidad (silíceas) son muy poco abundantes en la zona. Se pude afirmar la existencia de una tendencia a la disminución progresiva en la calidad y variedad de las materias primas utilizadas, siendo cuarzo blanco, filíta gris-verdosa y riolitas de procedencia local los materiales predominantes en tiempos tardíos, en cambio los materiales de buena calidad (silíceos) tienen una mayor representación en momentos tempranos. Los conjuntos artefactuales están compuestos por: lascas con sus filos utilizados, percutores, núcleos, yunques, raederas, cuchillos, puntas de proyectil, boleadoras, entre otros. Un elemento característico de los conjuntos líticos recuperados en sitios con cerritos, es la piedra con hoyuelo o "rompe-coquitos". Este artefacto consiste en un bloque de tamaño variable 10-15 cm. de diámetro, en el cual se pude observar el desgaste en forma de depresión (de no más de 1 cm. de diámetro), de una o varias zonas. La posible funcionalidad de estos artefactos se ha relacionado tanto con la talla bipolar (como yunque), como con actividades culinarias (extracción de la nuez del coquito de la palma de Butia. Otros artefactos de similar tamaño, lo constituyen las piedras con superficies pulidas (molinos) y cantos también pulidos (manos de moler). Como otro aspecto relevante de los artefactos líticos de esta cultura, se encuentra la confección de grandes piezas pulimentadas en granito (y otros materiales), como son los zoolitos y los rompecabezas. Algunos autores han querido ver en ellas, por su esmerado acabado y la dificultad de su elaboración el trabajo de especialistas, proponiendo para estas piezas la posible función de elementos de prestigio en amplias redes de intercambio (Andrade y López 1998).

El aumento en la extracción de energía (registro arqueofaunístico y florístico) la optimización de su aprovechamiento (cerámica) y la posible disminución en la movilidad del grupo (como demuestra la existencia de cerámica y la procedencia de los materiales líticos) parece coincidir con un proceso de monumentalización creciente del paisaje (mayor número de túmulos y mayor altura de los mismos), formas de apropiación del espacio que sugieren una *construcción activa del paisaje* en contextos cazadores recolectores (activa en el sentido de Criado 1993:45-47).

5) LA CONSTRUCCIÓN ACTIVA DEL ESPACIO: PAISAJE MONUMENTAL EN GRUPOS CAZADORES RECOLECTORES

Uno de los aspectos diferenciales más relevantes de esta cultura, son los propios cerritos (mounds). Dado el contexto cazador recolector que nos ocupa se entiende por *monumento:* el producto generado a partir de una serie de actividades y manipulaciones de materiales del medio circundante, reordenación de elementos que involucra una serie de técnicas, con el fín de obtener un artefacto visible y perdurable en el territorio del grupo. Es el ser un artefacto (producto cultural), a lo que se suma el destaque visual ("imperativo") y la perdurabilidad en el tiempo, lo que básicamente definiría a un monumento en un contexto cazador recolector (estas consideraciones contemplan los planteamientos realizados en (Criado 1993a,b)). Es en estas dos últimas características (la inevitabilidad de su percepción y la perdurabilidad en el tiempo), donde radica desde un punto de vista material su diferencia con el resto de objetos culturales. La actividad monumental no es precisamente lo que ha caracterizado a nuestra existencia como especie; la misma es un fenómeno relativamente reciente. El monumento como construcción antrópica, lo entiendo como la reordenación de materiales naturales que generan un espacio cultural visible y permanente en el paisaje, que altera en forma definitiva el espacio preexistente, y por consiguiente, la propia experiencia humana. Esto permite suponer, respecto a la sociedad que realiza estos monumentos, la existencia de un cambio en la percepción y valoración del tiempo y el espacio, por lo tanto, una nueva forma de pensarse (Criado 1989). Como acertadamente señala Bradley (1993, 1998), subyace en la definición de monumento el ser realizado para conmemorar. Conmemorar por medio de un monumento, pienso, puede ser entendido como la materialización permanente en el presente del recuerdo de un pasado. Siguiendo a Bradley (en Barrett et. al. 1991:8) el paisaje puede ser entendido como superficie o escenario en el que las personas se movían y congregaban, y por ende, como producto de su acción, un producto culturalmente significativo de la redundancia de su ocupación. Trasladando estas consideraciones al caso que aquí nos ocupa, podemos decir que en esencia (y esto es susceptible de controversias), un cerrito sería una construcción realizada básicamente con tierra; sedimentos removidos de las inmediaciones y depositados en sucesivas capas de acumulación que hacen que el túmulo gane en altura

(Bracco 1993, Pintos 1999), una dinámica que puede involucrar lapsos de miles de años entre la primera y última capa de deposición. Esta dinámica se inició en el caso de Uruguay alrededor del año 4000 bp. (Bracco et. al. 2000), cuando grupos cazadores recolectores comenzaron a remover porciones del suelo, generando acumulaciones de sedimento que disponían según una morfología relativamente constante[1] (Bracco & López 1987, López & Pintos 2000). Existe al parecer (como veremos en el punto siguiente) la intención de "perlar", de connotar monumentalmente un paisaje, mediante esta reordenación de sedimentos. La monumentalización como proceso que convierte al "sin lugar" en "lugar".

A su vez, los cerritos como monumentos, presentan otras dos particularidades suficientemente interesantes como para ser aquí destacadas:

a) su técnica constructiva,

b) su carácter funerario.

Los cerritos como lugar de enterramiento

Que un grupo cazador recolector entierre a sus muertos, aunque no es del todo frecuente, es plausible, pero de ahí a pasar a monumentalizar la muerte, existe ya una gran diferencia. A mi juicio, es de especial relevancia que estos monumentos no sean meras acumulaciones de tierra; éstos, presentan en su interior restos humanos, conformando un paisaje fundamentalmente connotado por la monumentalización de la muerte. El paisaje cultural monumental pasa a ser así un paisaje de la monumentalización de la muerte (Criado 1991). La presencia de enterramientos humanos en el interior de muchas de estas construcciones (Capdepont 2000, Gianotti 1998, Pintos y Bracco 1999), nos sitúa ante la materialización de factores ideológicos novedosos en relación con la tipología sociocultural tradicional de grupos cazadores recolectores. Su puede sugerir que el valor simbólico de un monumento diferirá dependiendo de si contiene, o no, los restos de un antepasado. En caso afirmativo, esto afectará a la relación de los individuos vivos para con ese monumento. Muerto y vivos, enterrado y "enterradores", configuraron en vida una serie de relaciones sociales (afectivas, políticas y económicas) que no pueden ser consideradas homogéneas en intensidad para el conjunto de los individuos del grupo. Aceptando esto, puede verse la monumentalización de la muerte de ciertos individuos, como la consolidación histórica de un cierto orden social; una sociedad que estaría dando un rol creciente a la figura del antepasado y al sistema de linajes (en el sentido que señala Vicent 1991,1998). Este autor plantea (Idiem:829-31) que las bandas de cazadores recolectores ("parentesco clasificatorio") establecen altos niveles de reciprocidad intergrupal como mecanismo paliativo en caso de crisis, lo que implica un acceso generalizado a los recursos y a los productos. La disolución del orden de banda se daría a partir de una transformación de la estructura de parentesco, que pasaría a poder definirse como "parentesco genealógico". El

---

[1] Los cerritos relevados muestran variaciones morfológicas considerables, en las que aquí no abundaremos. Un cerrito "tipo" se presenta como una estructura de planta relativamente circular de unos 30 m. de diámetro y entre el 1,5 y 2 m. de altura.

sistema de linajes se presenta así, como marco conceptual adecuado a partir del cual interpretar los crecientes niveles de reciprocidad negativa tanto a nivel intergrupal como intragrupal. Como argumenta Dillehay (1990) la actividad monumental puede ser entendida como expresión de una red social que en lo espacial regula las relaciones regionales con los vecinos y en lo vertical (construcción del túmulo y enterramiento) vincula el presente con los antepasados, los vivos con su historia. El caso arqueológico de los constructores de cerritos, quizá sea un aporte más para debatir como este proceso de creciente insolidaridad puede tener cabida en ambitos de caza y recolección.

La técnica constructiva

Un cerrito como construcción arquitectónica, consiste básicamente en la superposición de sucesivas capas de sedimento proveniente de los alrededores. Este proceso constructivo se extiende en ocasiones por lapsos mayores a los 2500 años de ritualidad acumulativa. Durante este período distintos eventos (capas) de construcción se suceden, relacionados (no siempre) con actividades de enterramiento humano. Se podría sugerir entonces que el cerrito como construcción planificada ya contempla en su esencia la proyección temporal, es desde su concepción "monumento-inacabado". Pensable más como un "proyecto monumental" que como hito o evento único. La ritualidad acumulativa de tierra vista, como reafirmación cultural y grupal en el presente, el monumento como proyecto monumental vinculando generaciones, vivos y muertos, genealogía y diacronía.

En contra de este *proceso o proyecto constructivo*, desde una óptica adaptacionista, se podrían argumentar impedimentos de orden energético y fuerza de trabajo para explicar tal dinámica. Dejando de lado las consideraciones acerca de lo aburrida y poco vistosa que sería tal hipótesis, cabe señalar además, el enorme etnocentrismo que supone negarles (también) a estos indios la capacidad de acumular algunos miles de kilos de tierra en varios siglos y/o milenios. No resulta disparatado pensar que la construcción no se hiciera en lapsos menores, sí este hubiera sido el objetivo y significación de dicho lugar y monumento para el grupo constructor. Hoy en investigación antropológica, el "¿cómo lo hicieron?" aparece con frecuencia como un objetivo un tanto anecdótico, frente a las potencialidades de un "¿por qué?" y sus posibles correspondencias estructurales con otras esferas de la cultura. Estamos frente a un gesto cultural (acumulación de sedimento) que se presenta con una redundancia de milenios. Se eligieron zonas muy específicas del paisaje para las cuales decenas de generaciones durante decenas de siglos mantuvieron su compromiso de actividad monumental; un gesto que aparece como un prolongado y efectivo mecanismo de negociación al interior de estas sociedades. Con esto, no quiero decir que durante 3000 años existiera la misma significación émica para con estas construcciones; mi deseo es, por el contrario, hacer hincapié en la idea de que lejos de ser olvidados, estos monumentos fueron tenidos en cuenta, acrecentados en tamaño, modificados en forma, enterrados sus muertos, resignificados.

6. LA MUERTE MONUMENTALIZADA, LA MUERTE VIOLENTA, LA MUERTE OLVIDADA

Que un grupo cazador recolector entierre a sus muertos, aunque no es del todo frecuente, es plausible, pero de ahí a pasar a monumentalizar la muerte, existe ya una gran diferencia. En la región Este de Uruguay (por ej.: en la Laguna de Castillos) el estudio sistemático de la distribución espacial de los túmulos, evidencia que no todos los espacios fueron igualmente valorados para el emplazamiento de los cerritos. La forma natural de la cuenca y las principales geoformas contenidas en ella, parecen actuar como unidad o plan directriz que inspiraría la semantización monumental de este paisaje. Se tomaron como prioritarias para su construcción formas de la geografía topográficamente destacadas, y fueron ubicados, por lo general, en verdaderos "balcones" desde los cuales se logra un dominio visual de amplias zonas más bajas (que suelen corresponder con altas concentraciones de recursos). La presencia de enterramientos humanos en el interior de un buen número de estas construcciones (Gianotti 1998), nos sitúa ante la materialización de factores ideológicos novedosos en relación con la tipología cultural tradicional de grupos cazadores recolectores (figura 5 y 6). Los posibles cambios en las estructuras sociales, parecen reflejarse en el registro de enterramientos humanos de los constructores de cerritos de Uruguay. Es decir, en mi opinión, hay evidencias en el registro arqueológico de estas sociedades de situaciones de desigualdad interpersonal, y en muchos casos restos humanos que sugieren "suertes sociales" muy distintas para los diferentes individuos integrantes de estos grupos.

Las evidencias exhiben al menos diferencias en tres niveles o aspectos del registro:

a) Modalidad de enterramiento y ajuares asociados.

b) Lugar de enterramiento: en los monumentos o fuera de ellos.

c) Huellas de violencia en la superficie de los huesos: marcas de corte, alteración térmica, orificios, entre otros.

Sobre la base de la documentación disponible, (Capdepont 2000, Gianotti 1998, Pintos y Bracco 1999, Pintos y Capdepont 2000, Sans 1999, Sanz y Solla 1992), es posible ver, para el registro mortuorio de la región, una serie de modalidades de enterramientos que pasaremos a caracterizar. Atendiendo al tratamiento del individuo se pueden establecer la presencia de los siguientes tipos:

a) Enterramiento primario. Con variantes: extendido, flexionado y fuertemente flexionado.

b) Enterramiento secundario: presentando mayoritariamente modalidades de:

• *Paquetes*: individuos prácticamente completos y cuya disposición refiere a un contenedor no preservado.

• *En urna*: cuenco de cerámica.

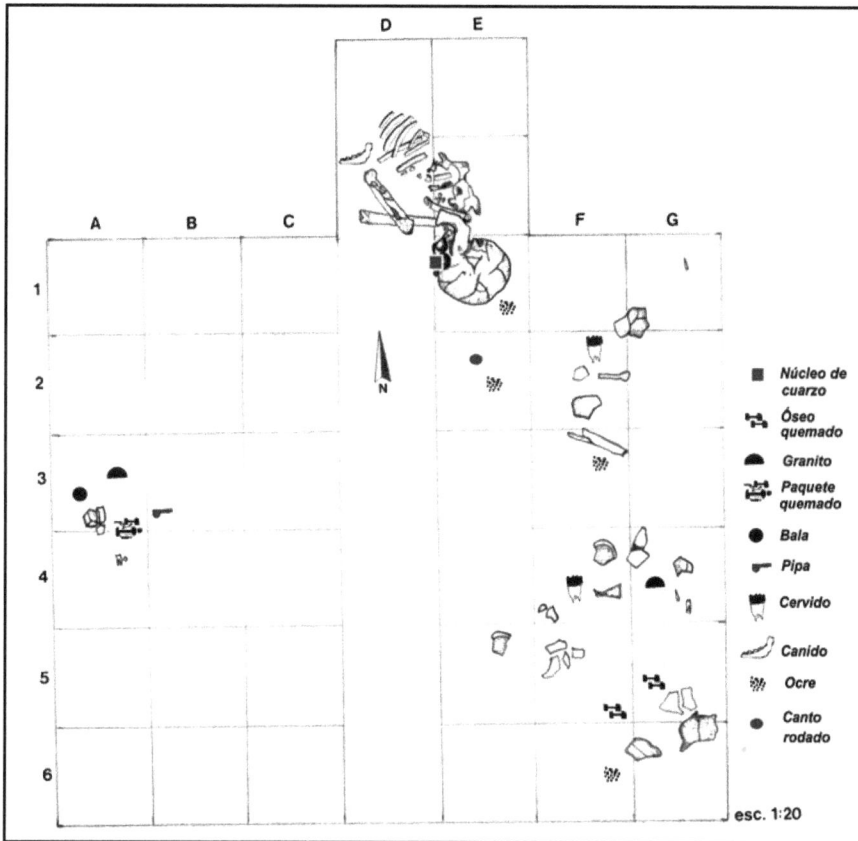

Figura 5. Escena funeraria, enterramientos humanos primarios y secundarios con sus correspondientes ajuares. Tercer capa de construcción del cerrito B, sitio Cráneo Marcado, Rocha-Uruguay.

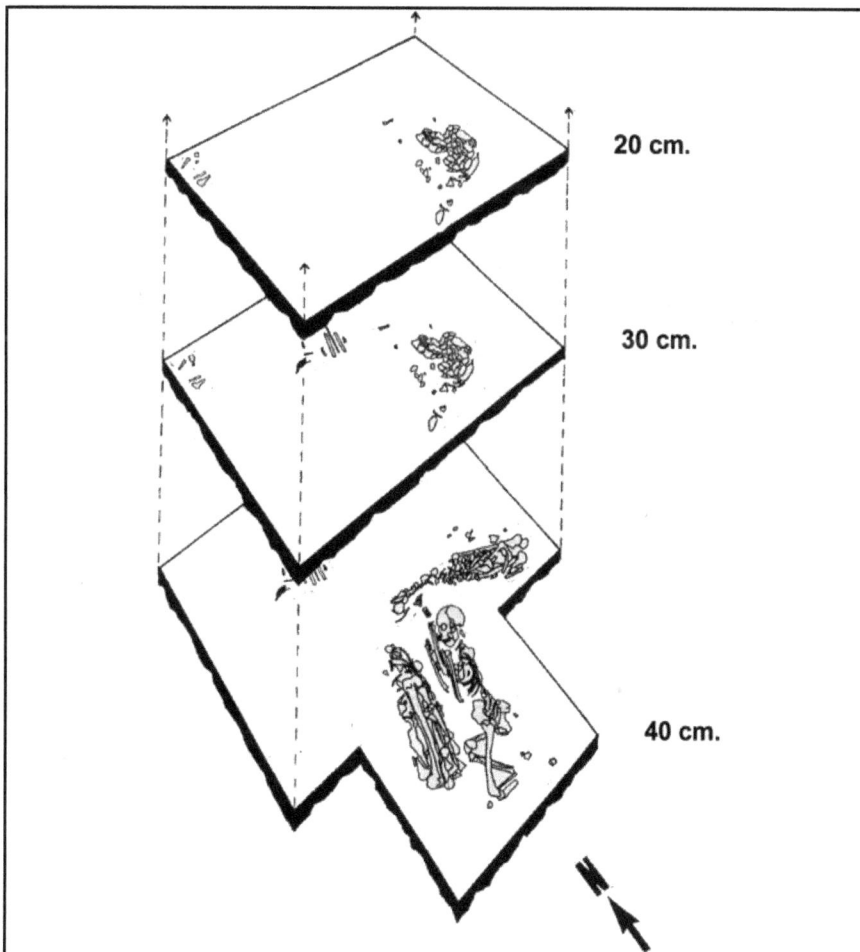

Figura 6. Conjunto de enterramientos, asociados a capa de construcción del cerrito A, sitio CH2D01, Rocha - Uruguay. Modalidades de enterramiento secundario (masculinos) y primario (femenino). (Tomado de Bracco et al. 2000).

Tabla: inventario de enterramientos humanos recuperados sitios con cerritos del Este del Uruguay.

SITIO	TIPO ENTERRAMIENTO	EDAD	SEXO	AJUAR / RESTOS ASOCIADOS	AÑOS BP.
CH2D01-A	Primario, flexionado	Adulto	?	-	2090 ± 90
"	Secundario cráneo roto	48	M	Artef. hueso pulido, valva.	400 ± 50
"	Secundario cráneo roto	40	M	Lito pulido, placa quelonio, valvas.	240 ± 50
"	Primario	42	F	Hueso pescado pulido.	400 ± 50
"	Primario flexionado	6	?	-	2090 ± 90
"	Indeterminado	45	?	-	2090 ± 90
"	Primario muy flex.	Adulto	?	-	2090 ± 90
"	Primario	55	M	Lito con hoyuelo	2090 ± 90
"	Primario levemente flexionado	45	M	-	2090 ± 90
"	Primario flexionado	55	M	Bivalvo perforado	2090 ± 90
"	Primario extendido	40	M	-	2090 ± 90
"	Primario levemente flexionado	49	M	-	2090 ± 90
"	Primario muy perturbado	6	?	-	2090 ± 90
"	Indeterminado.	Adulto	?	-	2090 ± 90
"	Secundario cráneo roto	17	M	-	2090 ± 90
"	Secundario solo cráneo, junto al enterramiento anterior	18	F		2090 ± 90
"	Primario flexionado	45	F	-	2090 ± 90
"	Indeterminado. Perturbado	25	F	-	2090 ± 90
"	Indeterminado. Sin contexto.	> 40	?	-	2090 ± 90
"	Indeterminado. Perturbado?	10 meses	?	-	2090 ± 90
"	Indeterminado. Perturbado?	10-15	?	-	2090 ± 90
"	Indeterminado. Perturbado?	Adulto	?	-	2090 ± 90
"	Indeterminado. Perturbado?	Adulto	?	-	2090 ± 90
"	Indeterminado. Perturbado?	Adulto	?	-	2090 ± 90
"	Indeterminado. Perturbado?	Adulto	M	-	2090 ± 90
CH2D01-B	Primario levemente flexionado.	Adulto	M	-	1090 ± 70
"	Primario levemente flexionado.	-	F	-	1090 ± 70
"	Secundario múltiple	Sub. Adulto y niño.	?	-	1090 ± 70
"	Secundario múltiple	Sub. Adulto y niño.	F	Óseo pulido (cuchillo).	1090 ± 70
CH1D01-B	Primario muy flexionado	Adulto	?	Lítico y ocre.	-
"	Primario muy flexionado	Adulto	F	Lenticular y ocre.	-
"	Indet. (femur, piezas dentarias)	Adulto	?	-	-
CH1E01-B	Primario levemente flexionado.	Adulto.	F	Colmillo de lobo marino, tiento, pequeño animal.	-
H1E01-A	Secundario, piezas craneales	10 meses	?	-	-
	Secundario, piezas craneales	10-15	?	-	-
"	Secundario, piezas craneales	Adulto	?	-	-
"	Secundario, piezas craneales y de post-cráneo	Adulto	M	-	-
CG14E01	Secundario urna	-	?	Cuentas de concha.	1500
"	Primario extendido	-	?	-	1500
"	Secundario paquete	-	?	-	1500
"	No determinado	-	?	-	-
"	No determinado	Adulto	?	-	-
"	Primario	-	?	-	1500
"	Primario	-	?	-	1500
"	Primario	-	?	-	1500
"	Perturbado	45	?	-	1500
"	Perturbado	> 20	?	-	1500
"	Perturbado	-	?	-	1500

SITIO	TIPO ENTERRAMIENTO	EDAD	SEXO	AJUAR / RESTOS ASOCIADOS	AÑOS BP.
LOS AJOS	Secundario. Cráneo.	Adulto	?	-	3350 ± 90
"	Secundario. Cráneo y Piezas de post cráneo	Juvenil	?	-	-
POTRERILLO	Primario fuertemente flex.	Adulto	F	-	2320 ± 50
PSLI	Secundario.	Adulto	?	Óseo pulido, conjunto lítico.	3430 ± 100
"	Secundario, cráneo y diáfisis.	Adulto	?	-	3430 ± 100
PSLII	Primario levemente flex.	Adulto	?	-	3550 ± 60
"	Secundario, piezas aisladas post-cráneo.	-	?	-	3550 ± 60
"	Secundario, piezas aisladas post-cráneo	-	?	-	1360 ± 100
"	Secundario, piezas aisladas post-cráneo	-	?	Conjunto lítico.	3550 ± 60
"	Secundario, cráneo y algunas piezas aisladas post-cráneo	30	M	-	3550 ± 60
"	Secundario, cráneo y algunas piezas aisladas post-cráneo	Niño	?	-	3550 ± 60
"	Secundario, cráneo y algunas piezas aisladas post-cráneo	Adulto	M	-	1390 ± 90
"	Secundario, cráneo y algunas piezas aisladas post-cráneo	25	M	-	3550 ± 60
"	Secundario pieza Cráneal	-	?	-	3550 ± 60.
LOS INDIOS	Secundario, restos parciales	25	?	-	-
"	Secundario, restos parciales.	40	?	-	-
"	Secundario, restos parciales	14	?	-	-
"	Secundario, restos parciales	Adulto	?	Fragmento de boleadora.	-
"	Secundario, restos parciales	Adulto	?	-	-
"	Secundario, restos parciales	> 40	?	-	-
"	Secundario, paquete.	Adulto	?	Rompecoco, diente de lobo, grandes piedras de granito.	-
"	Primario	40	M	Talla de cuarzo, esferoide.	-
"	Primario fuertemente flex.	> 35	M	Núcleo de cuarzo.	-
"	Primario fuertemente flex.	25-35	F	Gran bloque de granito.	-
"	Primario flexionado.	Adulto	?	-	-
"	Primario flexionado.	Adulto	?	2 núcleos de cuarzo y molino	-
"	Secundario paquete	Adulto	?	-	-
LC CRANEO M.	Secundario. Piezas del cráneo y post- cráneo.	Adulto	?	-	3050 ± 150
"	Secundario. Piezas del post-cráneo.	Adulto	?	Artefacto en filita.	2760 ± 60
"	Secundario. Piezas de cráneo	15-21	?	Artefacto granito, diente de lobo marino.	1660 ± 60
"	Secundario. Piezas de cráneo y post-cráneo.	25-35	?	Molar cérvido, ocre.	1660 ± 60
"	Secundario piezas cráneales	15-20	?	Artefacto granito, pipa, óseo quemado.	-
"	Primario semiflexionado, de cubito lateral.	35-40	F	Ocre, núcleo, lascas y cantos de cuarzo.	1660 ± 60
"	Secundario. Pieza dental.	4 - 7	?	-	-
"	Secundario. Piezas de cráneo.	-	?	Artefacto de granito, molares de cérvido.	-
"	Secundario. Piezas de cráneo.	-	?	Ocre.	-
LC GUARDIA DEL MONTE	Secundario. Piezas dentales.	-	?	Ocre	-
"	Secundario. Tíbia.	-	?	Artefacto, material de origen volcánico.	-
"	Secundario. Piezas de cráneo y post-cráneo.	-	F	-	4600 ± 60

(Fuentes: Capdepont 2000, Gianotti (1998), Pintos & Bracco (1999)).

• *Secundarios parciales*, compuestos por una o más piezas óseas humanas. Por lo general este tipo exhibe evidencias de tratamiento traumático (incisiones, quemado, fracturas).

Con relación al lugar de enterramiento:

a) En los monumentos: cerritos.

b) Fuera de los cerritos, en la planicie natural circundante.

En el interior de los monumentos se han evidenciado diferentes modalidades de enterramiento y tratamiento de los mismos: individuales, múltiples (simultáneos o en diacronía), primarios, secundarios, con ajuar o sin él. Existen túmulos como los excavados en la Sierra de los Ajos con un único enterramiento relevado por estructura (Pintos & Bracco 1999), mientras que para otros casos como los de San Miguel han sido recuperados hasta 26 individuos (Femenías et. al. 1990, Sanz y Femenías 1996), lo cual pude remitir a situaciones de jerarquía o importancia personal de quien fue enterrado. En cuanto a las modalidades de enterramiento, en muchos casos se ha depositado el cadáver en estado primario prácticamente "arrojándolo" sin mayor preparación o ajuar. Para estos mismos sitios, u otros, como es Puntas de San Luis (PSL) o Cráneo Marcado, se ha procedido a un cuidado y acondicionamiento secundario de los restos esqueletales (paquete o contenedor) de varios individuos a los que se acompañó de diversos ajuares (cuarzo, mandíbulas de cánidos, conchas, armas, etc.). En asociación con estos últimos enterramientos que podríamos denominar de más complejos, se registran enterramientos secundarios con claras evidencias de tratamiento traumático (marcas y agujeros) (Pintos y Bracco 1999). Estos últimos suelen ser de carácter

parcial, partes esqueletales atribuibles a elementos trofeo (cabezas, extremidades) (figuras 7, 8, 9, 10).

En cuanto al lugar de enterramiento surge otra marcada diferencia, ésta ha sido registrada muy recientemente para la Laguna de Castillos (sitios Cráneo Marcado y Guardia del Monte), donde se han recuperado restos humanos fuera de los túmulos, así como al interior de los mismos. Esto introduce una variable más en cuanto al tratamiento a los individuos, es decir, la monumentalización de su muerte o por el contrario la invisibilidad de la misma. La planicie asociada al lugar donde se encuentran los túmulos de ambos sitios (a 1 - 1.5 km. de distancia) se presenta como área de actividad claramente diferente a la de los alrededores inmediatos de los mismos, tanto en aspectos monumentales, topográficos, como en la concentración del registro material recuperado; indicios que permitirían pensar en posibles «zonas de habitación» (Pintos 1997, 1998). En la planicie del sitio Cráneo Marcado, fechada en 3050 + 150 años BP (URU 136), se evidencia la presencia de material óseo humano. El mismo consiste en un fragmento de cráneo correspondiente a un individuo adulto, con claras marcas de incisiones antrópicas y una falange anular con alteración térmica, asignables a una actividad de procesamiento del individuo. Estos restos se encuentran en un contexto donde predominan los restos de fauna descartados post – consumo, lo que permite inferir la posibilidad de prácticas antropofágicas (Pintos y Bracco 1999). Así mismo, en la planicie adyacente a los túmulos del sitio Guardia del Monte, fechada en 4600 ± 60 años BP (URU 205), se localizaron restos óseos humanos correspondientes a piezas cráneales y postcráneales (fragmento de coxal izquierdo y un fragmento de calota) (Pintos y Capdepont 2000) este material se

Figura 7. Cabeza trofeo, con marcas de scalping, y la tercer vertebra cérvical seccionada sitio PSL, Rocha-Uruguay . (Tomado de Pintos y Bracco 1999).

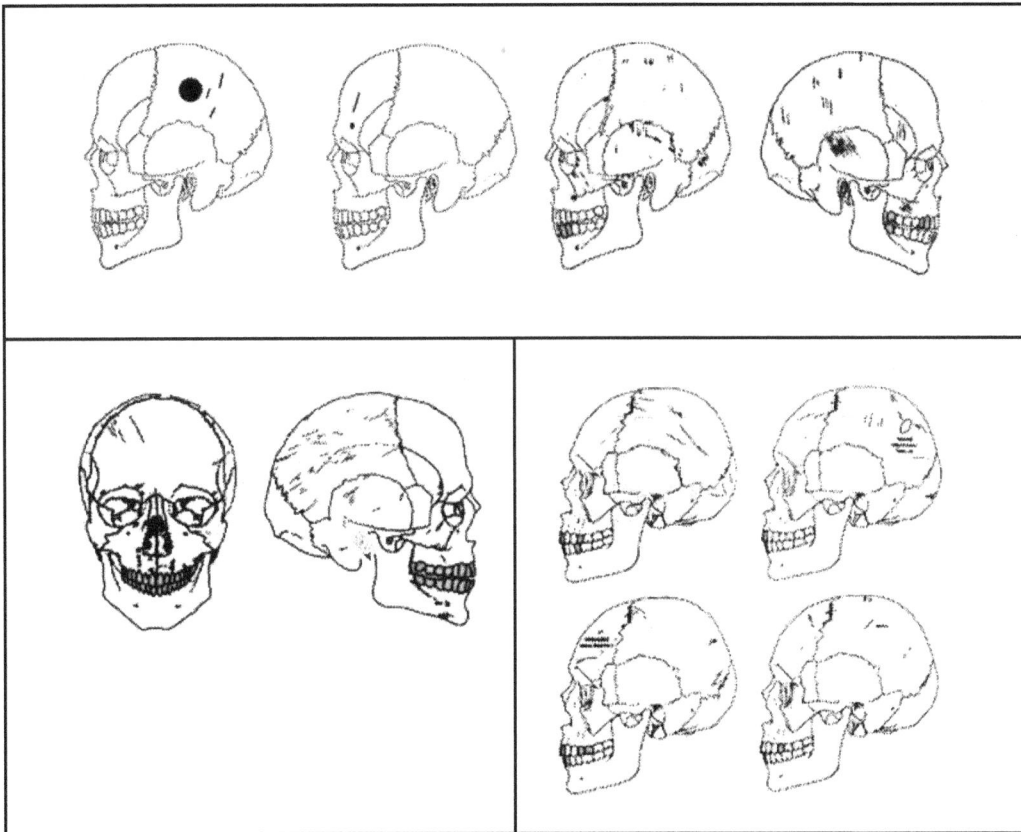

Figura 8. Patrones de marcas de corte y traumas perimorten, en craneos de PSL-Rocha- Uruguay (arriba) e "indios de las praderas" America del Norte. (Tornado de Pintos y Bracco 1999).

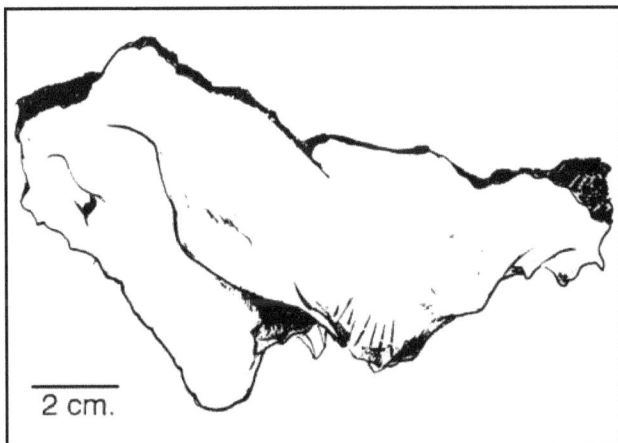

Figura 9. Marcas de corte en crimea del sitio "Crimeo Marcado" Laguna de Castillos, Uruguay.

encuentra asociado con restos de alimentación e industria lítica.

En resumen, atendiendo al repertorio mortuorio hasta el momento recuperado y al contexto cultural relacionado con el mismo, se pueden hacer una serie de puntualizaciónes:

• Existen túmulos con un único enterramiento y otros con múltiples.

• Hay individuos cuya muerte no fue monumentalizada (presencia fuera de los túmulos).

• Se aprecian marcadas diferencias en cuanto al tratamiento del cuerpo del individuo. Algunos exhiben un gran cuidado

Figura 10. Escena funeraria, de 6 enterramientos, asociados a la tercer capa de construcción del cerrito B, sitio Cráneo Marcado, Rocha - Uruguay.

en cuanto a acondicionamiento secundario y ajuar, mientras que otros son depositados primariamente en el túmulo. Otra diferencia la constituyen aquellas piezas esqueletales que presentan en su superficie huellas de tratamiento traumático, lo que remitiría a una suerte esencialmente distinta para estos individuos.

7. PUNTUALIZACIONES FINALES

Entre los grupos clásicamente caracterizados como cazadores recolectores, la muerte frecuentemente es ocultada mediante diversas prácticas. En el caso que nos ocupa se percibe una estrategia diferente en este sentido, existiendo extremados cuidados para con ciertos individuos. Una preparación del cadáver en donde se acondiciona el cuerpo, se le asocian ajuares, se realizan ritos y se monumentaliza la muerte (cerritos). Parece existir, dependiendo del individuo, una actitud diferencial ante el hecho de su muerte, pues, para con algunos, hay una monumentalización (recuerdo) de la misma, mientras que para con otros esta se oculta (olvida), es decir, no se jerarquiza el espacio donde el individuo yace (en la planicie).

Con el discurrir de la investigación en los humedales del Este del Uruguay, un número cada vez mayor de evidencias, me han obligado a replantearme toda la serie de preconceptos que llevaba a la hora de su estudio arqueológico. Atendiendo a las categorías de tiempo y espacio, como lineamientos básicos sobre los que una sociedad percibe y ordena su experiencia (Elias 1989, Hernando 1997ab, Kern 1983), cabe presuponer diferencias para estos constructores de túmulos en relación a la clásica caracterización de los cazadores recolectores "primitivos" (Lee y DeVore, 1968). El registro arqueológico al que me refiero, exhibe marcadas distancias (en comparación con otras sociedades cazadoras recolectoras) en cuanto a la utilización del espacio (territorialidad y explotación intensiva de recursos) y percepción del tiempo (monumentalidad y tratamiento de los muertos), lo cual invita a modelizar acerca de las diferentes correspondencias estructurales dentro de esta particular configuración sociocultural compleja.

Si algo ha quedado claro luego de los aportes de estas dos últimas décadas (Arnold 1992, 1996; Bender 1978, 1981; Binford 1980; Price y Brown 1985; Testart 1982a,b; Schnirelman 1992, 1994; Zvelebil 1986; entre otros), es que un gran número de sociedades cazadoras recolectoras, no concuerdan con la tradicional caracterización de bandas simples. Este "vacío" conceptual ha sido subsanado con la categoría de cazadores recolectores complejos, quienes presentarían un manejo social más intenso en cuanto a producción de individuos, uso del espacio (sedentarismo y explotación de recursos), jerarquización y especialización social. Es en este contexto de discusión en el que se incluye este texto, que no pretende sino presentar cuestiones que pueden ser de relevancia también a la hora de interpretar el registro arqueológico. Estos pobladores prehistóricos de los humedales del Este de Uruguay comenzaron alrededor del 4000 bp., ha realizar una verdadera *construcción activa del paisaje*. A diferencia de otros grupos cazadores recolectores que (siguiendo a Hernando 1999) exhiben una percepción de la realidad ordenada preferentemente en base a referencias espaciales naturales y con un fuerte sentido de presente y un escaso desarrollo de la linealidad temporal, para el caso de Uruguay, el paisaje se monumentaliza mediante la erección de monumentos en tierra, cerritos que entre otras funciones tenían la de lugar de enterramiento humano. La presencia de monumentos, y en este caso, la monumentalización de la

muerte de ciertos individuos, parecería indicar una percepción de la realidad diferente a la clásicamente atribuida a cazadores recolectores. La jerarquización de ciertos espacios (monumentalización) y el tratamiento diferencial de la muerte de los individuos (enterramientos, violencia y ajuares), aparecen como materialización ideológica de un estado de diferenciación y complejidad social (en el sentido señalado por Earle 1997).

La cultura de los constructores de cerritos, en mi opinión, presenta indicios de una sociedad que dista de la simplicidad atribuida al cazador recolector pleistocénico, pero en la cual sin embargo, aún no hay una plena "formación" de la mentalidad dividida o campesina. Constituyen ese tormentoso y heterogéneo pasado, en el que se dieron las condiciones (ambientales, sociales e ideológicas) para que grupos simples, igualitarios e indivisos, consintieran/convivieran con crecientes niveles de complejidad, desigualdad e intensificación. En aquellas sociedades que comienzan a protagonizar y consolidar una tendencia a la ruptura de la armonía social o de la reciprocidad positiva, concomitantemente, su registro material exhibe evidencias de algún tipo de jerarquización monumental del paisaje. A mi entender, el comienzo de la modificación de paisajes "naturales" mediante la construcción de túmulos, son en estas sociedades cazadoras recolectoras, la base material "escenográfica" y muchas veces catalizadora de un nuevo discurso sobre el ser social.

Lejos de constituir hechos puntuales y únicos (olvidables), estos monumentos fueron tenidos en cuenta por sucesivas generaciones durante miles de años. Siguieron agregándoles capas y junto con ellas restos humanos (tratados de muy diferente forma), acondicionándolas, reformándolas, en fin resignificándolas socialmente. Evidencias materiales de una ideología, que alude a procesos de negociación social en los que los antepasados, la historia, la profundidad temporal y el anclaje espacial del grupo, desempeñaron un rol destacado. En definitiva, parece ser que nos encontramos ante un manejo social del medio que presenta similitudes con lo que muchos autores han venido definiendo como cazadores recolectores complejos.

Authors address

Sebastian Pintos Blanco
Dpto. de Prehistoria, Universidad Complutense de Madrid, España.
Comisión Nacional de Arqueología, Uruguay.
salitres@teleline.es

Bibliography

ANDRADE, T., and LOPEZ, J., 1998. La emergencia de la complejidad entre los cazadores recolectores de la costa atlántica meridional Sudamericana. Lanata, J. (ed.) *Journal of American Archaeology*, OPHG/OEA. Washington.

ARNOLD, J., 1992. "Complex hunter-gatherers-fichers of prehistoric California: chiefs, specialist and maritime adaptation of the Channel Islands". *American Antiquity*,57:60-84.

ARNOLD, J., 1996. "The archaeology of complex hunter-gatherers". *Journal of Archaeological Method and Theory*, 3(2): 77-127.

BARRETT, J., BRADLEY, R. and GEEN, M., 1991. *Landscape, Monuments and Society.The prehistory of Carbone Chase.* Cambridge University Press. England.

BENDER, B., 1978. Gatherer-hunter to farmer: a social perspective. *World Archaeology* 10 (2): 204-222.

BENDER, B., 1981. Gatherer-hunter intensification. *Economic Archaeology.* J. A. Sheridaw y G. N. Bailey, eds., International Series 96: 149-157.

BINFORD, L., 1980. Willow smoke and dogs' tails: hunter gatherer settlement systems and archaeological site formation. *American Antiquity*, 45: 4-25.

BOSSI, J., BRACCO, R. and MONTAÑA, J., 1995. *Causas geológicas del paisaje Rochense.* PROBIDES. Uruguay.

BRACCO, R., 1993. Desarrollo cultural y evolución ambiental en la región este del Uruguay *UdelAR,* Uruguay:43-73.

BRACCO, R. and LOPEZ, J., 1987. Prospección Arqueológica y Análisis de Foto Aérea.Bañado de la India muerte y Bañado de San Miguel, Dpto. de Rocha. *CRALM-MEC.* Uruguay.

BRACCO, R., MAÑOSA, C., MATA V. and PINTOS, S., 1993. Análisis del conjunto cerámico correspondiente a la Elevación B del sitio CH2D01, San Miguel, Rocha. *Informe PROBIDES.* Uruguay

BRACCO, R., MONTAÑA, J., BOSSI, J., PANARELLO, H. and URES, C., 2000. Evolución del Humedal y ocupaciones humanas en el Sector Sur de la Cuenca de la Laguna Merín. Arqueología de las Tierras Bajas. MEC, Uruguay: 84-99.

BRADLEY, R., 1993. *Altering the Earth.* Society of Antiquaries of Scotland. Monograph Series, 8. Edinburgh.

BRADLEY, R., 1998. *The Significance of Monuments. On the shaping of human experience in Neolithic and Bronce Age Europe.* Routledge. London.

CAPDEPONT, I., 1997. Análisis cerámico en la Región Este del Uruguay. *Actas del IX Congreso Nacional de Arqueología.* Colonia, Uruguay.

CAPDEPONT, I., 2000. Manifestaciones Funerarias de los "constructores de cerritos". Laguna de Castillos. *Monografía.* FHCE, UdelaR. Uruguay.

CRIADO, F., 1989. "Megalitos, Espacio y Pensamiento. *Trabajos de Prehistoria*, 46. Madrid: 75-98.

CRIADO, F., 1991. Tiempos Megalíticos y Espacios Modernos., *Historia y Crítica, I,* España: 85-108.

CRIADO, F., 1993a. Visibilidad e interpretación del registro arqueológico. *Trabajos de Prehistoria*, 50 Madrid: 39-56.

CRIADO, F., 1993b. Limites y posibilidades de la Arqueología del Paisaje. *SPAL, 2.* Sevilla: 9-55.

CURBELO, C., CABRERA, L., FEMENIAS, J., FUSCO, N., LOPEZ, J. and MARTINEZ, E., 1989. Sitio CH2D01, área de San Miguel, Dpto. de Rocha, R.O.U.. Estructura de sitio y zonas de actividad. *V Reuniao da Sociedade Brasileira de Arqueología.* Santa Cuz, RGS, Brasil.

CURBELO, C. and MARTINEZ, E., 1992. Aprovechamiento de materias primas líticas para un área arqueológica relacionada con la Sierra de San Miguel, Dpto. de Rocha, R.O.U.. Ediciones del Quinto Centenario. Estudios Antropológicos. UdelaR, Uruguay: 121-139.

CHAGAS, L., 1995. Identificación y análisis del material óseo de los sitios costeros del litoral Atlántico. *Arqueología en el Uruguay.* Uruguay: 106-115.

DEL PUERTO, L. and CAMPOS, S., 1998. Silicofitolitos: un abordaje alternativo del registro arqueobotánico de la región Este del Uruguay. *Actas del Taller de Arqueología – En los Tres reinos: Prácticas de recolección en el Cono Sur de América.* Horco-Molle, Tucumán, Argentina.

DILLEHAY, T., 1990. Mapuche ceremonial landscape, social recruitment and resource rights. *World Archaeology*, 22(2):223-41.

EARLE, T., 1997. *How Chiefs Come to Power. The Political Economy in Prehistory.* Stanford University Press. California.

ELIAS, N., 1989. *Sobre el Tiempo.* Fondo de Cultura Económica. España.

FEMENIAS, J., LOPEZ, J., BRACCO, R., CURBELO, C., MARTINEZ, E., CABRERA, L. and FUSCO, N., 1990. Tipos de enterramientos en estructuras monticulares (cerritos) en la región de la Cuenca de la Laguna Merin (R.O.U.). Anais da V Reuniao Científica da Sociedade de Arqueologia Brasileira, *Revista do CEPA*, 17:345-358.

GIANOTTI, C., 1998. Ritual funerario y prácticas mortuorias en las Tierras Bajas. *Monografía*, FHCE, UdelaR, Montevideo.

HERNANDO, A., 1997a. Sobre la Prehistoria y sus Habitantes: Mitos, Metáforas y miedos. *Complutum*, 8. Madrid: 247-60.

HERNADO, A., 1997b. La identidad Q'eqchi. Percepción de la realidad y autoconciencia de un grupo de agricultores de roza de Guatemala". *Revista Española de Antropología Americana*, 27. Madrid: 199-220.

HERNANDO, A., 1999. *Los primeros agricultores de la Península Ibérica. Una Historiografía crítica del Neolítico.* Síntesis. Madrid.

IRIONDO, M. and GARCIA, N., 1993. Climatic variations in the Argentine Plain During the last 18.000 years. *Paleogeography, Paleoclimatology, Paleoeconomy*. 101. Elsevier Science Publisher. Amsterdam.

KERN, S., 1983. *The Culture of Time and Space 1880-1918.* Harvard University Press. Cambridge, Massachusetts.

LEE, R. and DEVORE, I. (eds.), 1968. *Man the Hunter.* Aldine, Chicago.

LOPEZ, J., 1994. Cabo Polonio: sitio arqueológico del litoral atlántico uruguayo. Anais da 7° Reunion Cintifica da SABB. *Revista de Arqueología 8(2).* Brasil:239-266.

LOPEZ, J. and BRACCO, R., 1994. Cazadores-recolectores de la Cuenca de la Laguna Merín: aproximaciones teóricas y modelos arqueológicos. Arqueología de Cazadores-Recolectores. Límites, casos y aperturas. *Arqueología Contemporánea*. Edición Especial: 51-64.

LOPEZ, J. and PINTOS, S., 2000. Distribución espacial de estructuras monticulares, en la Cuenca de la Laguna Negra. *Arqueología de las Tierras Bajas.* MEC, Uruguay: 49-58.

MARTIN, L. and SUGUIO K., 1989. International Symposium on Global Changes in South America during the Quaternary. *Special Publication* 2. Sao Paulo, Brasil

NAUE, G., 1968. Sitios arqueológicos no Municiopio de Rio Grande. *Pesquisas, Antropología, 18.* San Leopoldo, Brasil:141-152.

NAUE, G., 1971. Novas perspectivas sobre arqueologia do Rio Grande, R. S.. O Homen Antigo na America. Inst. de Pré-História da Universidade de Sao Paulo:91-122.

PINTOS, S., 1995. Manejo prehistórico de recursos faunísticos en los Humedales del Este. *Monografía de Grado.* FHCE, UdelaR, Uruguay.

PINTOS, S., 1996. Análisis arqueozoológico del sitio Potrerillo de Santa Teresa, Dpto. de Rocha-Uruguay. Segundas Jornadas de Antropología de la Cuenca del Plata. ARQUEOLOGIA II:118-127.

PINTOS, S., 1997. Arqueología en el Sitio "Cráneo Marcado - Laguna de Castillos" Dpto. de Rocha (R.O.U). *Actas del IX Congreso Nacional de Arqueología*. Colonia, Uruguay.

PINTOS, S., 1998. Actividad Monumental: la construcción del Paisaje entre los cazadores recolectores de la rergión Este del Uruguay. *Arqueología Espacial*, 19-20. Teruel:529-542

PINTOS, S., 1999. Túmulos, caciques y otras historias. Cazadires recolectores complejos en la Cuenca de la Laguna de Castillos, Uruguay. Complutm 10, Madrid:213-226.

PINTOS, S. and BRACCO R., 1999. Modalidades de enterramiento y huellas de origen antrópico en especímenes óseos humanos. *Arqueología y Bioantropología de las Tierras Bajas*. (López, J. y Sans M., eds.). UdelaR, Uruguay:81-106.

PINTOS, S. and CAPDEPONT, I., 2001. Arqueología en la Cuenca de la Laguna de Castillos - apuntes sobre complejidad cultural en sociedades cazadoras recolectoras del Este de Uruguay. *Arqueoweb*. Univ. Complutense de Madrid.

PINTOS, S. and GIANOTTI, C., 1995. Arqueofauna de los constructores de cerritos: "quebra" y requiebra. *Arqueología en el Uruguay*. Uruguay: 79-91.

PRICE, T. and BROWN, J. (eds.), 1985. *Prehistoric Hunter-Gathers. The Emergence of Cultural Complexity*. Accademic Press, Inc. London.

SANS, M., 1999. Pautas de adaptación en el Este del Uruguay a partir del estudio de los restos esqueletarios humanos. *Arqueología y Bioantropología de las Tierras Bajas*. (López, J. y Sans M., eds.). UdelaR, Uruguay:107-123

SANS, M. and FEMENIAS, J., 1996. Subsistencia, movilidad y organización social en el sitio monticular CH2D01-A (Rocha-Uruguay): inferencias a partir de las pautas de enterramiento y los restos esqueletales. *Arqueología de las Tierras Bajas*. MEC, Uruguay:383-394.

SANS, M. and SOLLA H., 1992. Análisis de restos óseos humanos del Este del Uruguay. Primeras Jornadas Antropológicas en Uruguay. MEC, Uruguay: 171-176.

SCHNIRELMAN, V., 1992. Complex hunter-gatherers: exception or common phenomenon?. *Dialectical Anthropology* 17:183-196.

SCHNIRELMAN, V., 1994. "Farming or fishing? On the unevenness of socio-economic development in Neolithic times. *6° Coloquio Hispano-Ruso de Historia*, Fundación Cultural Banesto, Madrid: 39-54

SCHMITZ, P., 1967. Arqueología no Rio Grande do Sul. *Pesquisas, Antropología N°16*. San Leopoldo, Brasil.

SCHMITZ, P., 1976. Sitios de pesca lacustre en Rio Grande, RS Brasil. *Tese de livre docencia*. RGS, Brasil.

TESTART, A., 1982a. The significance of food storage among hunter-gatherers: Residence patterns, population densities, and social inequalities. *Current Anthropology*, 23:523-537.

TESTART, A., 1982b. *Les Chasseurs-Cueilleurs ou L'origine des inégalités*. Société D'Ethnographie, Paris.

VICENT, J., 1991. El Neolítico. Transformaciones sociales y económicas. *Boletín de Antropología Americana*, Diciembre. Mexico.

VICENT, J., 1998. La prehistoria del modo tributario de producción. *HISPANIA, LVIII,3,200*. España:823-839.

ZVELEBIL, M. (ed.), 1986. *Hunter in Transition. Mesolitic Societies of Temperate Eurasia and their transition to Farming*. Cambridge University Press. London.

www.ingramcontent.com/pod-product-compliance
Lightning Source LLC
Chambersburg PA
CBHW061007030426
42334CB00033B/3394

* 9 7 8 1 8 4 1 7 1 5 9 6 4 *